Sylvia Rogers has an amazing gift for clear communication with a passion for God's Word. May *Healing Words* be a blessing to all who read it for specific health challenges.

—Scott Bradley
Lead Pastor of AS IS Church, Portland, Oregon
Author of *The Forgiveness Factor*

In the Gospels Jesus instructs us to speak to our personal mountains and tell them to move. This teaching was a mystery to me until I did a series of biofeedback sessions with Sylvia Rogers. Time after time I saw my biofeedback scores improve after speaking to "mountains" of physical and emotional stressors. It was astonishing! Even better is experiencing the freedom of no longer carrying those burdens. Speaking to our problems really works, no biofeedback computer necessary—just faith and belief that we have the power and authority to do so. Putting this principle into action has powerfully accelerated my journey toward health.

—Alison W.
Client

I have been a client at the Herbal Health Center and have been an avid believer in the power of the spoken Word over the body and one's life. I have done much personal work from her first book, *The Pearl Box*, and I can feel the results. I am one of Sylvia's biofeedback clients and have witnessed firsthand the power of prayer and speaking off emotions, trauma, and toxins from my being. I saw a dramatic shift in the computer report after treating myself with only two powerful prayers, and I could also feel the effects. I am excited about the message Sylvia is bringing and how she has made this information so easy to use and understand.

—Sharon Praus
Teacher at NW Bible Training Center Ministry
Portland, Oregon
Prayer Minister at Restoration Gateway Ministries
Beaverton, Oregon

Sylvia Rog⟨…⟩ ⟨…⟩nding of Scripture and
our maker'⟨…⟩ ⟨…⟩l dealing with medical

conditions and spiritual and psychological problems through God's principles. Sylvia's thirty-five years of continuing education in the caregiving field has provided her with the perfect blend of abilities, wisdom, education, and faith. Her understanding of the newest medical technology and nursing, and her exceptional knowledge as an herbalist and health educator enhance her ability to help others.

Her first book, *The Pearl Box*, is a journey into the depths of our physical, mental, emotional, and spiritual well-being from our Maker's point of view, which brings change to those who would apply the principles. Her new book, *Healing Words*, provides scriptural understanding of the importance of biblical principles for mental, physical, and spiritual health.

Sylvia's books are positive resources for both individual and group study. As a marriage and family therapist and an ordained minister, I find her approach, education, beliefs, and commitment to help others sound and exceptional. I recommend her new book for those seeking a better physical, mental, emotional, and spiritual life.

—Tom Newton, DMin, MDiv
Marriage and Family Therapist
Director of A Touch of Hope Ministries

Having been introduced to Sylvia Rogers several years ago through her first book, *The Pearl Box*, which was given to me as a Christmas gift by my sister who lives on the East Coast, I have been truly blessed by her teaching, as have countless others. After learning Sylvia's story, meeting her and her husband, Mark, at their Herbal Health Center, personally seeing the incredible results on the biofeedback computer after applying God's living Word to my circumstances, and later hearing her speak at a church retreat, I can personally attest to the fact that what you read in Sylvia's new book, *Healing Words*, is life changing.

As a women's ministries pastor and wife of a lead pastor of several large churches over the course of more than forty-two years, I have watched and experienced the transforming power of the Word of God restore good health and bring wholeness and healing to countless lives, not only physically but also mentally, emotionally, spiritually, and relationally. It is a privilege to highly recommend this uniquely detailed work of researched, proven, and practical principles that when applied or spoken over specific health challenges will immediately begin to bring positive, desired changes.

—BONNIE ERICKSON
WOMEN'S MINISTRIES PASTOR, PEOPLES CHURCH
SALEM, OREGON

This book is a must-read for anyone who wants to transform his or her life! It is for those just beginning their healing journey as well as those well versed in biblical and natural healing practices. Sylvia's book sheds light on biblical truths and hidden gems in Scripture that are there for all to partake in and experience healing. I'm so excited to put this teaching into practice for myself and use this information to help others transform their lives. I recently had a chance to hear Sylvia speak live to a large group of friends and colleagues. Afterward everyone was talking about her message. *Transformed, renewed, changed, enlightened, healed*—those are some of the words they were using to describe her talk. Read this book, apply the principles, and share it with others.

—GRETCHEN MENDELL
NATURAL HEALTH CONSULTANT
OWNER, NATURE'S REMEDY, ELLICOTTVILLE, NEW YORK

Healing WORDS

SYLVIA ROGERS

SILOAM

Most CHARISMA HOUSE BOOK GROUP products are available at special quantity discounts for bulk purchase for sales promotions, premiums, fund-raising, and educational needs. For details, write Charisma House Book Group, 600 Rinehart Road, Lake Mary, Florida 32746, or telephone (407) 333-0600.

HEALING WORDS by Sylvia Rogers
Published by Siloam
Charisma Media/Charisma House Book Group
600 Rinehart Road
Lake Mary, Florida 32746
www.charismahouse.com

This book or parts thereof may not be reproduced in any form, stored in a retrieval system, or transmitted in any form by any means—electronic, mechanical, photocopy, recording, or otherwise—without prior written permission of the publisher, except as provided by United States of America copyright law.

Unless otherwise noted, all Scripture quotations are from the Holy Bible, Modern English Version. Copyright © 2014 by Military Bible Association. Used by permission. All rights reserved.

Scripture quotations marked DARBY are from the Darby Translation of the Bible (Public Domain).

Scripture quotations marked ESV are from the Holy Bible, English Standard Version. Copyright © 2001 by Crossway Bibles, a division of Good News Publishers. Used by permission.

Scripture quotations marked JUB are taken from the Jubilee Bible, copyright © 2000, 2001, 2010, 2013 by Life Sentence Publishing, Inc. Used by permission of Life Sentence Publishing, Inc., Abbotsford, Wisconsin. All rights reserved.

Scripture quotations marked KJV are from the King James Version of the Bible.

Scripture quotations marked NAS are from the New American Standard Bible, copyright © 1960, 1962, 1963, 1968, 1971, 1972, 1973, 1975, 1977, 1995 by The Lockman Foundation. Used by permission. (www.Lockman.org)

Scripture quotations marked NIV are taken from the Holy Bible, New International Version®, NIV®. Copyright © 1973, 1978, 1984, 2011 by Biblica, Inc.™ Used by permission of Zondervan. All rights reserved worldwide. www.zondervan.com. The "NIV" and "New International Version" are trademarks registered in the United States Patent and Trademark Office by Biblica, Inc.™

Scripture quotations marked NKJV are taken from the New King James Version®. Copyright © 1982 by Thomas Nelson. Used by permission. All rights reserved.

Scripture quotations marked YLT are from Young's Literal Translation.

Copyright © 2016 by Sylvia Rogers
All rights reserved

Cover design by Lisa Rae McClure
Design Director: Justin Evans

Visit the author's website at www.equippedtoheal.com.

Library of Congress Cataloging-in-Publication Data:
Names: Rogers, Sylvia H., author.
Title: Healing words / Sylvia Rogers.
Description: Lake Mary, Florida : Siloam, [2016] | Includes bibliographical
    references.
Identifiers: LCCN 2016011908| ISBN 9781629987309 (trade paper) | ISBN
    9781629987316 (e-book)
Subjects: LCSH: Medicine, Psychosomatic. | Mind and body. |
    Healing--Psychological aspects.
Classification: LCC RC49 .R64 2016 | DDC 616.08--dc23
LC record available at https://lccn.loc.gov/2016011908

This book contains the opinions and ideas of its author and is not intended to diagnose or prescribe. It is solely for informational and educational purposes and should not be regarded as a substitute for professional medical treatment. The nature of your body's health condition is complex and unique. Therefore, you should consult a health professional before you begin any new exercise, nutrition, or supplementation program or if you have questions about your health. Do not make any changes to your current medications without the advice of your doctor. Neither the author nor the publisher shall be liable or responsible for any loss or damage allegedly arising from any information or suggestion in this book.

The statements in this book about consumable products or food have not been evaluated by the Food and Drug Administration. The publisher is not responsible for your specific health or allergy needs that may require medical supervision. The publisher is not responsible for any adverse reactions to the consumption of food or products that have been suggested in this book.

While the author has made every effort to provide accurate Internet addresses at the time of publication, neither the publisher nor the author assumes any responsibility for errors or for changes that occur after publication.

First edition

16 17 18 19 20 — 9 8 7 6 5 4 3 2 1
Printed in the United States of America

CONTENTS

Part I
Prepared for Healing Victories:
Building a Strong Foundation of Health

Part II
Equipped to Heal:
Using Your God-Given Authority

Part III
Healing Hands:
Ministering to Others

ACKNOWLEDGMENTS

I WOULD LIKE TO thank my family for their support and my clients, who have contributed in unique and wonderful ways to the content of this book. I also give my utmost praise and gratitude to our marvelous, supernatural God, who took a copy of my first book, *The Pearl Box*, from a conference sale on the East Coast and put it in the hands of a pastor and his wife on the West Coast, who shared it with a local businesswoman, who then gave a copy to a book scout, who read it and then sent it to Charisma House in Florida. This book is a product of that miraculous journey.

PREFACE

*I*MAGINE YOU PICKED up an ancient book at an antique store and tucked it under your bed. That night you awake to a mysterious glow coming from under your bed. You wipe the sleep from your eyes and bend down to take a look, and there it is, larger than life, emanating a brilliant light. You open it, and inside the front cover are glowing letters:

WARNING: Supernatural power contained within. Read at your own risk of receiving the gifts it imparts.

Would you start reading?

This isn't just a make-believe story. There is, in fact, a wonderful, ancient book that contains great power. It is authored by a loving, supernatural being, and its truths can change your life *and your health*. We know this book as the Holy Bible, and it proclaims some startling revelations, including the fact that *you do not have to be sick!*

The remedies within its pages may shock and surprise you, as they are very different from the mainstream health remedies that are popular today. This Book explains that you have been created with the potential and ability to speak powerful, healing words that unleash the power of God and greatly impact the health of your body, mind, emotions, and spirit.

Can you envision a life in which you do not have to expect or experience colds, flu, depression, headaches, arthritis, diabetes, or even cancer? Your Creator can, and that life is what He desires for you.

I have written this book you hold in your hands to show you how to join forces with your loving Creator and experience a supernatural life of victory. If you choose to partner with Him, you can find freedom from illness, trauma, heartbreak, all of your past mistakes, and more.

The psalmist proclaimed that the Scriptures are a treasure, saying, "I rejoice at Your word as one who finds great treasure (Ps. 119:162, NKJV). And Apostle Peter wrote that Christ's "divine power has given to us all things that pertain to life and godliness through the knowledge of Him" (2 Pet. 1:3).

These are glorious truths that point to an immense promise. All things pertaining to life—*your life*—have been given. It has already been done. It is in the Book! "All things" includes every part of life, from our body systems all the way down to our cellular blueprints. The promise found in 2 Peter 1:3 is not one that is waiting for you in heaven. This promise is here for you to discover right now.

Will you embrace this truth and journey with me to discover the life-giving power of God's Word? Don't waste another moment in ill health of any sort. Join me on an adventure that could change your life. Are you ready?

INTRODUCTION

*W*HAT IF YOU could actually see the spoken Word of God impacting the health of your body systems? What if speaking God's Word and praying its principles over your body acted as a healing medicine the very moment you spoke them? That would be pretty awesome, wouldn't it? Actually this can happen, and the technology exists to view this amazing phenomenon. I am privileged to see this occur almost daily with my clients, family, and, yes, even our family dog through my creative use of a unique biofeedback computer, which has the capacity to detect over eight thousand stress patterns throughout the body and allow for creative treatment of them.

I have an education in Western medicine, but I have spent the majority of my career—more than thirty-four years—in the study, education, and teaching of natural methods of health and healing. Biofeedback has been one of my most fascinating tools.

During a biofeedback session, sensors are attached to the client's skin, usually by way of conductive bands placed around the person's head, wrist, and ankles. These sensors send signals to a monitor, which displays various images that represent the person's stress patterns and their response to treatments for them. The gathered data originates from body responses that are involuntary, and seeing these responses displayed on a computer screen often helps clients become more aware of what is happening inside their bodies.

The biofeedback device then helps to treat stressful patterns in clients by introducing computer-chosen frequencies into the body. The frequencies replicate the vitality within the unique molecular patterns contained in health-imparting herbs, flowers, vitamins, minerals, amino acids, and other natural elements. The body absorbs

1

these frequencies, which one might think of as healthy, body-healing blueprints, in much the way the body absorbs light waves from the sun and frequencies of sound from music. The body uses these life-giving frequencies to release stressful patterns, thereby assisting healthy body functions in much the same way nutritious food yields up energy that assists our body's ability to complete tasks. During each session, my clients are able to see fascinating changes occurring on the computer screen and feel the positive changes that are occurring in their bodies.

AN AMAZING, PIVOTAL EVENT

After using biofeedback technology for years to help people improve their health, I met with a turning point in the way I approached health one day when a client chose to pray aloud for two minutes, taking powerful authority over a specific emotional stress she saw reflected on the biofeedback screen. Using healing, scriptural words and promises, she commanded off all the stored anger and unforgiveness she perceived she was carrying toward a coworker.

Together we watched a dramatic and instant shift take place on the screen, indicating a significant release of stress. This was a profound moment of discovery for two reasons. First, the release of stress has far-reaching, positive effects on the body. Many medical professionals consider reducing stress key in preventing a majority of diseases. Second, this result occurred when the client treated herself verbally by praying truths from Scripture.

Since then most clients have chosen to participate in similar exercises. As they engage scriptural principles to command and release old emotional and traumatic baggage from the confines of their bodies, they witness similar stress-freeing results. These clients have literally treated themselves with minimal use of the computer, and the screens and graphs have responded in a profound manner!

This caused me to wonder whether holding unresolved hurts, toxic thinking patterns, and unsettled emotions inside our bodies can cause those stressful patterns to set up house within us—within our systems, our organs, our cellular blueprints, and even within the expression of our genes. Could these be at the root of imbalance, the storage of toxins, and disease? Could the simple act of commanding them out in faith remove them? I found some interesting food for thought on this possibility in the Book of Jeremiah:

> How long shall your evil thoughts lodge within you?
> —JEREMIAH 4:14

Lodge within you? That doesn't sound very good. Could ungodly thoughts and stressful emotions be contrary to God's will because of the damage they cause our bodies, our tissues, and possibly even the blueprints within our genes and DNA? I believe the answer is a resounding yes.

A multitude of scriptures declare that ungodly thoughts and poorly processed and buried emotions make us sick. As Proverbs 23:7 says, as we think in our hearts, so are we. My biofeedback computer's responses appear to agree. When clients use scriptural principles to verbally release toxic, stressful mind-sets and emotions from different parts of their bodies, they consistently and immediately experience fascinating results.

Once these unwanted patterns are evicted from specific parts of the body, I teach clients to fill those vacancies with the promises of divine health, healing, and victory found in God's Word. Leaving a vacant zone in the body, mind, or emotions opens it up to unwanted invasion that we may never full understand. Matthew 12:43–45 tells us:

> When an unclean spirit goes out of a man, it passes through dry places seeking rest, but finds none. Then it says, "I will return to my house from which I came." And when it comes, it finds it empty, swept, and put in order. Then it goes and brings with itself seven other spirits more evil than itself, and they enter and dwell there. And the last state of that man is worse than the first.

This is why clients fill the vacancies left with God's life-giving, healing truths that oppose and are resistant to the stress they have released. The goal is to prevent even worse stresses and oppressions from reentry and to gain long-term success.

As I began to join clients in praying over these unwanted patterns, I saw their faith in God's provision begin to grow rapidly, as did mine. I witnessed many wonderful and diverse results. Over time I settled upon a fairly consistent method to verbally release stressful patterns with the healing words of Scripture, and I am happy and blessed to share it here with you. I can tell you without a doubt that you have access to tremendous authority and power that can transform your health.

In this book we will look at many specific ways to receive and partake of God's treasure of healing as it relates to the following body systems:

✦ Immune	✦ Sensory	✦ Reproductive
✦ Lymphatic	✦ Digestive	✦ Circulatory
✦ Respiratory	✦ Excretory	✦ Nervous
✦ Endocrine	✦ Urinary	✦ Skeletal
✦ Muscular		

Some of these systems are regrouped and combined in specific ways to make the study and application of the principles easier. Bible verses that mention specific organs and healing principles are included. The goal is to help you learn to see, embrace, and speak these powerful healing verses over yourself (and others) and envision yourself able to receive the healing treasures God has already provided for you. Daily study of God's Word will keep you hungry for comprehensive and lasting results.

Seeing the improvement in my clients after they applied Scripture to their particular situation left me with many questions: Didn't miraculous healing die out two thousand years ago with the apostles as I had been taught for years? Could it still be available today? If so, how do we connect to and partake of these healing provisions? Are fear, doubt, and lack of knowledge getting in our way? Is unrepentant sin one way the devil gains legal access to our bodies, minds, and emotions to inflict oppression and disease? How many methods of healing has God given us to use? Has God given us answers to all diseases?

My biofeedback and these questions propelled me to study afresh what the Bible says about God's will to heal. What more amazing discoveries were waiting in God's Word? My excitement grew as I discovered documentaries that provided both medical and visual evidence of people who experienced wonderful and miraculous healings after learning to apply God's Word to their health.[1]

In August 2014 I attended an intensive healing conference titled "Healing Is Here," which was held in Woodland Park, Colorado. Instructors shared more than forty years of study into the scriptural basis for healing. I observed many people who, hungry for knowledge, found the courage to believe God's promises and received healing that week. A pile of crutches and braces was left by the stage, and I witnessed a paralyzed man rise out of a wheelchair.

In conversing with him later, I learned he had received partial healing of his upper spine two and a half years earlier when he received prayer and had hands laid on him by a faith-filled believer. He came to the healing conference after using those years to study God's promises related to healing and allow his faith to incubate and grow. He told me that he had come to the event confident and ready to receive the rest of his healing from God. There was a great stir in the audience as he rose to his feet with the aid of a few friends, slowly placed one foot in front of the other, and then crossed the room in front of the stage.

It was a privilege to witness knowledgeable, faith-filled teachers testifying of the progressive and miraculous results they'd experienced in their own lives. They were dedicated to growing in their understanding of how to use God's Word and promises as powerful healing tools for themselves and others.

I have grown to believe that every believer is called to be in health and assist others in their pursuit of wholeness. This should be a part of our normal, everyday lives. It is a growth process. The methods presented in this book provide many ways to unwrap different types of healing provisions from the Lord. Some require a minimum of spiritual growth and faith-building, and others require much more. Begin where you are comfortable and let the teachings meet you where you are.

WE MUST GAIN KNOWLEDGE

The potential for us to be healthy and whole would be so much greater if, from the time we were children, we learned in church about how to use God's healing promises so we could develop spiritual muscles of knowledge, trust, and faith. If that were part of most Christians' spiritual foundation, it would be much easier to understand how we can use God's Word to experience true wholeness.

Today's crisis is that the majority of our sick don't realize the victories they could be experiencing. Many Christians face the same depression, anxiety, obsessions, traumas, emotional bondage, addictions, and physical ailments as the rest of the world. Most look to the world's remedies and experience the world's results. Frustrated with their pain and suffering, the masses spend vast amounts of money trying to manage their illnesses at pharmacy counters or in the operating rooms of their surgeons.

It's not that those methods don't provide some relief. The problem is that the root issue is often elusive, and there are risks of harmful side effects with surgery and traditional approaches to treat disease. It is time for us to explore another doorway and embrace what God has already provided and promised in His Word.

Don't dwell in the barren desert of illness and infirmity. God wants you to be in health. It is time to make a life choice to move toward the healing rivers of victory that await all of us. You are important to God. He loves you to pieces! He wants you to be confident in His road to victory. He has given you amazing promises in Scripture to receive, feed upon, take a stand upon, and declare. These promises can lead you into a life of exciting, supernatural living!

> Do not remember the former things nor consider the things of old. See, I will do a new thing, now it shall spring

forth; shall you not be aware of it? I will even make a way in the wilderness, and rivers in the desert.

—ISAIAH 43:18–19

The Bible is a tremendous, comprehensive book on health. It is a mistake to put any limitations on it. If people knew what power was available to them, they would never leave the Bible on a shelf gathering dust. Investigating its truths will open up a thirst-quenching river of healing. The fruit of divine health is ripe and bountiful upon the healer's tree. The prophet Ezekiel wrote:

> By the river upon its bank, on this side and on that side, shall grow all kinds of trees for food, whose leaf shall not fade nor shall its fruit fail. They shall bring forth fruit according to their months, because their water issues out of the sanctuary. And their fruit shall be for food and their leaves for medicine.
>
> —EZEKIEL 47:12

God is a good Father. He provides for us and equips us for every good work—every one!—when we receive and activate His promises over our lives. Scripture tells us:

> All Scripture is inspired by God and is profitable for teaching, for reproof, for correction, and for instruction in righteousness, that the man of God may be complete, thoroughly equipped for every good work.
>
> —2 TIMOTHY 3:16–17

Is it a good work to have a healthy body so you can be in service to the Lord? The answer is yes! Sickness is never a blessing from God's point of view, but it may follow us around until we take a stand against it. Sickness is a vehicle used to kill, steal, and destroy our lives. That is the life mission of the devil (John 10:10). He gains access to oppress us when we live in ignorance and sin. That is not what God wants for you. He wants you free.

On our quest for knowledge we must first stand on a firm

foundation and learn to see our world, our lives, and God from His perspective. I had to do some intensive study to become more confident in many of the techniques you will learn in this book. I hope to make the learning process easier for you by condensing many of these foundational truths. Be prayerful as you begin this journey and ask the Holy Spirit to assist you in your learning process.

IT'S TIME TO TAKE
RESPONSIBILITY FOR YOUR HEALTH

I have been a Christian for the majority of my life, and I have always believed that God gave me—not just the doctor or dentist—the responsibility of investigating the best tools to achieve and maintain my health. Since I was the one having to live with the results of my choices, I wanted to be involved and knowledgeable.

My tender heart toward others propelled me into nursing school. However, after a few years I found more satisfaction in the pursuit of natural health techniques and in sharing information on the use of herbs, essential oils, and healthy lifestyle with others. I hated seeing the harmful side effects of drugs, and the more body-friendly tools were a joy to use and share.

I readily embraced a lifelong pursuit of God-given healing techniques that work without harming the body. I remained true to what I taught others, and I reaped the benefits. My pregnancies were healthy and my labors short (two were only four hours from start to finish!). My children grew to adulthood without requiring any prescriptions for illness.

My husband and I wanted to share our knowledge. The Herbal Health Center was the result. Here we teach and demonstrate God's strategies for optimal health to equip clients to take personal responsibility for their own health choices. God continually and generously shows us new and more excellent ways as we grow.

It is important to understand that all healing techniques that originated in the Bible may be placed under the umbrella of Christian spiritual healing, as it emanates from God's Word and is therefore God's will. If He has provided these techniques in His Word, I do not want to ignore or show disdain for any of them. These include important principles on the use of healthy food (including herbs), water, and essential oils, along with all God's other wonderful promises in Scripture.

"But what about my doctor?" When people begin expanding their knowledge base and become excited about new healing possibilities, this question often comes up. Let's face it. If we didn't have doctors, many people who are alive today would be dead. However, an unfortunate paradox is that a significant percentage of people who go to a doctor for healing die prematurely from unnecessary procedures, the side effects of prescription drugs, and the risk factors of surgery.

People who have conditions and no time to investigate other options often rely on emergency procedures and drastic measures to improve their health. Western medicine typically looks for the right drug or surgery to cure the vast array of complex diseases that plague people today. But the cause of most diseases is not a deficiency of medication or surgery. It is not even completely rooted in a poor diet or a lack of herbs and essential oils. Our ailments spring from not understanding the many promises for our health and healing present in the Word of God.

Jesus said, "It is written, 'Man shall not live by bread alone, but by every word that proceeds out of the mouth of God'" (Matt. 4:4). God's Word is life and health. It feeds our bodies certain life-giving properties they require. If we want to experience health and wellness, we must learn to balance and apply this truth.

Now, before I go further, I want to give a word of caution. Please do not stop taking your medications without consulting with your doctor. I expect you to feel better after applying the techniques in this book, but it is important that you have your doctor's guidance before changing or eliminating any medications. Any time you believe it wise to allow a trusted professional to monitor your progress, please do so.

The title *doctor* means *teacher*. Is your doctor teaching you how to become healthy, or is he or she simply suppressing your symptoms? Symptoms are not your enemy. They are your body's voice asking you to seek out the root cause of a problem. Always be informed about any medical procedures your doctor prescribes.

I often encourage people to find a Christian health professional who incorporates biblical principles for healing and is encouraging, positive, and supportive of your goals to not rely solely on prescription and surgical routes to experience good health. Be wary of anyone who speaks negativity over your future or places limitations on what you want to accomplish. If you hear the words *you can't, you'll never,* or *you won't,* stop and think. If you believe those words, they will likely become your reality. Always remember that nothing is impossible with God.

The next section will lay a strong foundation of understanding for addressing your healing. Don't skip it. Take time to apply it to your life and allow the Holy Spirit to be your guide as you move forward.

Part I

PREPARED FOR HEALING VICTORIES

---

*Building a Strong
Foundation of Health*

CHAPTER 1

YOUR RIGHT TO DIVINE HEALTH

*P*ORTIONS OF WHAT is contained in this book will work for everyone, but some of the most powerful truths within these pages cannot take effect unless you are in alignment with God's purpose for your life. That purpose is a truly wonderful one—it is to walk with the Lord and abide in Him, His Word, His strength, and His supernatural power as a son or daughter of God. Jesus said:

> I am the vine, you are the branches. He who remains in Me, and I in him, bears much fruit. For without Me you can do nothing.
>
> —JOHN 15:5

Without Him we can do nothing—that is, nothing of true consequence. On our own we are broken, mangled, sick, traumatized, marred, and unable to fulfill our true purpose in this life. We carry scars and baggage that weigh us down. We can't make ourselves good or holy enough to be in the presence of God, no matter how wonderful we appear to ourselves in the mirror. Our lives, when we choose to manage them by ourselves and live in our limited knowledge and strength, will always pale in comparison to the vision and power God has in mind for us.

Knowing this, God did something that didn't make sense. He sent His precious Son, Jesus, to suffer and die so we could be made righteous in His sight. He is willing to take mankind "as is," with all our faults and shortcomings, and make us part of His family. If we will surrender our lives to Him, our amazing God will transform the plainest lump of clay into a masterpiece. He has something more marvelous in mind for us than we could ever imagine. In fact, He loves us so much that He has prepared a place in heaven so that we may spend eternity with Him.

When we respond with a confident *yes* to God's invitation to receive the gift of salvation Jesus purchased on the cross, we say good-bye to a self-governed life and the shortsighted limitations this world provides, and say yes to a supernatural life governed by the principles in God's Word. When we as God's children believe His Word and embrace its truth as *the* truth, we can begin to walk in the promises of God—promises that yield supernatural results in our lives that cannot be fully explained.

Everything Jesus endured—being beaten and then crucified on a cross—was so we could walk in freedom and victory right now. If we embrace His forgiveness, power, gifts, and promises, we can use those supernatural powerhouses against sin, disease, demonic influences, mental and emotional bondage, and even premature death.

In our forgiven and reconciled state, we can begin to experience who our wonderful heavenly Father truly is: our Creator, our provider, our protector, our Redeemer, our deliverer, our healer, our hope, and our life. He is holy and glorious, gracious and merciful, wise and understanding. He is our power and our strength, and He is always good and faithful to fulfill all His promises. We must learn to stand in confidence upon His Word. He has anticipated every need we could ever have from the beginning of creation.

If you have not yet experienced God's gift of salvation, it is available to you now. Turn to appendix A to discover how to receive this free gift of eternal life and all the benefits that will flow into your life as a result. Your future victories depend on this.

As we come to know Him, we respond in love, gratitude, and praise. And we learn to lean into His love, power, and might. This opens our hearts to receive healing from God. You are to be the confident victor, not the helpless victim of your circumstances.

As God's child, He defines who you are. You are renewed (2 Cor. 4:16), accepted (Eph. 1:6), forgiven (Col. 1:13–14), spiritually transformed and sealed (Col. 1:21–22; 2 Cor. 1:21–22), a new creation (2 Cor. 5:17), a citizen of heaven (Phil. 3:20), anointed for a purpose

(1 John 2:27; 2 Tim. 1:9), the salt of the earth (Matt. 5:13–16), clothed with Christ's righteousness (Gal. 3:27), loved completely (Zeph. 3:17; John 3:16), part of a royal priesthood (1 Pet. 2:9), a saint (Eph. 1:18), His workmanship created for good works (Eph. 2:10), a member of His body (Eph. 3:6), His bride (Rev. 21:9), His church (Eph. 5:30; Col. 1:18), seated with Christ in a position of authority (Eph. 2:6), complete (Col. 2:9–10), set apart from the world (John 15:19), lacking nothing (James 1:4), thoroughly equipped (2 Tim. 3:17), more powerful than the devil (1 John 2:13–14), a temple and dwelling place for His Holy Spirit (1 Cor. 3:16), justified by Christ (Rom. 5:1), freed from bondage (Gal. 5:1), blessed with every spiritual blessing both coming in and going out (Eph. 1:3; Ps. 121:8), inseparable from the love of God (Rom. 8:37–39), able to heal the sick and cast out demons (Mark 16:17–18), and wholly able to remove the mountains in your life through the power of your words (Mark 11:23). What promises these are! What power and authority you possess! Align your mind and emotions with these truths and let go of everything else.

Jesus summarizes this amazing love that our God has toward us::

> I give them eternal life. They shall never perish, nor shall anyone snatch them from My hand.
>
> —John 10:28

I encourage you to memorize these wonderful words and read them aloud daily. They declare who you are in Christ, and they are incredible medicine for every cell in your body. God has you right in His hands. That means you are in the healer's hands and you are to see yourself there!

Christ followers have a special gift available to them that the world doesn't have: the Holy Spirit. It was the Holy Spirit—the power of God—who raised Christ from the dead, and it is the Holy Spirit who empowers the believer. That means you! If you have not yet asked for the gift of the Holy Spirit in your life, you have yet to claim the promised power that is available to you. But it is easy to claim God's gifts and promises. All it requires is that you ask:

If you then, being evil, know how to give good gifts to your children, how much more will your heavenly Father give the Holy Spirit to those who ask Him?

—LUKE 11:13

Ask now and know that it is done. Here is a sample prayer you can use as a guide.

Father, I thank You for sending Your promised Holy Spirit. I want to experience His power and presence in my life. You said all I need to do is ask for Your promises, so I ask You to fill me now with Your Holy Spirit. I praise You now that it is done because I have faith in Your Word. From this day forward I will walk in Your power and declare Your Word with boldness. In Jesus's name I pray. Amen.

It takes time to see ourselves as God sees us and to understand the authority we have over our lives and bodies. This knowledge is empowering and freeing. We have been given authority to speak powerful healing words over our bodies. Jesus has made us to be free of bondage and sickness.

TAKE YOUR SPIRITUAL VITAMINS DAILY

Once I roll out of bed in the morning, it is nonstop. A dozen things flood my mind that I need to do. The house always seems to need cleaning. So do the garage and the closets. All kinds of people want me to do something for them. They ask me to volunteer or to assist at events. Oh, and the kids need attention and the dog needs walking. I may have to skip lunch today if I'm not near any fast-food restaurants, and the doctor visits need scheduling. Somewhere in there I need to get the groceries. Exercise—what's that? Surely you jest!

Does this sound like your life? Do your days go by in a whirlwind, with an overflow of tasks that must be pushed into the next day?

This busyness is typical in many homes. We compensate by starting the day with a double latte and ending it with a cocktail of high-blood-pressure pills, antidepressants, and sleeping medications.

When a day is less busy, sometimes we take a moment to cram in our Bible reading and then go several days, weeks, or months before doing it again.

We would be in terrible trouble if we applied this same philosophy to our dental hygiene. I brush my teeth twice daily. What if I reasoned that I would get it over with for the week and in one day brushed my teeth fourteen times? Maybe I could brush them sixty times in one day, fulfilling the quota required for the month.

Am I starting to sound a little crazy? We all know the daily routine yields the best benefit for the health of our teeth. Likewise, a daily routine of being in the Word gives us essential spiritual vitamins suitable for our physical, mental, emotional, and spiritual health. We need our muscles in these areas to be strong. We shouldn't wait until we are sick and exhausted to begin studying God's Word for what it says about health and healing.

Consider this: How we feel each day depends on what we choose to magnify. If we choose to see ourselves as an equipped victor, daily exploring God's tools for success, we can more easily frame our day as an overcomer, reaping peace and joy with these efforts. Others, unaware or resistant to their spiritual source of nutrition, may choose to revel in the junk food of the negative, falling into the victim role and magnifying the problems of life in their thoughts, actions, and emotions. You have a choice. Your physical chemistry and emotions respond to what you think and magnify each day. Even your hormonal balance depends on how you interpret your world. This means that if we want healing from the Word and power of God, we have to make a conscious choice to regularly feast on the nutrient-rich sustenance of His Word. This is how we grow to our full strength and maturity.

Here is a convicting lesson on this point from Scripture:

> As they went, He entered a village. And a woman named Martha welcomed Him into her house. She had a sister called Mary, who also sat at Jesus' feet and listened to His teaching. But Martha was distracted with much serving, and

she came to Him and said, "Lord, do You not care that my
sister has left me to serve alone? Then tell her to help me."

Jesus answered her, "Martha, Martha, you are anxious
and troubled about many things. But one thing is needed.
And Mary has chosen the good part, which shall not be
taken from her."

—LUKE 10:38–42

Mary understood that the most critical thing she would do each
day was to get her daily spiritual nutrition, and Jesus validated her
important decision. However, His opponent, Satan, is committed
to our daily malnutrition and lures us toward it in the most creative
ways. He hates God's solutions for wholeness.

He nods his encouragement when we are too busy to study and
learn what God said in Scripture. If he can lure us away from God's
Word and entice us with mindless TV, video games, online surfing,
and other diversions, he can keep us from what he fears above all: our
growth in the knowledge of God's Word that leads us to receive our
healing promises and neutralize Satan's power.

The devil has never been a good sport about being defeated. He's
banking on you staying uninformed. He hopes you will believe God
is too busy to notice you challenges and that you turn instead to fear,
faithlessness, and frenetic energy when disaster strikes. He promotes
the lie that God has forgotten to provide any more than what the
world offers for our health. If he can get us to doubt that God's Word
has the power to bring health and wholeness due to our lack of knowledge, he knows he can increase our stress and sabotage our results.

This wavering is called being double-minded, and it breaks an
important connection with our heavenly Father, as the following
verse attests:

Let not that man think that he will receive anything from
the Lord. A double-minded man is unstable in all his ways.

—JAMES 1:7–8

Without knowledge, we lack belief, and without sound belief, we
become vulnerable:

My people are destroyed for lack of knowledge.

—Hosea 4:6

God wants everyone to be saved, but not everyone is:

The Lord is not slow concerning His promise, as some count slowness. But He is patient with us, because He does not want any to perish, but all to come to repentance.

—2 Peter 3:9

He wants everyone to be in good health, but not everyone is:

Beloved, I pray that all may go well with you and that you may be in good health, even as your soul is well.

—3 John 2

Wonderful people perish all the time from deficiencies of life-saving spiritual vitamins. We cannot be strong for battle when we are starving. So let us feast upon His Word each day, speaking it over our bodies to nourish, grow, and maintain our health. If our commitment to study God's Word determines how much we grow, I pray that we all become like spiritual oak trees, not flimsy twigs.

Nothing grows properly in God's universe apart from God's strength and nutrition. That's why the Bible tells us to "study to show yourself approved by God, a workman who need not be ashamed, rightly dividing the word of truth" (2 Tim. 2:15).

I want to challenge you to pull out your Bible each morning with your cup of tea, and start reading three to four chapters a day. Put a star by any verse that offers any health promise. Copy your favorites to a journal. Take time to ponder and digest what you are reading and how you can apply these truths to your life.

As an act of faith, open your mouth and declare (out loud) Psalm 1:2–4, which I have personalized for you:

My delight is in the law of the Lord, and in His law I meditate day and night. I shall be like a tree planted by the

rivers of water that brings forth its fruit in its season. My
leaf also shall not wither, and whatever I do shall prosper.

Now give the Lord praise for this wonderful promise because it
is fully yours!

GOD WANTS YOU TO BE IN GOOD HEALTH

Healing is a controversial topic in many churches. If we ask God to
heal us and don't see results, we might assume He doesn't want to
heal us, that our illness is meant to be a lesson, or that the healing
gifts stopped long ago. I believed some of these things too, until
I saw amazing and miraculous recoveries occur with people who
stopped listening to what others told them and began doing some
serious Bible study for themselves.

Let's turn to God's Word to discover God's will on healing:

> My son, attend to my words; incline your ear to my say-
> ings. Do not let them depart from your eyes; keep them in
> the midst of your heart; for they are life to those who find
> them, and health to all their body.
> —PROVERBS 4:20–22

> Jesus went throughout all the cities and villages, teaching in
> their synagogues, preaching the gospel of the kingdom, and
> healing every sickness and every disease among the people.
> —MATTHEW 9:35

> God anointed Jesus of Nazareth with the Holy Spirit and
> with power, who went about doing good and healing all
> who were oppressed by the devil, for God was with Him.
> —ACTS 10:38

> Beloved, I pray that all may go well with you and that you
> may be in good health, even as your soul is well.
> —3 JOHN 2

Jesus came to do His Father's will, which was to deliver people
from all forms of bondage and oppression in their bodies and souls.

Healing was a part of that deliverance. He never denied anyone or told anyone they were unworthy. God's will is the same yesterday, today, and tomorrow.

Jesus, the Word of God, demonstrated firsthand how healing works. All of God's words are for us today. Proverbs 4:20–22 promises that His words are life to all your body. There is no tissue or body system that the words and promises of God cannot penetrate to minister life and health. He says so!

I believe the reason some are healed and some are not is because of how they handle the Word of God. God's ways are different from our ways. It takes study and knowledge to claim the promises available to us. Look, for example, at the promise of this passage:

> Bless the LORD, O my soul, and all that is within me, bless His holy name. Bless the LORD, O my soul, and forget not all His benefits, who forgives all your iniquities, who heals all your diseases, who redeems your life from the pit, who crowns you with lovingkindness and tender mercies, who satisfies your mouth with good things, so that your youth is renewed like the eagle's.
>
> —PSALM 103:1–5

When it says God heals *all* your diseases, it means all of them—no exceptions.

Furthermore, do you see an order implied in this passage? I believe this is important, and we will use it as our guide.

+ When you come to God to accept His treasures of healing, first bless—speak well of—Him and praise Him from your heart. Praise Him for all His benefits and blessings, no matter what your circumstances.

+ Then become your best self by repenting and confessing any of your sins, especially any unforgiveness you carry toward yourself, others, or God.

+ Lastly acknowledge the healing promises God has already given you and the specific scriptures in which

you are placing your trust. Declare your belief that
these scriptures are now at work within your being,
imparting life and healing. See His healing power
flowing through you and Jesus the healer nourishing
each cell of your body and restoring it to wholeness.

God is eager for you to be well. He has done His part already and
puts the receiving of it into your hands. See God's healing power as
a well of living water within you. You simply need to draw from it
on a daily basis.

We do this by walking in love toward God and man, and
releasing and forsaking any sin that tries to ensnare and distract us.
Then, standing on His promises of healing and restoration, with no
wavering or unbelief, we withdraw healing power by declaring His
promises to us and believing them. This turns the waters of healing
loose to permeate our lives.

If you continually beg for healing as if it were a whim of God's or
something "out there somewhere" that you don't have access to, you
will invite emotional stress, and God is going to wonder why you
don't take hold of what has already been provided for you. He has
already said yes to your healing. I can plead for fresh tomatoes all
day to appear in my kitchen, but I can usually get better results if
I just go out back and pick them from my garden. The same is true
for you. God's promises of healing are yours and available for the
taking. They are scattered as pearls throughout the Scriptures. You
only need to pick them up.

Let's Dig Deeper

A tremendous gift was given to mankind that many only understand and receive in part. We are taught that forgiveness of sin is
available, but many of us have not been taught that healing is also
available for the body, mind, and emotions. In case you believe the
word *healed* applies to only our spirits or the forgiveness of sins, let's
dig a little deeper.

Nirpā[1]

First, consider this passage in Isaiah:

> Surely he has borne our grief and carried our sorrows; yet
> we esteemed him stricken, smitten of God, and afflicted.
> But he was wounded for our transgressions, he was bruised
> for our iniquities; the chastisement of our peace was upon
> him, and by his stripes we are *healed*.
>
> —ISAIAH 53:4–5, EMPHASIS ADDED

The word *healed* here, in the original Hebrew, is *nirpā*. This
Hebrew word occurs just four times in Scripture, with the three
additional uses being found here:

> But if the scale appears not to have changed and there is
> black hair growing in it, then the scale is healed.
>
> —LEVITICUS 13:37

> And the priest shall go out of the camp, and the priest shall
> examine him and see if the disease is healed in the leprous
> person.
>
> —LEVITICUS 14:3

> If the priest comes in and examines it and sees the disease
> has not spread in the house after the house was plastered,
> then the priest shall pronounce the house clean, because
> the disease is healed.
>
> —LEVITICUS 14:48

Notice that each of these references refers to physical healing.
God is concerned about our bodies!

Have you ever wondered why before Jesus was crucified, God
allowed Him to be scourged, the most painful of all whippings
during which flesh is torn? It is because this scourging is where
Jesus received His physical stripes, and our physical healing was
purchased by those stripes.

Sōzō

Additionally we find a wonderful Greek word, *sōzō*, used more than 110 times in the New Testament. It is often translated *save*, *saved*, *healed*, *delivered*, or *made whole*. Strong's Concordance defines it "to save," "deliver or protect," "heal, preserve, save (self), do well, be (make) whole."[2]

Clearly this includes more than the forgiveness of sins. Yes, it is true that *sōzō* is translated *save* and *saved* many times in reference to the forgiveness of sins. However, this same word is also translated as *healed* in the account of Jairus, whose daughter Jesus raised from the dead (Mark 5:23). He asked Jesus to heal (*sōzō*) his daughter. In Luke 8:36 the same word is used to describe a deliverance from demons. Paul healed (*sōzō*) a lame man in Acts 14:8–10. James 5:15 mentions physical healing and the forgiveness of sins together by saying the prayer of faith shall *sōzō* the sick.

Sōzō is a wonderful, comprehensive term that includes the forgiveness of sins, the healing of the body, wholeness, and deliverance from evil oppression. This is true healing.

Thorns in the flesh

Many times people point to the Apostle Paul to "prove" that God didn't remove what Paul called his thorn in the flesh:

> And lest I should be exalted above measure by the abundance of the revelations, a thorn was given me in the flesh, a messenger of Satan, to torment me.
>
> —2 CORINTHIANS 12:7

This thorn in the flesh has often been assumed to be a physical ailment, and some may conclude that this proves it isn't God's will that everyone be healed. You might believe that if God allowed Paul to suffer some physical ailment, He may want you to suffer this in kind. This could lead you toward doubt and confusion about your health and why you are suffering.

I have hope to offer you. In the Old Testament certain terminology was used—references to "thorns in your sides" and "thorns in your eyes"—to refer to the ungodly people of the land, their evil deeds, and their harassment. See, for example:

> But if you do not drive out the inhabitants of the land from before you, then those whom you let remain will be like thorns in your eyes and thorns in your sides. They will show hostility to you in the land in which you live.
>
> —NUMBERS 33:55

> Know for certain that the LORD your God will no longer drive out these nations from before you. But they shall be snares and traps to you, a whip on your sides and thorns in your eyes.
>
> —JOSHUA 23:13

Now, please consider this. Paul dealt with hostile people all the time. He was beaten, stoned, shipwrecked, left for dead, jailed, and suffered all kinds of persecution. He no doubt looked awful after most of these incidences. People were concerned about his eyes at one point. Do some further reading on Paul's life and note how quickly he seemed to miraculously recover after incidents that would put the average man in the hospital for weeks, if not months.

Is it possible Paul's "thorn in the flesh" referred to those who did him harm—those he was asking God to remove from his life—rather than any physical ailment? After all, he suffered many physical ailments, as we have just seen, and yet he continued on in a marvelous, potentially miraculous way. I share this with you so you can be sure the "thorn in the flesh" argument against God's intent to heal isn't necessarily sound or foolproof.

FEASTING AT THE LORD'S TABLE

Once we believe God wants us healthy and whole, we must build an arsenal of promises we can use to do battle when the need arises. This takes time, and it may frustrate us when we want healing to come faster than we can gain the knowledge of how to receive it. This is why it is best to study God's ways *before* we get sick. Fear, unresolved sin, feelings of unworthiness, and other blocks can distort our view of God and how we trust Him, and these must go in order for us to be receptive to complete health and wholeness.

Our spiritual health and relationship with our Lord will always be the cornerstone upon which we build everything. Physical healing flows from this. Wouldn't our children grow into powerful, equipped adults if they were given this foundation from the time they are toddlers?

Now, I want to walk you through the process of receiving a promise that I have seen wipe out many types of stress in biofeedback. It often works quite quickly, to my delight!

To begin, let's look at a few foundational verses. The first is from 2 Peter:

> Grace and peace be multiplied to you through the knowledge of God and of Jesus our Lord.
>
> His divine power has given to us *all things* that pertain to life and godliness through the knowledge of Him who has called us by His own glory and excellence, by which He has given to us exceedingly great and precious promises, so that through these things you might become partakers of the divine nature.
>
> —2 PETER 1:2–4, EMPHASIS ADDED

In this passage we see that God has given us *all things* pertaining to life and godliness. They are ours now; they have already been given. We can count on them:

> For all the promises of God in Him are "Yes," and in Him "Amen," to the glory of God through us.
>
> —2 CORINTHIANS 1:20

Now this is a promise that has a great effect. It is true that while we are on this planet, we face enemies of our health and welfare. God is aware of this and made a safe place for us, right at His supernatural dining room table:

> You prepare a table before me in the presence of my enemies.
> —PSALM 23:5

Our part is to choose to take a seat and to see ourselves there. This table is a place of rest and safety from the intrusion of the world—that is, if we choose to stay seated and keep our eyes focused on God and His provisions. In 2 Peter we just read that we can rest in His divine power that is available now, giving us *everything*—all things!—pertaining to life and godliness. This "life" includes our physical life, mental life, emotional life, and spiritual life. No exceptions are named.

Psalm 23:5 makes it clear where we receive this life. It is at the table God has prepared for us in the very presence of our enemies. God invites us to take a seat at the most incredible table you have ever seen, conceived in the mind of God thousands of years before we were even born. This table isn't meant for our future in heaven—notice that the passage speaks of enemies being present, and you have no enemies in heaven. This is a promise for you now.

Take a moment and visualize what this table might look like. In my mind it is encrusted with brilliant gems and has comfortable, plush velvet chairs. Spiritual power and life shine from every delectable morsel lavished upon it. Remedies housed in gemstone bowls promote a healthy body, a healthy mind, and healthy emotions. No expense was spared in the setting of this table. There are wondrous things here to partake of—everything pertaining to my life and godliness, as well as yours. He says so! The enemies to your life and health cannot touch you here.

Now envision yourself taking a seat at this table. Once you are comfortable, you are invited by your dad to dine to your heart's content. Don't turn your chair around. Don't get up. You can't dine properly in those positions, and they will only make you vulnerable to the enemy's attack.

Look at the table for what you need. What if you said, "Please pass the vials of joy, peace, patience, faith, and confidence. *Mmmm,* those are wonderful! Now please pass my perfect heart remedy, my freedom-from-addiction smoothie, my perfect thyroid remedy, and

those new genes to replace any defective elements." I like to visualize each one of these in the form of a delectable golden liquid. I
take my time drinking each one until I see them filling my entire
being completely from my toes to the top of my head.

What do you need for your mental, emotional, and physical health? What do you need for absolute wholeness? Envision
yourself gratefully receiving these into your cup and thoroughly
quenching your thirst. Really feel and see yourself doing this.
Sometimes my clients use a cup as a prop, imagining it filled and
pressing it to their lips. See this cup filled to overflowing with
everything you need, crowding out all impurities because of the
powerful name of Jesus.

Your heavenly Father nods His approval as He passes His delicacies to you. This supernatural food never runs out. We can trust in
its goodness, and it tastes fantastic!

> Oh, taste and see that the LORD is good; blessed is the man
> who takes refuge in Him.
>   —PSALM 34:8

I hope you eat and drink to your heart's content at this table
each day. Here you can visualize any sickness melting away and
being replaced with wholeness, love, forgiveness, and the perfect
markers of health. If you are sick, don't just spend a minute on
this. Spend an hour each day if you need to do so. This table is
a place of life, and the biofeedback graphs echo the wonderful
changes that can result.

Don't take your eyes off the table, no matter what distracting
report you get from man. The devil would love to distract you from
the table. He is waving his arms and doing a song and dance in the
corner, trying to get your attention so you will stop eating. Quote
scripture back at him and declare the promises that are yours in the
name of Jesus—he hates that and will leave to find someone else to
torment. Then settle in and enjoy another serving!

Here are some of the wonderful morsels you'll find on the Lord's
bountiful table:

+ A hope and a future (Jer. 29:11)

+ Power over weakness, renewed strength, release from fatigue, the ability to run and walk (Isa. 40:29–31)

+ Life to all your flesh (Prov. 4:22)

+ The ability to conquer obstacles (Rom. 8:37)

+ God's love (Rom. 8:39)

+ Peace for your heart (John 14:27)

And these are just the appetizers!

There are many more courses in this meal prepared for you, and this table is available to you each and every day, all day long. God has said yes to you. Partake each day until you are whole.

We will discuss the power of seeing things before they exist in chapter 4. But for now remember that our God spoke everything that exists into being. The earth and everything in it was real in God's mind before it ever became real in the physical world. In much the same way I believe God wants us to exercise our faith and visualize Him moving in our lives to bring healing. This is why throughout this book I will encourage you to see yourself at the King's table, drinking of His healing remedies. And it is why I include diagrams of the various body systems in part 2—so you can see exactly which part of your body needs to come into alignment with God's Word.

Now that we understand it is God's will to heal, we must realize our authority as sons and daughters of God. Read on to discover the power at your disposal through the mighty name of Jesus.

CHAPTER 2

KNOW YOUR AUTHORITY

*T*HE BIBLE STATES that Christ is our head and we are His body—His hands and feet on this planet, equipped and empowered by Him, with His authority and power that flows through us. He intends for us to follow in His footsteps and accomplish His will on earth. Many aspects of your health may have been turned over to you to address. This is truly a provocative thought and we need to take a look at it.

We have been given a position of authority over the created life God put on this earth:

> Then God said, "Let us make man in our image, after our likeness, and let them have dominion over the fish of the sea, and over the birds of the air, and over the livestock, and over all the earth, and over every creeping thing that creeps on the earth."
>
> —GENESIS 1:26

Do various germs, bacteria, parasites, worms, amoebas, and other nasty plagues that can attack our bodies creep upon the earth? I have seen them under a microscope, and they definitely move (and many are certainly creepy!). They are most certainly included in our realm of dominion. We have been placed above them in creation. They are our subjects; we are not theirs.

As Christ's body, we, the church, also have been given the authority to operate in the powerful name of Jesus, as He is our head. We may boldly speak according to His will in His name. What is so special about His name? It's more powerful than anything on this earth that can rise against you.

> Therefore God highly exalted Him and gave Him the name
> which is above every name, that at the name of Jesus every
> knee should bow, of those in heaven and on earth and
> under the earth.
>
> —Philippians 2:9–10

I use the powerful name of Jesus when taking authority over my body. Sickness, virus, bacteria, fungus, plague, depression, anxiety, fear, grief, Satan—any foe that could possibly oppress me has a name. I have the authority to command each one to bow and be subject to Jesus's name and be placed under His feet. They must bow to His power and authority, which is enveloped in His name and what He has said in His Word.

Please take note, as I mentioned at the start of the previous chapter, we must first abide in a healthy relationship with the Lord and have His Word abiding in us in order to exercise this authority:

> If you abide in Me, and My words abide in you, you will ask
> what you desire, and it shall be done for you.
>
> —John 15:7, nkjv

Has an unknown illness reared its ugly head in your life? You have the authority to name it. Just as you name your children and your pets, which have also been placed under your authority, so you can give name to your disease and place it under your dominion too. You may even name any mysterious, perplexing syndrome the doctor can't figure out and place it under the name of Jesus and under your feet. Then give it the stomping of a lifetime! One woman named her illness Bill. She named it and embarked on a journey to command her body to kill it each day, and it worked!

While you are at it, take authority over the devil also. This works only after you have closed the doors of your life to him by confessing and turning away from any sin you may entertain. The issue that is often the biggest mountain to conquer is unforgiveness and its resulting guilt, bitterness, and hatred. We do not have to bear this burden. Verbally give the injustice to the true and righteous judge, the Lord, and let the weight slide from your shoulders. God will take care of all injustices at the right time. When we hold on to unforgiveness, which we have no legal right to in the sight of God, Satan walks right in that unguarded door and wreaks havoc, claiming his legal right to kill, steal, and destroy your life. The way to stop him is to understand that he is our chief opponent; submit ourselves to God's truth, making it our chief weapon; and subject Satan to hearing the Word of the Lord from our lips.

> For our fight is not against flesh and blood, but against principalities, against powers, against the rulers of the darkness of this world, and against spiritual forces of evil in the heavenly places.
> —EPHESIANS 6:12

> Perhaps God will grant them repentance to know the truth, and they may escape from the snare of the devil, after being captured by him to do his will.
> —2 TIMOTHY 2:25–26

> Therefore submit yourselves to God. Resist the devil, and he will flee from you.
> —JAMES 4:7

> You are of God, little children, and have overcome them, because He who is in you is greater than he who is in the world.
> —1 JOHN 4:4

Satan is on an aggressive mission to kill, steal, and destroy everything God loves. You are a prime target. He is angry and miserable over the punishment awaiting him, and he wants you to suffer in kind. He seeks those who are vulnerable, who passively let sin take hold in their lives, and those who are unarmed, ignorant of God's powerful tools, so he can devour their lives in creative, terrible ways.

Acknowledge the power of God within you. Pick yourself up. Get off Satan's menu and out of his dinner plate. It is a sick, ugly place.

The sad part is that we tend to blame God if we fall onto Satan's dinner dish when Christ has given us the power to escape. Christ disarmed and defeated the devil over two thousand years ago through His death and resurrection:

> Having disarmed principalities and powers, He made a public spectacle of them, triumphing over them in it.
> —COLOSSIANS 2:15, NKJV

Historically defeated kings were paraded publicly through town, sometimes naked, with their thumbs cut off to show they could no longer grasp a sword and with their big toes removed so they could no longer charge forth in battle. Their power was stripped away, and that dissolved any fear the people had of them.[1]

Similarly Satan has been thoroughly disarmed—publicly conquered through the death and triumphant resurrection of Christ. But he will act as if he isn't defeated unless we fearlessly and boldly take authority over him and put him in his place.

This is why it is also important to study the armor of God—and wear it. We have a very real opponent whom God says we must deal with in our battles. In any case of illness you must proclaim Satan's defeat through Christ and resist him with Scripture.

> Finally, my brothers, be strong in the Lord and in the power of His might. Put on the whole armor of God that you may be able to stand against the schemes of the devil. For our fight is not against flesh and blood, but against principalities, against powers, against the rulers of the darkness of this world, and against spiritual forces of evil in the heavenly places. Therefore take up the whole armor of God that you may be able to resist in the evil day, and having done all, to stand. Stand therefore, having your waist girded with truth, having put on the breastplate of righteousness, having your feet fitted with the readiness of the gospel of peace, and above all, taking the shield of faith, with which you will be able to extinguish all the fiery arrows of the evil one. Take the helmet of salvation and the sword of the Spirit, which is the word of God.

Pray in the Spirit always with all kinds of prayer and
supplication. To that end be alert with all perseverance and
supplication for all the saints.
                                          —EPHESIANS 6:10–18

Remind the devil of your righteousness in Christ and proclaim
that it is written that he is disarmed and helpless before you because
of what Jesus accomplished on the cross. Then believe and boldly
act like you have victory over the enemy. Have a good laugh at his
expense. Resist him with powerful scriptures you verbally proclaim
to express who you are and who he is—conquered and defeated!—
and he will flee from you.

PASSING THE HEALING ON

Jesus taught His followers their authority, and they did the works
Jesus did, which included using the power of the Holy Spirit in
laying hands on and healing the sick. Paul taught the churches to
do the same:

Imitate me, just as I also imitate Christ.
                                    —1 CORINTHIANS 11:1, NKJV

Just before Jesus left this earth, He commanded His disciples to
go teach others what He had taught them. He left instructions that
His work was to be passed on:

Then the eleven disciples went away to Galilee, to the mountain to which Jesus had directed them....Jesus came and
spoke to them, saying, "All authority has been given to Me
in heaven and on earth. Go therefore and make disciples of
all nations, baptizing them in the name of the Father and
of the Son and of the Holy Spirit, teaching them to observe
all things I have commanded you."
                  —MATTHEW 28:16, 18–20, EMPHASIS ADDED

Again, *all things* means *all things*. Jesus sent His followers to cast
out devils, raise the dead, heal the sick, free the sinner, and preach

the entire gospel of good news. Healing was taught to new believers, as it was expected they would take hold of this teaching:

> Truly, truly I say to you, he who believes in Me will do the works that I do also. And he will do greater works than these, because I am going to My Father.
> —John 14:12

You are to be Jesus with skin on in this life. You are to both receive healing and pray for others to receive healing.

If you were taught as I was that only the apostles or those they laid hands on could heal, then take a look at this interesting account of a person who ministered in the area of healing with no special qualifications. He wasn't an apostle—he didn't even physically associate with their group—yet he was a believer, doing miracles in Jesus's name:

> John answered Him, "Teacher, we saw one who does not follow us casting out demons in Your name, and we forbade him because he was not following us."
> But Jesus said, "Do not forbid him, for no one who does a miracle in My name can quickly speak evil of Me. For he who is not against us is for us."
> —Mark 9:38–40

This example should silence any argument that we cannot pray for people to receive healing or that healing is a work of the devil. Healing in Jesus's name is always an act for the Lord.

The same power that raised Jesus from the dead is available to us who believe. What God says is true. Take Him at His Word. See the wisdom, knowledge, understanding, hope, riches, and greatness of His power that He wants you to possess:

> That the God of our Lord Jesus Christ, the Father of glory, may give you the Spirit of wisdom and revelation in the knowledge of Him, that the eyes of your understanding may be enlightened, that you may know what is the hope of His calling and what are the riches of the glory of His inheritance

among the saints, and what is the surpassing greatness of
His power toward us who believe, according to the working
of His mighty power, which He performed in Christ when
He raised Him from the dead and seated Him at His own
right hand in the heavenly places, far above all principalities,
and power, and might, and dominion, and every name that is
named, not only in this age but also in that which is to come.
—EPHESIANS 1:17–21

Notice the immensity of power that is available to us who
believe—the same power that raised Christ from the dead. Now
envision yourself sitting with Jesus. He is sitting at the right hand
of God, a place of authority, and we are sitting there with Him as
His body. We are actually living in two places at once—here on
earth and at the right hand of God the Father:

But God…even when we were dead in sins, *made us* alive
together with Christ (by grace you have been saved), and
He raised us up and seated us together in the heavenly
places in Christ Jesus.
—EPHESIANS 2:4–6, EMPHASIS ADDED

Here, the phrase *made us* is in the past tense. That means it has
already happened. We are now sitting with Him in the heavenly
places, and we are in Christ.

We are the living body of Christ the healer, and we have been
given charge to speak in Christ's name on this planet. What He has
spoken we may echo as we are joined to Him. He is the source of
our power over illness. It is my intention through this book to wake
up that power within us all!

Don't frustrate the Holy Spirit by keeping Him locked in a closet.
He has work to do in your life and in the lives of those you touch.
As you work on your own healing, daily pray the prayer we just read
in Ephesians 1, starting at verse 17, until it drops into your very core,
becoming one with your heart and mind.

As you discover your authority as a follower of Christ, it is also important that you realize you have the power and authority to come into agreement with another person regarding anything that is the will of God, such as your wellness, and have it done for you. Jesus said,

> Again I say to you, that if two of you agree on earth about anything they ask, it will be done for them by My Father who is in heaven.
>
> —MATTHEW 18:19

You also have the authority to cast out demons (who can cause illness) and act as a vehicle of God's power as you lay hands on the sick. Remember, this is a work done in Jesus's name, not of yourself:

> He said to them, "Go into all the world, and preach the gospel to every creature. He who believes and is baptized will be saved. But he who does not believe will be condemned. These signs will accompany those who believe: In My name they will cast out demons...they will lay hands on the sick, and they will recover."
>
> —MARK 16:15–19

We are positioned far above any power of the devil, far above the power of any name that is named on this earth. Christ is seated in a position of authority, we are seated with Him and in Him, and He, the healer, is in us. It is important that you see yourself in this way to understand the authority you have right now.

We become conquerors through the power of Christ (Rom. 8:37). We can do nothing without Him, but with Him all things are possible. When this truth becomes locked inside your heart, you will have many victories. Expect them!

THE IMPORTANCE OF DAILY PRAISE

The Bible tells us to "rejoice in every good thing which the LORD your God has given to you and your house" (Deut. 26:11). And we read in the New Testament, "But you are a chosen race, a royal priesthood, a holy nation, a people for God's own possession, so that you may declare the goodness of Him who has called you out of darkness into His marvelous light" (1 Pet. 2:9).

Our daily praise, thanksgiving, and joy in the Lord are good indicators of our spiritual health. He deserves our gratitude and adoration, and we can find many examples of praise throughout the Bible, especially in the Book of Psalms. Consider favorites you can call upon, whether in word or song, to build your joy and master your emotions so you may live in a state of peace. Here are just a few:

> Enter into His gates with thanksgiving, and into His courts with praise; be thankful to Him, and bless His name.
>
> —PSALM 100:4

> Glory in His holy name; let the heart of those who seek the LORD rejoice.
>
> —1 CHRONICLES 16:10

> All the people came up to see him and played flutes and greatly rejoiced, so that the earth shook at the sound.
>
> —1 KINGS 1:40

A beneficial side effect of daily praise is a calmer emotional response to emergencies when they arise. Praise is a powerful medicine against fear, which is the enemy of faith. We are not to be anxious for anything. See yourself entering His gates as a beloved son or daughter, full of boldness and confidence in your dad. See your heart open to Him and His compassion for healing. His hand and scepter are outstretched toward you in welcome. Can you visualize this promise happening? Imagine the impact on you for peace, confidence, and steadfastness if you continue to do this!

Begin all your prayers with praise, no matter how difficult your circumstances. If you received news that a loved one was in an accident and in critical condition, what would it be like for you to first stop, calm your emotional response, and praise the Lord for His love, power, and mighty promises of healing for fifteen minutes before going forth, armed with the good reports of scripture and God's promises to proclaim over your loved one? I realize this reaction flies in the face of our natural response to traumatic news, which is to become fearful. But praise is extremely valuable because of the way it can focus our hope and faith in the face of worldly events.

I have heard some wonderful testimonies of the supernatural trumping the natural during dire situations when the person first approached the Lord in a state of praise, acknowledging His power and goodness until their volatile emotions gave way to confidence, boldness, and peace. Praise creates a strong, loving connection between us and our Lord, allowing the door to open for miracles to occur, even in the darkest of hours.

I am reminded of the account of Thurman Scrivner, a Bible teacher and healing minister, who received news while teaching a course on healing that his wife and daughter were killed in a car accident and that his granddaughter was severely injured and on life support.[2] Before going to Cook Medical Center in Fort Worth, Texas, he spent twenty minutes in prayer. He didn't echo the finality of the event. He didn't blame God. He remembered what Job did when he worshipped the Lord after hearing that a tragedy had befallen his family and all ten of his children had died:

> Then Job stood up, tore his robe, and shaved his head. He fell to the ground *and worshipped*.
> —JOB 1:20, EMPHASIS ADDED

Thurman chose to do likewise. He proclaimed God to be a good God, the King of kings, and he praised God for His promises. Then he went to the hospital, determined to fight for his granddaughter's life.

At the hospital he was confronted with *the report*. The doctor's stated that his granddaughter would never breathe on her own due to multiple fractures, organ damage, and a completely severed brain stem. Her head was twice the proper size and covered with cuts and bruises. The nerves attaching her eyes to her brain were totally disconnected. She was a shocking sight.

Thurman was able to resist fear and stand up to the doctors prognosis because he was already prepared through his study of the promises of God. He stood upon these promises and reminded God of His faithfulness to His Word, citing 2 Corinthians 1:20: "For all the promises of God in Him are 'Yes,' and in Him 'Amen,' to the glory of God through us."

Thurman reminded God that he, Thurman Scrivner, was a faithful follower. He reminded God of his devoted study of the Word and said he believed he walked in love toward others, as Christ commanded. He reminded God of His promises.

Then, in steadfast belief that God would fulfill His promise, he asked God for a full recovery for his granddaughter—that she would have no brain damage or scars and that she would breathe on her own when taken off the respirator. Then he did something extremely bold. He put his faith to work by guaranteeing to her doctor that his granddaughter would breathe on her own when taken off the respirator.

Thurman made his reality God's Word, and he was unwilling to accept anything other than the vision of what God said. And for the next ten hours he sat by his granddaughter's bed and praised and worshipped, thanking God for His provision. Through the week that followed, he and his family stood patiently firm, declaring God's promises. The entire situation was steeped in praise and the promises of God.

Thurman's granddaughter, about whom the doctor declared no hope of recovery, confounded science. Against all natural law, she began to breathe on her own when taken off the respirator. After thirty days in intensive care, that little girl went home. Every cut, bruise, and scar was gone, and she functions normally today.

We can have this type of triumph in our lives if we are diligent to prepare ourselves properly, as Thurman did. A key piece of his victory was his confidence and mastery of emotions through praise. The Scriptures proclaim that God inhabits the praises of His people. His diligence allowed Thurman to have unwavering belief and rest in God's promises. Beginning with praise calmed his emotions, pushed out fear, and drew him and the Lord together as a unified force.

We can learn from this wonderful account to apply praise too as we approach God confidently with our personal concerns.

What We Have Learned

We have covered a lot of ground in these first two chapters, but it is the most important foundation you can build in this process of learning to speak God's healing words and promises into reality within your life. We've seen the importance of having an abiding relationship with Christ to begin, then added the importance of daily Scripture reading to build your arsenal of promises for battle, then confirmed God's will for you to be in good health. We saw that God's desire for your healing extends to all your life—body, mind, spirit, and emotions—and we sat down at the bountiful table of God to visualize and partake of the feast of healing blessings God lays out for us. We confirmed the truth of our authority over illness, over Satan, and over any illness encountered in others we might be invited to counter on their behalf. Lastly, we studied how praise pushes out fear, calms our emotions, and draws us to the Lord for our healing.

Are you seeing the beautiful picture that is beginning to take form? Are you ready to step into the fullness of life God has for you? Will you say "yes" and "amen" to the words God has spoken over you that bring life and length to your days? If so, let's move forward and discover the power contained in our words.

CHAPTER 3

THE POWER OF YOUR WORDS

*Y*OUR WORDS HAVE a supernatural component that is a special gift from God. They do more than communicate. Words contain a God-given vitality with frequencies and vibrations that can be scientifically measured. Voice analysis technology is now showing that our voices can reveal certain important facets of our health.[1] Though the technology is relatively new, we have long known that our voices change in subtle ways when we are well and when we are sick, and even more dramatically when we are young and when we are old. This is God's work as a master physicist. He has designed our voices to not only reflect our health, but also to produce language and words that can medicinally target and penetrate our bodies at their cellular core.

Words are one of the most powerful spiritual tools available to us. What we say can promote life and health or depression, hopelessness, and despair. Think of words as invisible containers into which we can inject meaning, intention, power, boldness, confidence, faith, and more. If we use them according to God's will, we will literally speak His encouraging, life-giving, healing words into our bodies. Healing sound frequencies and vibrations are already being used to treat the physical body.[2] Speaking God's healing Word, whether to ourselves or others, can have the same effect.

The Bible affirms that words can be used to promote life or death. We have an awesome responsibility to use them properly. We can feel confident that we have His approval when we apply His Word as a healing medicine to our bodies, speaking His truth and His promises over our entire being and over others who are in need.

Death and life are in the power of the tongue: and they
that love it shall eat the fruit thereof.

—PROVERBS 18:21, KJV

For the word of God is alive, and active, and sharper than
any two-edged sword, piercing even to the division of soul
and spirit, of joints and marrow, and able to judge the
thoughts and intents of the heart.

—HEBREWS 4:12

Words penetrate into our joints and marrow. When we are
speaking to someone, we are impacting them at the level of their soul,
spirit, and body. Do you see how our words can powerfully affect us
and others—physically, emotionally, mentally, and spiritually—in
ways we may not consciously realize?

When godly words and principles of health and healing have
been spoken during biofeedback sessions, I've seen them trigger a
dramatic release of stress. They appear to be functioning as a powerful treatment. Stress release, by its very nature, triggers positive
change in our cells, tissues, and body systems. Healing can't help
but be a side effect—and this makes sense, as God promises His
Word is healing to all our flesh (Prov. 4:22).

This is why we should be very careful what we say. Through our
words we are bringing either life and healing or curses and death.
"You can't," "You won't," and "You'll never be" work as destructive
forces, whether spoken to others or directed toward ourselves. We
have the power to dish out doubt, fear, and venomous, crushing words
that, if received, may contribute to depression, sorrow, fear, addiction,
obsession, worry, and all types of stressful manifestations.

We are not to curse others or ourselves with negative proclamations. God's Word says:

Bless those who persecute you; bless, and do not curse.

—ROMANS 12:14

However, this doesn't mean we shouldn't curse disease, infection,
infestation, or the like. This is the proper use of speaking "death"

to the arsenal of the devil. My clients curse their diseases, tumors, infections, and whatever they feel may be attacking their health. I have seen this work beautifully. God wants us to use our words properly and skillfully. Healing words can shape our lives in many positive ways—and it doesn't cost you anything!

BE A LION!

> The wicked flee when no man pursues, but the righteous
> are bold as a lion.
>   —PROVERBS 28:1

I was a pretty timid kid. I used to hide behind my mother when she introduced me to someone new. But God does not mean for us to be shy. We are to develop the boldness of a lion! This means being confident—not arrogant—in approaching the things of God and sharing them with others.

I would encourage you to adopt a technique that will help you boldly address your particular health concern. Find a healthy picture of that body system or part of the body and pin it up in your bathroom. This can help you to clearly see what you are speaking to, and it can help you visualize a healthy pattern, which is your goal. Daily command out of your selected body part anything that does not have the appearance of the health and wholeness your picture represents. Daily replace the vacancies left by declaring God's perfect cellular patterns from His table of life, allowing them to fill you up each day.

Being bold is stepping up and taking control over whatever may be attacking your life and persevering until you see breakthrough. Mind-sets and emotions you wish to change for the better will also respond favorably to this technique and should be included.

We maintain humility because of God's grace to us in what He has provided, but we stand boldly in His authority to address anything that comes in to kill, steal, or destroy what is ours. Ask God for His help in increasing your boldness:

> In the day when I cried out, You answered me, and made
> me bold with strength in my soul.
> —Psalm 138:3, nkjv

> So they continued there a long time, speaking boldly for
> the Lord, who bore witness to His gracious word, granting
> signs and wonders to be done by their hands.
> —Acts 14:3

> In this way God's love is perfected in us, so that we may
> have boldness on the Day of Judgment, because as He is, so
> are we in this world.
> —1 John 4:17

Notice what that last passage says—that as Christ is, so are we in this world. What a profound statement with profound meaning! We have authority from heaven standing behind our bold use of godly truths.

In biofeedback sessions I am bold when demonstrating how I declare God's truths over the body. I encourage clients who are beginning this journey to see themselves as a general in the military talking to a newbie in the ranks when they command out any obstacle of stress. It works!

Speak to Your Mountains

God charges us with the responsibility of speaking faith-filled words to any obstacles standing in the way of our health and commanding them into the sea:

> For truly I say to you, whoever says to this mountain, "Be
> removed and be thrown into the sea," and does not doubt
> in his heart, but believes that what he says will come to
> pass, he will have whatever he says. Therefore I say to you,
> whatever things you ask when you pray, believe that you
> will receive them, and you will have them. And when you
> stand praying, forgive if you have anything against anyone,
> so that your Father who is in heaven may also forgive you

your sins. But if you do not forgive, neither will your Father who is in heaven forgive your sins.

—MARK 11:23–26

God told *us* to speak to the mountain. He has given us authority; now we must stand up and make a move. How? Remove any encumbrances in your life by repenting of any sins you may have committed and verbally forgiving those you need to release, and then go to work. God certainly gives miraculous promises for emergency measures, but He wants us to grow into victorious beings by using all the tools He has put at our disposal. Speaking to any "mountains" regularly can make a powerful difference between whether you are well or sick.

Jesus took all our suffering—past, present, and future—so we could come to Him, receive what He has given us, and be made free when obstructive mountains rise up in front of us. In the face of any obstacle in life we are more than conquerors in Christ. Use your voice to command your body and its cellular programming—from your DNA to your genetics and all your created parts—to release their mountains and come in line with Scripture and be free:

Therefore if the Son sets you free, you shall be free indeed.

—JOHN 8:36

When I demonstrate this technique to others, I speak boldly to the particular mountain by naming it and commanding it to be vaporized and cast into the sea. In faith, *without doubting,* I see it happen in my mind and emotions before I feel it. Then I boldly declare it *gone* right afterward! There may be time lag involved, and you may feel some persistent symptoms for a while. Be patient and keep focused on the healthy pattern that is replacing the unhealthy one.

When you speak to your mountain, it is important that you stay focused on the end result, not on the current circumstance. Your mountain may completely disappear, or it may break off in chunks if you forget to name some of its important parts. Sometimes we must speak to several elements to get it all out—emotional baggage, demonic oppression, trauma, accidents, or unforgiveness toward yourself or others. If you neglect to speak to all the elements of the mountain, you may experience partial and periodic rumblings from remnants of your obstacle as portions of connected memories and emotions continue to erupt periodically.

You may need to spend some time in prayer to discern what additional elements need to be included in your command. Do some soul-searching in this area. Ask God for wisdom and keep speaking to the obstacle regularly and in different creative ways until it is gone for good. Again, images can be powerful. Put a picture on your wall of how you and your life will be when your mountain is gone.

I conduct this exercise regularly with my clients. It is not difficult to complete an entire therapy session without even using the treatment mode on my computer! This is done simply by coaching my clients to speak to the "mountains" they believe are getting in the way of their health. My clients often become creative, speaking to specific toxins, organs, traumas, unhealthy mind-sets, and more. They sometimes speak to their disease by name. Sometimes as they do this, they immediately feel sensations in their physical bodies. Others simply feel more relaxed. Lots of yawning occurs, especially when large releases are happening.

My clients often address a provided list of common emotions and trauma/accidents, and we see incredible shifts to the positive when they do. You will find this list in appendix B for your own use.

When you do this yourself, do not doubt that it is working. It works because God says it does! Again declare that the mountain you spoke to is completely vaporized and gone!

Now remember that we never want to leave a vacuum. We speak life-giving declarations into the vacancy that instantly occurs so no demonic oppression or anything else gets in there. We might say, "I declare this new vacancy that was just made be filled with God's perfect cellular programming, healthy tissue, perfect immunity, love, peace, faith from His bountiful table," and so forth.

Again, we are not told in the Bible to instruct God to do the work on our mountains. He has empowered *us and our words* with that ability. What an honor to see the faith God has in us and how He has made us to be powerful in His might!

ONE SUCH MOUNTAIN

Once I became empowered with this knowledge, I decided to boldly take a stand after fighting yearly winter bugs, which I believed I contracted while flying across the country for intensive, all-day speaking engagements. I was beset with laryngitis several times. But when I started using God's tools to deal with these inconvenient mountains, I stopped getting sick.

How would you respond to a news flash that flu season is fast approaching and that record outbreaks are expected? Is your first response programmed by the media and today's current beliefs about the flu, or is your first response in line with the Word of God? I used to be stuck at the level of the world's report, but now I am starting to look at God's report first. The following is my new response:

> In the name of Jesus, the name that has authority over all names, including the flu and all sickness, I speak life and health to my immune system and protection from any type of weapon formed against me. I take up my authority and command that no plague shall come near my dwelling—my body, my home, or my workplace—because Psalm 91:10 states, "No evil shall befall you, neither shall any plague come near your tent." As a member of the church, the body of Christ, I receive and implant this truth into every cellular blueprint of my being and my immunity. I, therefore, command my body to continually reject all these pathetic, infective obstacles, and I command them straight into the sea. Now, I praise God for giving me this wonderful power and authority over my circumstances. I am healthy, well, and strong! Amen.

I can't tell you how abruptly my immunity shifted when I grabbed hold of a verse I could stand on—in this case Psalm 91:10—and made it part of my life.

Don't be surprised when you do this if some time goes by and all at once you feel like you are coming down with something. The devil will test you.

If this happens, don't agree with the sickness or say you are getting sick. Simply spend about five minutes verbally reaffirming your position, cursing any disease and repeating the verse you're standing on.

Three different times after I made my initial declaration, something tried to attack me during my travels. I stood my ground, and it left within the hour. Refute any words from others proclaiming you are getting sick. Clients frequently apologize for coming in sick and tell me they hope I don't catch their bug. "I've decided not to catch bugs anymore," is my reply.

Never agree with negative proclamations of sickness. Instead say, "No way am I getting that. No weapon formed against me shall prosper, including any and all illness!" My biofeedback program is brilliant for assessment and therapy, but I have observed over and over that we can learn to treat ourselves just as easily—and with more power—using the Word of God in the name of Jesus. When we learn to speak powerful healing words to the varieties of stress-filled mountains, the stream of health flows.

This magnificent principle of God's Word should be a fundamental tool in our daily lives. Are you feeling more powerful now?

MAN'S REPORT VS. GOD'S REPORT

If you just received a bad health report, what would you do first? React in shock? Retreat into fear and anxiety? Plan on that outcome becoming a reality? I hope you would do none of those things because of the powerful information you are learning.

However, almost by default most people become fixated on the doctor's report, the chemistry report, the CT scan report, the Internet report, and what family and friends report. Before we get too excited or go into shock, we should always ask ourselves a few questions: What is God's report? What does He have to say? Am I going to include Him and what He is offering in my healing journey?

What if you automatically reacted to man's report with the following: "I respect your education, your findings, and that you are trying to help, but I serve a powerful God, and He has something to say about my health also." This is not about disrespecting your doctor or well-meaning family and friends. This is about respecting God.

What if, after you received the report and any accompanying prognosis, you proclaimed this personalized verse?

> "No weapon formed against me shall prosper, and every tongue that rises against me in judgment I shall condemn. This is the heritage of mine and all servants of the Lord, and our righteousness is from God," says the Lord.
>
> —ISAIAH 54:17, PARAPHRASED

Do you see the mountain being spoken to? How powerful would it be to put these mountains into their proper place at the very beginning of a crisis? Remember, your body reacts to the words coming at it. Make sure it receives the right words for your health's sake so it can react in harmony with your goals and God's Word. When anyone tells me I can't, wont, don't have, or will never, I condemn those words. I call them *voodoo curses*, and I absolutely refuse to receive them. I command them out of my being and counter them with "I can, I will, and I am able to do all things through Christ who strengthens me. Nothing is impossible with God." Why would I allow man's words to govern my cells instead of the superior power of God's Word?

Do you need a little practice countering any negative proclamations made over your life? What would you put in these blanks if any person—your spouse, family, doctor, teacher, employer, or anyone else—spoke a negative proclamation over your body or your person? Proclaim this aloud with boldness!

"You say to me _____, but my God says _____."

Do you see why you need to be equipped with the Word of God to take your stand? You need to know what God says in order to counter any false words with truth.

What's more, this type of response usually quiets the conversation pretty quickly. People don't like to argue with God and His Word. Neither does the devil. But again you have to be knowledgeable of

Check Out Receipt

Port Orchard
360-876-2224
http://www.krl.org

Friday, September 4, 2020 10:56:14 AM

Item: 203736261
Title: Healing words
Call no.: ILL
Material: Interlibrary loan
Due: 09/25/2020

Item: 204119040
Title: Spirited
Call no.: ILL
Material: Interlibrary loan
Due: 09/25/2020

Total items: 2

Choose your own adventure, something new
Read 10 to 100 hours, it is all up to you!
Visit KRL.org weekly for more summer fun
Virtual events to enjoy, out in the sun.
Dive in to Summer Learning 2020!

God's truth and bold to adopt this stance. Sometimes you may be the only one saying anything life-giving in the situation.

Can you come up with ten healing verses or promises you could boldly declare if you were challenged? I asked several Christians this very question and they sheepishly admitted that they could not. Don't be caught unprepared. Make a list of all that God says about you, your health, and your circumstances as you read this book. Keep your focus, faith, and speech centered on those healing words.

Moving From the Natural Into the Supernatural

As we shift our mental focus to the wonderful promises of God, we must also shift our thoughts away from the limited science of this natural world and how it appears to function around us. This focus and dependence on the natural world—what we see, hear, taste, smell, and feel—is called "living in the flesh," or being carnally minded. It is shortsighted at best. We must change our focus to the supernatural universe out of which God operates above and beyond our worldly reality. We have already taken a big step by learning about the power of our words. This new focus will continue to grow our belief in God's provision and allow us to peacefully trust in His Word. The result is supernatural living, which enables God's supernatural results to occur.

Supernatural events are those that defy our brain's logical reasoning. We may scratch our head, trying to figure out how they work, as they may not fit with our natural understanding of things. Now that doesn't mean the supernatural is not scientifically sound. It just means we don't yet understand it from our natural point of view.

Some folks immediately attach a New Age label to anything they don't understand or that sounds even remotely mysterious. This may be premature in many cases. Some principles of the relatively new quantum physics, for instance, defy some of the old rudimentary teachings of physics and are replacing them. That doesn't mean quantum physics should be placed in a questionable category. It simply means we are catching up with God's truth that has been there all along. I believe there is much more to come and that God provides these delightful gifts for our discovery and His glory.

Let's compare the difference between living in a natural state and living in a supernatural state:

WHEN WE LIVE IN A NATURAL STATE, WE…	WHEN WE LIVE IN A SUPERNATURAL STATE, WE…
Focus on the worries, cares, sorrows, and betrayals of life	Focus on the great and precious promises of God
Get sick and frustrated	Think about what is good, lovely, and of good report while going about daily tasks
Declare the stress that has happened or will happen	Declare praise, gratitude, and the good plans God has for us to prosper
Vent or suppress our feelings	Release emotions through gentle, truthful conversation and expression
Go on mental overload focused on what is seen	Remain in mental peace focused on His truth
Believe it only if we can see it	"See" God's promises fulfilled in faith, even before they're experienced
Pass this pattern on to others	Pass this pattern on to others

You have a choice on where you are going to live. Trusting in man's worldly and limited wisdom is not God's best. It is often what the world says about life and health that causes us to be in fear and turmoil. If we stay in that place, divine health and healing won't make sense to us, and we may doubt. We must remember that nothing is impossible with God! All things are possible to those who believe. This brings us up from the fleshly realm ("I have to see to believe") to access the supernatural power provided by God ("I believe what I can't yet see based on His promises"). This is a conscious choice we make; it doesn't happen by accident. We must make our choice each and every day until it becomes automatic.

The supernatural realities of God are a fascinating frontier of study. The true remedies and solutions for our lives are in this invisible, powerful realm. God earnestly compels us in Scripture to make this important step upward into true life and peace.

> Thus says the LORD: Cursed is the man who trusts in man and makes flesh his strength, and whose heart departs from the LORD. For he will be like a bush in the desert, and will not see when good comes, but will inhabit the parched places in the wilderness, in a salt land and not inhabited. Blessed is the man who trust in the LORD, and whose hope is the LORD.
>
> —JEREMIAH 17:5–7

> For those who live according to the flesh set their minds on the things of the flesh, but those who live according to the Spirit, the things of the Spirit. To be carnally minded is death, but to be spiritually minded is life and peace.
>
> —ROMANS 8:5–6

What powerful statements from our God! When we make our primary reality His reality, we open up in our natural lives power and might that we would never otherwise have access to. His power trumps any opposing force on this planet.

We transform as we adopt true supernatural living. Our minds and hearts align with the Word of God, and rivers of healing begin to flow from that well within that God has provided through His Son. Visualize this happening as you apply the Scriptures. A nice side effect is a mind-set of victory.

When people approached Jesus with blindness, deafness, leprosy, and even dead bodies, did He ever flinch at what he saw? He viewed all of them from a supernatural, spiritual perspective and treated them differently than the physicians of that day. He is our example for how we might look anew at ourselves, informing us that our health is more than what appears in our mirror. As we see our situation through the teachings of Jesus, our minds expand to include possibilities we may have never before considered.

The average person is being bombarded with a worldly, natural point of view from many sources. Let's move past this shortsighted, limited focus. There is more to God's creation than meets the eye. Even science is starting to peer more closely into this marvelous realm, and some startling facts have been revealed.

For instance, scientists have now found that only 5 percent of creation is what we see around us. They calculate that 95 percent of everything else created cannot be seen in the light of day. Because of this, science has chosen to call these invisible substances *dark matter* and *dark energy*.[3] (Yes, I know—as believers, we would likely call it something else, perhaps God's matter and God's energy.)

If you need a proper definition for energy, science can easily provide this. Physics teaches that all matter is comprised of molecules that contain large amounts of energy. The dictionary defines *energy* as the "the capacity of acting or being active" and "usable power."[4]

Dark matter comprises 27 percent of what exists.[5] It is not visible with any telescope. It exerts gravitational effects on what can be seen, on radiation, and on the overall structure of the universe. It is considered to be a great mystery by astrophysicists. Dark energy comprises the remaining 68 percent.[6] This is the invisible energy that permeates all of what seems to be empty space.

Now think for a moment. We have empty space between the atoms in our bodies. These spaces contain created energy. We might call it our God-given life force or vitality. Could God's divine healing tools be used to imprint and impact our being at this very foundation? I believe they can.

> I will praise You, for I am fearfully and wonderfully made;
> marvelous are Your works, and that my soul knows very well.
> —PSALM 139:14 NKJV

God's knowledge far surpasses what we see each day with our eyes. He sees all of His creation while we see only 5 percent of it. And yet most people typically make major health decisions based on only a fraction of the information available to them—only what they see, hear, smell, taste, and feel. God's power is much greater than these resources and confounds the current teachings of science. This is why His tools of healing for our bodies don't always make sense to our minds when our primary focus is on the natural world around us:

> For My thoughts are not your thoughts, nor are your ways
> My ways, says the LORD.
>   —ISAIAH 55:8

Let's see if we can put this all together and apply it. Just what are we made of? We have just been informed there is more to creation the 5 percent than meets the eye. Do we have invisible components that can be influenced by the Word of God? Apparently we do. Can these, in turn, dramatically affect our body and its health? I believe they can. Our complexity is fascinating, and we are definitely more than what we can see. We agree with our God that we are a wonder of His creation. So let's see how we can choose God's supernatural report over man's limited natural one and experience even greater healing power in our lives.

CHAPTER 4

SEE YOURSELF HEALTHY

*B*IOFEEDBACK DOESN'T HAVE all the answers, but through it I am able to discern a great deal. In its work of detecting and treating stress patterns, my computer allows me to "see" how healing can move from an invisible beginning to a visible manifestation.

If we had a powerful microscope, we would see that our bodies are made of tissues, which are comprised of cells, which are comprised of molecules, which are made of atoms, which are held together with an invisible vital force, which I believe is the power of the spoken Word of God, set in motion during the creation of this world. There are many types of stressors that are antagonistic to our vitality. These may arise from many sources—toxins, trauma, accidents, poor lifestyle choices, and the unresolved emotions of bitterness, fear, anger, anxiety, and grief are just a few examples. Every form of stress contains antagonistic forces that may war with our vitality. Our bodies react with fatigue, pain, and tension.

In contrast, joy, peace, love, and praise support our vitality, as do healthy lifestyle choices, godly thinking, trust in God's promises, and speaking God's Word. As we support our vitality in these ways, we support our bodies. These things make us feel wonderful and feed our health.

Now each type of stress has a unique blueprint that is antagonistic to our being. A liver stress, for example, which may manifest as a diagnosable disease, might consist of a tangle of stressful blueprints created from chemicals, infections, toxins, pollutants, and excessive fat. These, in turn, might be tethered to the liver through buried, improperly processed anger, hatred, depression, unforgiveness, and more. Stress happens as the organ diverts its own vitality and function in an attempt to remove these elements. We then manifest all types of symptoms if the body doesn't have the means or strength to eject them.

This means that when we address our bodies at their core level of vitality by dealing with our thinking patterns and buried emotions, and by believing and speaking God's Word, meditating on it, and applying it, we see powerful changes at all levels, including in our cells, tissues, organs, and body systems.

Are you growing in your understanding of how speaking the healing Word of God over your body, mind, and emotions may be one of the most powerful of all remedies for your entire being? The good news is that you don't need twelve years of medical school to do this.

Here is a simple illustration that sums up these principles beautifully.

Mental Illness   Hormonal Imbalance
Infections   Diabetes
Cancer   Arthritis
Stroke   Allergies
Asthma   Heart Attack
High Blood   Digestive Disease
Pressure   Tension
                   Pain
                   Stress

Disconnection from God   Sinful Thinking
Wordly Standards   Buried Emotions   Sinful Actions
     Parental Sin   Demonic Oppression
     Ancestral Sin   Sinful Speaking

+ **Roots.** Healthy vitalities at our foundation shift into stress through invisible mechanisms, including sinful thinking, sinful speaking, sinful actions, worldly standards, buried emotions, disconnection from God, side effects of parental sin and ancestral sin, and demonic oppression. We can't see these in most cases, nor can we remove them through surgery (though that would be nice!), but their impact is very real and powerful.

+ **Trunk.** The infection at the roots builds into multiple types of stressful patterns, which manifest as tension, pain, and a lack of well-being at the physical, mental, and emotional levels.

+ **Leaves.** The unresolved stressful patterns in the trunk build to infect the leaves as well, resulting in disease manifestations of all types, such as stroke, high blood pressure, heart attack, asthma, cancer, infections, allergies, digestive disease, hormonal imbalance, diabetes, arthritis, and mental illness.

Biofeedback is generally designed to target the middle level—the trunk—when treating stress, but clients who choose to address the first level—the roots—will receive the most lasting benefit. God graciously allows us to receive healing at any of these levels, but addressing the core issues with the Word of God makes the most sense and is the more excellent way to experience true wellness. We don't have to deal with complex disease names or expensive treatments. We use the simplicity of God's Word. And when we cut off the root, the whole tree is conquered.

We are free to take any approach to our health that we wish, but let's also include this powerful tool and address our body systems from the root. We must walk by faith, speaking God's powerful promises to replace our own dysfunctional programming, allowing new, holy, invisible blueprints to form and take hold until our physical bodies begin to manifest the health we seek.

The Western medical model does not yet see the body as a wonderful tree with a root of God-given vitality that can be influenced on each level with godly forms of healing. Therefore, the root issues are rarely addressed. Instead, the outward illnesses residing in the branches and the leaves of the tree are targeted. With this Western approach, some of us have had so much pruning we don't even look or feel like a healthy, beautiful tree anymore. Our "healing" has consisted of medicating the affected organ so we don't feel the stress, suppressing the response of the organ so we don't experience symptoms, or, in extreme cases, removing the organ altogether. Suppressing symptoms doesn't really make us well; it just makes us suppressed. This is quite similar to dealing with a car's warning light by cutting the wires to it.

When I work with clients in biofeedback and watch what happens when they speak the principles of God's Word into their bodies to target their stress, no suppression occurs. Instead, the supernatural remedies from God's medicine chest unravel and peel away these stressful patterns, allowing their bodies to move toward the health their Creator intended them to enjoy.

Make Your Case

When an obstacle presents itself to you, notice it for the powerful moment that it is. Remember your authority. These mountains give you opportunities to exercise your spiritual muscles with the Word of God.

The question becomes: Do you have a case to stand upon? Have you done the necessary preparation? What scriptures will you use to support your actions?

When I was first starting to believe in my authority, and understand the powerful name of Jesus and my ability to speak to my mountains, a flea infestation moved into my home and attacked my dog. It was worse than I could have ever imagined. Each time I bathed the dog, I would count at least fifty fleas. My son left a glass of water on the floor by his bed one night, and the next morning when he brought it to me it had fifteen to twenty fleas in it.

I put flea medicine on my dog, which made him deathly sick—and still the fleas remained. I put diatomaceous earth into my carpet for a month and then vacuumed it up. The fleas reappeared shortly, alive and well.

I refused to bomb our home and subject everyone to those

chemicals, so I felt at a loss for what to do next. But sometimes it is good to come to the end of our rope. We may be more open to new ideas and strategies that we would have never otherwise considered. And that is what happened with me.

One day a client told me about someone she knew who had fleas in her home. The person had a shaman come and curse the fleas, and the fleas left. I thought, "Really?" Then I decided, "Well, if they could do that with their words, then certainly I can too—and best of all, I have God as my partner!"

I pondered what case I could present to take authority over the situation and get rid of the fleas. I felt the nudge of the Holy Spirit, and then I knew. As we have already seen, Jesus is the name above all names, and His name is more powerful than the name *flea*. I reminded myself that I served a mighty God and that the might and power of His Holy Spirit was available to me.

The infestation was a definite mountain that needed to go. I recalled a favorite scripture:

> Because you have made the LORD, who is my refuge, even the Most High, your dwelling place, no evil shall befall you, nor shall any plague come near your dwelling.
> —PSALM 91:9–10, NKJV

Do you recognize this passage? It is the same one I used to deal with sickness during travel.

Next I remembered:

> Come now, and let us reason together, says the LORD.
> —ISAIAH 1:18

God likes to reason with us and partner with us in agreement. So I reasoned with God that I didn't believe He wanted me, my family, or my dog to suffer any sort of plague, and this infestation of fleas certainly qualified as a plague. Then I went home ready for battle.

No one was home yet, so I went through each room of my home, full of righteous indignation that these invaders had dared set up residence in my dwelling. I was armed with my scriptures. Though we are certainly not supposed to curse men, fleas were fair game in my mind. I cursed them boldly in each room and commanded them to bow to the name of Jesus. I wasn't very quiet about it as I bellowed forth my dominion over any flea that dared to be in my home. I just couldn't stand another day of them. I commanded them to not open their mouths in my home and told them they were to go. We have a doggy door and I envisioned them heading there in hoards, stumbling over one another in their haste to evacuate.

A week later I saw one flea on our dog, but to my satisfaction, it was thin and puny. I walked through my house again and did a repeat performance. After that they disappeared.

Three times over the next three years I saw a flea or two attack the dog. I didn't wait to see if their numbers would increase or if they would go on their own. I cursed the fleas, and each time they disappeared within a few days.

What is interesting is that shortly after the initial flea invasion a client came in, complaining about a flea infestation in her apartment. She had two small dogs that were miserable, and nothing had helped.

"Make your case and curse them," I encouraged.

I shared my story and that I had discovered my authority over my home and over my flea problem. She was a strong believer and took up the challenge. She made her case, took up her authority, placed the name of Jesus over her home, soundly cursed the fleas, and to her great satisfaction, they soon disappeared. The last few she saw were scrawny and skinny also.

Did you know that disease is no more powerful than a flea in God's eyes? If it is more powerful in your eyes, you must challenge yourself to change that line of thinking. God wants you to be in health with a prosperous soul and to experience the promises of His Scriptures. Give Him all praise and glory. Gather your scriptures, build your faith to make your case, take authority over your body and your home, and boldly speak to your mountain. Persevere until it is only dust under your feet.

SEE IT BEFORE IT EXISTS

Our God is a faith God. He envisioned and spoke into existence the invisible framework for the created world before He made its parts appear:

> In the beginning God created the heavens and the earth.
> The earth was formless and void.
> —GENESIS 1:1–2

Void means empty. If the earth was empty and formless, what was it? He called it the earth before it wholly existed. I believe God spoke the invisible pattern before He created the matter to fill it. Everything we see in this world was first a spoken word—an invisible, living blueprint:

> Declaring the end from the beginning, and from ancient times the things that are not yet done.
> —ISAIAH 46:10

> By faith we understand that the universe was framed by the word of God, so that things that are seen were not made out of things which are visible.
> —HEBREWS 11:3

God always sees the end result before it is a reality. He wants us to see in this manner also. A simple parallel to this, but on a much lesser scale, is when we create clothing. We develop a pattern before the fabric is cut to fill it, whether on paper or in our minds. God has spoken many invisible patterns in Scripture for us to grab hold of in faith. This is the invisible substance that forms the reality that manifests as physical health within our bodies.

When we reach toward the truths of God and speak His Word over our lives, the Holy Spirit partners with us by responding to our faith, and His power is released. This new, living blueprint begins to move toward a physical form.

The formation of a child within the womb is an example of this phenomenon. Even science is puzzled over just how it happens, as it defies explanation. The fertilized egg divides, and several cell divisions occur that are all identical under scientific examination. Then something unexplainable happens: the cells begin to change into specific, unique cells to form organs, eyes, the brain, the spinal cord, and more.

Why does this happen? We can't really *see* why. There is no *natural* explanation. Something invisible and supernatural is taking place. The organs and parts are following an invisible blueprint, and a child is formed. What is seen is being influenced by an invisible force that science cannot see under any microscope. But we who read the Word are allowed to understand that our God created a living blueprint of us in His mind even before He made our physical parts.

> Before I formed you in the womb I knew you.
> —JEREMIAH 1:5

Let's take a look at a fascinating account of a man and woman who received a startling revelation from the Lord and how they responded to it. It is the story of Abraham and Sarah, who had a definite part to play in bringing God's promise to life.

In this story God had promised Abraham, who was ninety-nine years old, that he would become a father for the first time and that God had already made him the father of many nations. Do you see the living blueprint being created here? The final result was already there in the mind of God.

Now, Abraham's wife, Sarah, was ninety years old. Let's stop here for a moment. What if you were given this promise at that age and you told your friends and doctor? The words would just barely clear your lips when you'd likely hear—"Have you been drinking?"; "That's impossible—no way!"; "You would have to take a lot of hormone injections to have even a remote possibility."; or, "Have you talked with your pastor about this—or better yet, a psychiatrist?" You'd have to find the energy to climb out from under the oppressive weight of unbelief that would be hurled upon you.

In the natural world starting a family was impossible, but Abraham focused on God's promise, not on what he heard from others, saw, or felt in his aging body. He banished all unbelief, allowed the spiritual blueprint of God's words to penetrate him to his core, and a miracle occurred! Abraham and Sarah did have a son, but it didn't happen right away. There was a significant time lag before Sarah became pregnant. They had to have patience and faith to receive the promise.

When God makes us a promise, His Word never returns void if we are willing to persevere and take a stand. Look at what is said of Abraham's part:

> Against all hope, he believed in hope, that he might become the father of many nations according to what was spoken, "So shall your descendants be." And not being weak in faith, he did not consider his own body to be dead (when he was about a hundred years old), nor yet the deadness of Sarah's womb. He did not waver at the promise of God through unbelief, but was strong in faith, giving glory to God, and being fully persuaded that what God had promised, He was able to perform. Therefore "it was credited to him as righteousness."
>
> —ROMANS 4:18–22

Abraham allowed hope and faith to take hold within him, he gave the glory and praise to God (I believe he did this verbally), and he saw the results in his own mind before it was a reality. He didn't rely upon his senses, and he didn't waver. To God, this is a right and expected response.

In the same way, when we are declaring God's Word over our own life challenges, the Word has the power to overcome what our senses report, as well as all the reports of the authority figures in whom we so often place our faith. We must believe, see, and speak the fulfillment of God's report, even before it happens. That is what we hold in our hearts and minds on a daily basis. We praise and thank God daily for performing His Word, which never returns empty when we use it properly. We visualize the result, not what we are experiencing now.

Invisible, supernatural changes are occurring, sparking physical shifts and healing. Do not let a time lag discourage you. Your senses may scream as time ticks by that declaring God's promises over your life is not working. You may be forced many times to reaffirm what you have chosen to believe. Remember God's timing is not the same as ours. He will manifest the result when the time is right.

With that said, if you are suffering from a serious condition, please do what brings you peace. Some people receive complete healing solely by speaking to the mountains affecting their bodies. Others, strongly believing that the Lord has provided many ways of healing, choose to incorporate a variety of healing strategies. This is my personal position. I have attacked many challenging issues in my life by doing everything I know to do: speaking to my mountains, utilizing herbs and essential oils, purposefully eating healthily, and dealing with factors creating stress in my life. If you at any time feel that you should include other treatment modalities, please do so. The Lord can bring healing in many diverse ways.

Keeping God and what He says in our sights is wise in any circumstance and builds our spiritual strength. Listening to man and the devil can make us weary, but God sees and calls things real before they come into existence. We need to do the same as we read His promises:

> The righteous shall be glad in the LORD, and trust in Him.
>
> —PSALM 64:10, NKJV

> But those who wait upon the LORD shall renew their strength; they shall mount up with wings as eagles, they shall run and not be weary, and they shall walk and not faint.
>
> —ISAIAH 40:31

> Then the LORD said to me, "You have seen well. For I will hasten My word to perform it."
>
> —JEREMIAH 1:12

> God…who raises the dead, and calls those things that do not exist as though they did.
>
> —ROMANS 4:17

PICTURE YOURSELF VICTORIOUS

What we think in our hearts, we are. I want to challenge you to reverse a common mind-set, especially if it is still trying to cling to you. See yourself as a well person, evicting sickness with boldness and righteous indignation, not as a sick person struggling to get well.

Sickness is like a big, ugly spider that has invaded your home. It is not the boss or authority over your dwelling. It is not there to be your pet. God does not intend it as a punishment for your past. Jesus already took your punishment on the cross, if you'll let Him have it. It is not God's will for you to live with a toxic, poisonous spider!

You are the owner of your home and body, and you have authority to evict any trespasser that would make you sick. Get mad and slay your challenger with Scripture. It is trying to steal your precious living space and hurt your family.

Keep in mind, before you begin evicting this creature, to check any unguarded door. Take care of any unforgiveness or conscious sin that might have opened the door to illness in the first place:

> Therefore, since we are encompassed with such a great cloud of witnesses, let us also lay aside every weight and the sin that so easily entangles us, and let us run with endurance the race that is set before us.
> —HEBREWS 12:1

> Confess your faults to one another and pray for one another, that you may be healed. The effective, fervent prayer of a righteous man accomplishes much.
> —JAMES 5:16

You wouldn't announce, "Hey, family, a big, ugly, poisonous spider is going to live in our house!" That would be a ridiculous statement to make, especially when you can put on your stomping boots and destroy this toxic creature. Agreeing with a sad fate that accompanies a diagnosis lays a blueprint for its fulfillment. It is like inviting that ugly spider to invade your home and set itself up as the master. If you let it, the "spider" will continue ruling the situation until you start to believe the truth—that you have power and authority over it, due to what Christ has already provided for you.

God wants you out of a weak, victim-based belief pattern as soon as possible. He has told you that you are more than a conqueror through Christ. If you don't quite see yourself that way yet, God says to speak strength to yourself:

> Let the weakling say, "I am a warrior!"
> —JOEL 3:10

But you also have to want to be well, enough to be diligent to do your part. Jesus asked this very question of one man He encountered:

> When Jesus saw him lying there, and knew that he had already been in that condition a long time, He said to him, "Do you want to be made well?"
> —JOHN 5:6, NKJV

If you receive more attention because of that spider, part of you may wish to keep him. I once knew a minister who would not proceed in praying for someone until the person looked him square in the eye and answered, "Yes, I want to be well!" Sometimes a client of mine will appear to be searching for wellness but prove resistant to suggestions or support. In this case I've learned it comes down to a single question: "Do you want to be well?"

See your position of victory before you begin. Do you have a picture of what that looks like in your mind? See that big boot of yours raised above that spider! Now say, "*Adios*," and do what needs to be done. Then speak from the Scriptures what your wellness looks like as often as you need to. We already know that this is necessary and powerful. Know that there is always a profitable return. God's Words always bring results:

> So shall My word be that goes forth from My mouth; it shall not return to Me void, but it shall accomplish that which I please, and it shall prosper in the thing for which I sent it.
> —ISAIAH 55:11

> For I the LORD will speak, and the word that I speak shall
> come to pass.
>
> —EZEKIEL 12:25

God's healing Word is there for us to use, and it never returns empty-handed when we echo its truths because God is the guarantor of His promises. Enter God's court with well-deserved praise. Keep your vision of your wellness and the scriptures that support them constantly in front of you. Remember that pictures are powerful. Use them in your bathroom, kitchen, office, and car. Do your due diligence to understand His will and the part you are to play. Make a solid case. And rest in the fact that you have made your heavenly Father and all of His gems of spiritual healing your source. In this knowledge you can inwardly be in perfect peace and see yourself healed and whole as Isaiah 26:3 says: "You will keep him in perfect peace, whose mind is stayed on You, because he trusts in You."

CHAPTER 5

THE FIVE FOUNDATIONS OF OPTIMAL HEALTH

*O*UR HEALING AND how we maintain it includes how we care for and maintain our physical health. Wouldn't it be ideal if you didn't end up in dire need of a miracle in the first place? Let's explore some solid rocks mentioned in Scripture upon which we can build to provide basic care for our bodies.

FOUNDATION #1: HEALTHY, REAL FOOD

"Let food be thy medicine and medicine be thy food." Hippocrates, the father of modern medicine, proclaimed this centuries ago. He understood the healing power God placed in healthy, real food. Most of today's common diseases can be positively influenced by adopting and committing to a diet of real food, consumed as God designed it, not processed beyond recognition. We are wonderful, complex beings, and if we don't give our bodies the proper fuel, we risk internal disharmony, stress, and illness. This is all too evident today. The leading causes of death in the United States are heart disease, cancer, chronic lower respiratory disease, and stroke.[1] How we eat and the lifestyle we keep are significant factors in our health.

Our standard American diet (SAD) has drifted far from what God designed for us. It is adulterated with refined, processed foods, unhealthy fats, and an overload of sugar and salt. As a result, diabetes and obesity are epidemic.

Big business is obsessed with toxic pesticides and the genetic modification of our produce. It supports raising animals quickly in unhealthy conditions, due to our insatiable desire for fast, cheap "food." In the midst of all of this our life expectancy is lagging behind that of other developed countries, many of which have life spans well over eighty years. According to the American Council on Science and Health, "It is also possible that the *rate of increase in life expectancy* in America is beginning to lag, possibly because of obesity."[2] It does not surprise me that science is not ready to state the reason for the lag, but it is pretty obvious our lifestyle and resulting maladies are a huge factor. We have more obesity in children than ever before.

I consistently observe better biofeedback readings—meaning, less stress—among the clients who do a few simple things:

1. Develop sound habits of health by eating real, life-giving food. (Junk food or processed food is not real food by any biblical definition.)

2. Consume reasonable portions so they are comfortable, not stuffed, after meals.

3. Eat in a peaceful atmosphere—not in front of the distressing television news or scenes of violence, horror, nudity, or profanity—after speaking prayer and thanksgiving over their food.

God showed us an example of what real food is when He created the Garden of Eden. A beautiful array of organic, fresh, unmodified, non-radiated, unrefined, unprocessed fruits, vegetables, grains, nuts, and seeds were presented to Adam and Eve as their perfect diet. God later added more real food—proteins from specific meat, fowl, fish, and, yes, a few healthy insects. In the New Testament God allows all living creatures to be eaten as food when received with thanksgiving:

> For everything created by God is good, and not to be refused if it is received with thanksgiving, for it is sanctified by the word of God and prayer.
> —1 TIMOTHY 4:4–5

> Therefore let no one judge you regarding food, or drink, or in respect of a holy day or new moon or sabbath days.
> —COLOSSIANS 2:16

God doesn't impute sin to us over what we eat today. Man is not to judge us either. However, our bodies might judge us mightily if we drift off the path of real food and into the ditch of processed and devitalized junk food. It will always remain true that there is value in certain healthy principles that God has taught in Scripture. Let's push aside our misplaced cravings for nonfood and embrace real food again.

If you are ready to consider laying aside the standard American diet and eating instead what your body needs to live and heal properly, you will be laying a solid foundation for good health. Take a discerning look inside your cupboards and refrigerator. Are you eating real food? I hope you will throw out the nonfoods today that are processed and depleting to your body. When possible avoid refined sugars, flours, salt, modified foods, and trans fats, as well as sodas, candies, and corn syrups. These are some of the most fattening nonfoods in our supermarkets.

The following is a simple example of how one might embrace a healthy lifestyle with real, life-giving food. Below I've listed common, nutrient-rich foods that I emphasize when teaching. Ideally those you choose would be organic and not genetically modified:

+ Fresh vegetables and fruits

+ Healthy fats, such as fresh, raw, or lightly roasted nuts and seeds; butter from grass-fed cows; avocados; and grape seed, olive, almond, walnut, flax, fish, and coconut oils. (Note: When raw nuts and seeds are soaked overnight, they become easier to digest. In this form they are wonderful in smoothies or in blended soups to create a creamy texture.)

+ Grains, such as brown and wild rice, buckwheat, quinoa, millet, farro, teff, and amaranth

+ Yellow potatoes, red potatoes, sweet potatoes, and yams

+ Beans and legumes, such as black beans, lentils, and peas. (Note: Legumes are encased in some sort of pod.)

+ Fresh vegetable juices, fresh-squeezed lemonade, and herbal teas sweetened with a little raw honey or stevia

+ Nutrient-rich cheeses produced from raw milk (Note: Goat and sheep cheeses are easier to digest than cheeses made from cow's milk. The more we process our cheese, the more it loses certain valuable properties of the raw product. How well you tolerate and digest cheese may depend on how it is processed and made.)

+ Meat, fowl, and fish raised without chemicals or additives (Note: Grass-fed, humanely treated pastured animals should be the norm, as grass-fed animals have different nutrient components in their meat, butter, and eggs, which contributes to our better health. Bone broth is also a healthy component for our diet, as well as organ meats, which contribute to the health and mineralization of our teeth. Fish such as salmon and trout should be taken from clean rivers or the ocean, where they feed on natural food sources.)

+ Pure water without chemicals or additives (See appendix E for reasonably priced alkaline water purification systems.)

+ Herbs such as garlic, parsley, kelp, capsicum, turmeric, oregano, green tea, horseradish, mustard, and fennel

Have you ever spoken to the "mountains" in your food? All kinds of pesticides and toxins exist in our food today, but we don't have to be passive eaters. We can take authority over our food. I often command any harmful component in my food, such as pesticides or germs, to vaporize and be gone into the sea—I do this especially when eating in restaurants—and I believe it may be another reason I don't get as sick as I used to in the past. (Note: I am not advocating speaking over obvious poison, such as chemicals in your garage, then drinking it. That is not smart and tests God. Don't do it.)

We shouldn't put all of our trust in our diet, but we shouldn't neglect it either. Everything must be kept in its proper context.

Remember that a long, healthy, productive life is also fed by the Word of God.

FOUNDATION #2: HERBS

> By the river upon its bank, on this side and on that side, shall grow all kinds of trees for food.... Their fruit shall be for food and their leaves for medicine.
> —EZEKIEL 47:12

I have used herbs on a daily basis for decades. Quality organic herbs have been a key in nourishing my family's health for thirty-four years and counting. These gifts from God have been a major factor in keeping my family free of medical bills. They are a normal part of our personal prevention program and provide support for our bodies' healing and maintenance. I have also seen countless people cure themselves of all sorts of ailments when using herbs properly.

Herbs are typically therapeutic and nutrient-dense plants. They are used by many people and cultures for cooking and medicinal purposes. China and India have used herbs as medicine for thousands of years. In America they are legally classified as food. They are part of God's pharmacy, and His Word makes many references to them. The people in biblical days understood the divine, healing gift of herbal medicine. Some wonderful examples of herbs referenced in Scripture are spikenard (used to anoint the feet of Jesus), saffron, calamus, cinnamon, frankincense, garlic, bitter herbs, mint, anise, cumin, and myrrh. (See Exodus 12:8; Numbers 11:5; Song of Solomon 4:14, 5:1; Matthew 23:23.)

I believe God intended herbs as healthy, nutrient-rich medicinal foods for regular and daily use to support the optimal functioning of our bodies:

> He causeth the grass to grow for the cattle, and herb for the service of man: that he may bring forth food out of the earth.
> —PSALM 104:14, KJV

Dosage of a dried herb can range from one capsule to twelve capsules daily. A capsule is about a ¼ teaspoon. Smaller amounts are used for bitter herbs, as they have a cleansing effect. Some popular bitter herbs include goldenseal, milk thistle, and dandelion. Larger amounts are used for the soothing mucilants such as slippery elm (which benefits the colon), fenugreek (which benefits the sinuses), and chickweed (which aids the skin and digestive organs).

Herbs can help warm, cool, dry, moisten, loosen, detoxify, and tone the body. A good portion of the herbal kingdom supports the body's natural functions of building, energizing, and healing. They have virtually no side effects. However, when we begin to use herbs, we may feel temporary discomfort as our sluggish body parts energize, allowing toxins and cellular wastes to loosen and begin moving toward the eliminative organs for release. When the body expels a toxin that may be at the root of a symptom, we can feel it, just as we can feel when our bodies are fighting and expelling a cold or the flu. Symptoms of toxic expulsion may include headache, diarrhea, lethargy, digestive disturbances, skin breakouts, and irritability. Gentle walking, drinking plenty of water, taking essential oil baths, and eating nourishing soups may ease this detoxification phase and shorten it.

Herbs are a part of God's divine treasure trove for all to enjoy. But unfortunately the American culture has paid lobbyists to move our focus elsewhere. Some of the most powerful lobbyists exist solely to advance pharmaceutical sales. When herbs are maligned in the news, such disparaging information sometimes comes from insidious sources that seek to drive the consumer toward the pharmaceutical market. Even harmful outcomes from pharmaceuticals proven through scientific testing have been withheld from the public at times in order to advance the agenda of pharmaceutical sales.[3]

Despite the lobbyist agenda, herbal popularity is rising with laymen and health professionals alike due to the overall lack of serious or life-threatening side effects that are common with pharmaceuticals. I meet people every day who are looking for natural health care because their disease care is not satisfying them. Our heavenly Father created herbs, and He proclaimed His creation good. That settles it for me.

Note: Herb quality and safety is important. Please find a reputable company that utilizes organic raw product, tests each batch, and bottles the product in its own facility. (See appendix E for suggested quality herbal products.) Also later in this book, when we look at the care and healing of each bodily system, you will find some of my favorite herbs listed that assist in the care of the different body systems.

FOUNDATION #3: ESSENTIAL OILS

There is treasure to be desired and oil in the dwelling of the wise, but a foolish man squanders it.
—PROVERBS 21:20

And when they came into the house, they saw the young Child with Mary, His mother, and fell down and worshipped Him. And when they had opened their treasures, they presented gifts to Him: gold, frankincense, and myrrh.
—MATTHEW 2:11

Yes, essential oils are a wonderful treasure indeed! There are more than two hundred references in Scripture to oils. They were used as gifts, medicine, perfume, for mood and emotional elevation, to anoint the sick, and to embalm the dead.

Essential oils are concentrated aromatic extracts from many kinds of plant material—seeds, rinds, bark, leaves, twigs, flowers, and some types of nuts. They are different from the common vegetable and nut oils we buy for cooking. Only small amounts—anywhere from one to twelve drops—are usually needed for daily use. They easily penetrate the cells when inhaled or applied to the skin, often absorbing in seconds. Essential oils such as lavender and jasmine are known for their positive and sometimes dramatic effect on mental and emotional health. They reduce stress by promoting healthy cellular function and vital well-being.

Amazingly these delightful tools contain more vital energy than most food and herbs. This is why I love making them into powerful bath recipes that I use as catalysts to assist my body in its healthy detoxification processes and relaxation.

When used externally, essential oils may be safely applied to the soles of the feet either straight or diluted with a carrier oil, such as grapeseed oil. A carrier oil reduces the potential for skin irritation that can result from some of the stronger oils, such as cinnamon, lemongrass, and oregano. Once diluted with a teaspoon or two of carrier oil, essential oils may be applied to the skin over various organs, *excluding* most of the face, the inner ears, the eyes, and the sensitive tissues down south. Applying and layering oils down the spine can result in tremendous health-giving benefits. Educate yourself as you go and have fun with these.

Essential oils may be inhaled by putting four to five drops in the palms, rubbing them together a few times, and cupping the palms over the nose for five to six minutes twice daily with very effective results. This method especially supports health in the brain, respiratory system, and mood. A few popular essential oils are frankincense, lavender, clary sage, lemon, Bulgarian rose, and pine needle. The best oils will be pure and organic. (See appendix E for suggested products that have the SureSource guarantee of purity and authenticity.)

In the body system chapters that follow in part 2, I provide personal recipes for how I use essential oils to enhance the healthy function of each body system. If you have any questions or concerns about using essential oils, consult a qualified aromatherapist, as some essential oils carry certain precautions, such as photosensitivity. Citrus oils have the potential to enhance sunburn up to twelve hours after applying them. And pregnant and nursing women should avoid using essential oils. Most people, however, have great results with a little study and common sense. Essential oils are useful tools to assist you in your healing journey.

FOUNDATION #4: PURE WATER

Water is a miraculous gift. Our bodies need it to function properly. If you wish to know how much water you should consume, take your weight and divide it by two. That is the number of ounces you need daily. If you divide that number by eight, you will find how many eight-ounce cups of water you need to drink each day. (Please note that coffee, soda, sugared drinks, caffeinated energy drinks, and alcohol do not count toward our daily intake of water; however, green tea, herbal tea, and fresh juices can be included as a portion of our daily water intake.)

The bad news is, water today is not as the Lord created it to be. In most of the United States the water is treated with a cocktail of toxic chemicals before being released into our water supply, whereas in many European countries the more body-friendly ozone is used to treat water. Additionally, certain water supplies in the United States have been found to contain carcinogens from factory runoff— and that's not all. According to an Associated Press investigation, in very small amounts, "a vast array of pharmaceuticals including antibiotics, anti-convulsants, mood stabilizers and sex hormones have been found in the drinking water supplies of at least 41 million Americans."[4] It's shocking, but it's true. No wonder some of us have an aversion to tap water!

It is time to take responsibility for what we drink and return as much as possible to God's original design: water that is pure and chemical free. Consider finding some way to purify your family's water. Reading food labels and choosing food with care while drinking a glass of chemically laced water makes no sense. We need to be wise and informed and adopt a plan to make our water healthy for our families. My family has done this through investigating alkaline water purification systems for our home. (See appendix E for suggestions.)

Drinking pure water is a pleasure. When we are well-hydrated, our cells take in nutrients and expel wastes more efficiently. We also carry less stress.

Imprinting water

I was fascinated to learn that water has the ability to take on an imprint, a type of unique blueprint, from various substances, flowers, nutrients, and—it shouldn't surprise you to learn—our spoken words. This was the subject of many careful, creatively designed experiments using water crystals recorded in the book *The True*

Power of Water by Masaru Emoto. Through Emoto's amazing discoveries, we learn we may be able to make our water into medicine.

In Emoto's experiments the word *gratitude* was presented to water
and was shown to imprint the water in a surprising, unique, and
beautiful manner, causing it to form a one-of-a-kind, delicate snowflake pattern when it froze and crystallized. He also experimented
with other positive words, including *love* and *happiness*. Each of
these words formed a unique and beautiful snowflake pattern too.

© Office Masaru Emoto, LLC

Thank You   You Fool

On the other hand, imprinting the hateful words *you fool* appeared
to prevent any snowflake pattern from forming and instead yielded
a chaotic pattern. Other negative words such as *unhappiness* and
stress created deformed crystals.

Photographing crystalized water revealed many unique individual patterns that formed in response to the imprint of the word
or words. I believe that when Emoto first viewed these under a
microscope, he discovered some of the wonderful physics of God.

Emoto discovered that words imprint water, whether offered in
verbal or written form. Furthermore, words not only impact our
water, but also our food, possibly because our food contains water.
In one of Emoto's experiments two identical jars of rice were placed

on a counter. Each jar had the same rice in it, but one was subjected to the words *you fool* and the other to the words *thank you.*

The reaction within the chemistry of the rice was amazing. The jar of rice that received the words *thank you* fermented with a mellow smell, while the rice in the jar that received the words *you fool* turned black and began to rot.

You Fool   Thank You

Doesn't this make you wonder how much healthier we might be if we imprinted our food and water with gratitude to our Lord through spoken prayer and praise before we eat and drink it? In reading and observing Emoto's work, we can deduct that speaking words of thankfulness and love over our meals appears to impact the water within it with the unique blueprint of those words before we ingest it. This may function as a type of medicine, depending on the type of words we use and how they impact our bodies. Though the Lord did not share the reasons He asked us to receive our food with thanksgiving, I believe we gain blessings when we do it. Emoto's research offers proof enough.

> In everything give thanks, for this is the will of God in Christ Jesus concerning you.
> —1 THESSALONIANS 5:18

Healing water

Now let's take this a step further. What if, simply by holding a jug of water and speaking over it, you could create a sort of medicine by infusing your water with a blueprint of the Scriptures, especially the principles of God's will for your health? In other words, what if you could program your drinking water to promote health within your body?

Think about it this way. Our bodies are at least 70 percent water. We've already established that God wants us to speak and read His Word and swallow it into our core so that its blueprint becomes our own. What if water and the Word of God combined can impact our physical challenges in a positive and effective way?

With this idea in mind, I decided several years ago to try an experiment. I wanted to see what would happen if I spoke scriptural health principles over a container of water that I held in my hand for about five minutes, then drank some of it. Furthermore, what would happen if I declared aloud my whole family's health goals—divine health and healing—while holding a jug of water and then we all used that jug of water for the next three days? What would water imprinted with those words do?

My family remembers this experiment because we felt the results of it within the first three days. My son noticed immediate changes in his digestive system, as it started speeding up and doing some cleansing. My daughter had none of those cleansing symptoms in her digestion system, but her thyroid, which had been exposed to an X-ray before birth and was significantly enlarged, felt hot after drinking a few glasses of the water. Her throat also felt sore. Now, inflammation is part of how the body ejects toxins. Interestingly enough, today doctors consider her thyroid normal. For myself, I noticed several emotions surfacing after I started drinking the water. As an introvert I was used to swallowing those emotions down—suppressing them—but the water seemed to be working as a catalyst in the areas where a healing needed to begin.

I call this blueprinted water *healing water*. Now, let's be clear: it is the words of God's truth that do the healing here. The credit always goes to Him. The water is simply a carrier that holds the blueprint of those healing declarations within it.

If you would like to experiment by making your own healing water to assist the health of your body systems, here is an example of my formula:

+ Hold the jug on your body and in your hands and take a seat.

+ Be as specific as you wish, and be clear with your words. Don't use slang. I spoke the words over my water in a quiet room that was free of the TV and other distractions.

+ Spend a good five minutes speaking over your water to attain a good blueprint. Don't rush.

+ Declare boldly—and aloud—the following about seven times while holding the jug of water: "My entire head and its parts are functioning in divine health. These parts are all fearfully and wonderfully made."

+ Envision what this declaration looks and feels like while you speak. This helps you be focused and truly believe what you are speaking regarding God's will for your health. If you speak words but your mind is on some other distraction, the process may not work properly— and you don't want your water to be inadvertently programmed with thoughts of pizza for dinner, what a friend said that day, or the dog's need for a bath!

+ When you are finished declaring the first statement seven times, move to another statement: "My entire neck and its created parts are functioning in divine and perfect health and wellness. My entire chest and arms and their created parts are functioning in divine and perfect health and wellness. My entire midsection...my entire pelvis...my legs and feet..." You get the idea. You may also choose to speak to the health of specific organs and cells. It might be a good idea to write it all out first so you can stay focused. Tape your words on the jug of water too.

+ Make enough of this water to have a few glasses daily for three days before remaking it. Store the water away from any interfering electrical fields, such as digital clocks, microwave ovens, TVs, refrigerators, computers, and the like. Also avoid fighting or arguing around your wonderful healing water.

The key to long-term success is to listen to what your body is telling you through its symptoms and speaking specific portions of the Word of God that the Holy Spirit brings to your mind as your therapy. God has programmed your body to appeal to you for help by emitting symptoms. As stressful patterns begin to emerge from storage sites in the tissues, it is not uncommon to feel them through this process of elimination, just as my son and daughter did. With this in mind, you may wish to modify your words with each new jug of water, addressing any physical, emotional, or mental symptoms that begin to emerge and stating aloud that the Son of God has set you free of these, that they release easily, and that they are no longer allowed in your being. Your body was made for perfect function. It knows what healthy function is. It reacts to and obeys your words. You have authority over your body. If any other program has snuck in, eliminate it!

Personalized scriptures and their principles are perfect to write out, affix to, and declare over your healing water. Here are a few examples of what you might use:

> I am awesomely and wonderfully made. I am full of joy and praise for the Lord. My body systems and all my created parts are filled to overflowing with the vitality God intended for me.

> All my fear and timidity is gone. I can do all things through Christ who strengthens me. I am overflowing with peace and forgiveness toward all. I have perfect faith and belief in all of God's promises. Every molecule of my being overflows with God's rivers of healing.

Use the scriptures that resonate with you presently, and change them as desired. You will soon have scriptures to use with each body system. Read them, speak them, and put their blueprint into your water, then see how your body responds.

As one last word of encouragement for you around this, I will share a story from my daughter-in-law, Cathy, who used healing water when she and my son hit a wall after struggling for a few years with infertility. Here is her testimony:

> My husband and I were ready to have children two and a half years ago, but doors seemed to be closed for our success. We went down a road of trying natural remedies, such as herbs, vitamins, chiropractic care, and even acupuncture. The disappointments kept mounting. I felt broken, lost, and out of sync with God's will for my life.
>
> After much prayer my husband and I began fertility treatment at a local clinic nine months ago. Through the clinic I was finally diagnosed with PCOS [polycystic ovarian syndrome] and could visualize the place we were and the place we needed to be.
>
> After three more failed pregnancy tests, I called my mother-in-law on August 21 for encouragement. She reminded me of God's faithfulness. We discussed scripture about Jesus's living water and how He promises He is my ultimate healer and in control of my life.
>
> I wrote scriptures on a container of water and drank from it every day. On the container I wrote praises to God and declared His blessings to be mine! Some verses I used included 1 Samuel 1:27, Philippians 4:13, 1 Peter 1:6, Luke 17:21, John 15:7, and Psalm 43:4.
>
> On September 11, 2015, we got the news we had been waiting years to hear. Though I was still taking fertility treatments, this successful pregnancy is God's victory in our lives, and we will continue to give Him glory and praise throughout this whole journey.
>
> —Catherine Rogers
> September 20, 2015

After Cathy studied God's Word on fertility and took steps of faith to apply it, she was pregnant the following month. Drinking God's Word has the powerful potential to drive out whatever opposes it. Along the way you may feel some detoxification symptoms and the release of old buried emotions. We may be toxic from many sources—polluted air and water, food additives, X-rays, heavy metals, overgrowths of pathogens, and side effects of medications, not to mention any of the seventy-five thousand chemicals produced in the United States. Go slowly. One or two glasses daily of imprinted healing water may be all you need each day.

In America we spend thousands of dollars on health care when our heavenly Father has blessed us with the simplicity of His water that He created with amazing scientific properties and potential. Water may be a powerful remedy at a price everyone can afford. What if we routinely used this technique before we ever got sick?

And just in case it still sounds a little crazy to speak to water or write scriptures on paper and tape them to the side of water jugs, just remember that Moses was instructed to speak to a rock, Balaam spoke with a donkey, and Jesus spoke to wind, waves, food, a fig tree, and the dead!

Of course, this wonderful tool is not a substitute for reading God's Word or your regular prayer life. Continue to spend time each day with the Lord to "chew" well and "swallow" His scriptures into your core—your very heart—so they become part of your life. This is called meditating on the Word.

You might just pour yourself a glass of water first.

FOUNDATION #5: LIFESTYLE

When we are diligent to set aside time each day to read and frame our day with the Word of God, we get a healthy dose of what true reality is and what are His true reports. Here is where we develop a resistance to the limited point of view this world offers and develop a peace and rest in the Lord.

Mental health

An important factor in this process is in the monitoring of our thought life. I am continually having to monitor my reactive response to thoughts that are not in my best interest. Taking time to pause and ask myself if I will be better off without that thought has been a helpful step to take before allowing that thought down into my core and owning it. Thoughts have little power until you welcome them in and make them a part of your being.

What you think about, you become. Discard any thoughts that misalign you with the mind of Christ and that lead you off your path and purpose, and into the dark places of unbelief. God's power and promises do not dwell in this wilderness:

> Do not be conformed to this world, but be transformed by the renewing of your mind, that you may prove what is the good and acceptable and perfect will of God.
> —ROMANS 12:2

> Casting down imaginations and every high thing that exalts itself against the knowledge of God, bringing every thought into captivity to the obedience of Christ.
> —2 CORINTHIANS 10:5

> Finally, brothers, whatever things are true, whatever things are honest, whatever things are just, whatever things are pure, whatever things are lovely, whatever things are of good report, if there is any virtue, and if there is any praise, think on these things.
> —PHILIPPIANS 4:8

Allow God's Word to keep you a believing believer—stable and grounded. This is especially important when facing health challenges. When you have health challenges, many things may come your way—doubts, fears, negative proclamations, expiration dates, and so forth. Keeping God's words foremost in your thoughts and continuing to read His Word each day will keep you in a state of faith and peace. When we are in a state of peace, our nervous system is less stressed, and we have greater potential for sharper focus, better memory, more optimal cellular intake of nutrition, and more efficient elimination of wastes.

Be a faith builder by speaking and visualizing the promises of God daily. Speak them to your friends and family so often that they think of you when any emergency arises. Begin to teach them how they can take a stand. Renew your mind daily and align with the mind of Christ, where true mental health resides. Reject everything else.

Emotional health

We have learned praise is a way to calm our emotions in times of stress. Additionally any emotional trauma may play a huge factor in our wellness. I am convinced we should be taught from a young age how to master our emotions and how to frame our lives so we don't take our challenges too seriously. This would keep us from piling up so much emotional and traumatic baggage and having to spend so much time releasing it. I would never want to minimize the impact of anyone's pain and suffering, but we must remember that even these pale in the light of eternity and its wonders if we are willing to adjust our focus.

Let's examine a workable model for emotional health that has brought victory to many of my clients in their personal healing journeys. We will use this model frequently when we work through each body system.

Emotional energy is powerful. When clients pursue emotional health by addressing suppressed emotions and the trauma often buried with them during biofeedback, it is the norm for a powerful release of stress to occur. We don't want these buried stresses to control our bodies.

To begin, let's agree together that God created emotions when He created mankind and pronounced His creation good. Emotions are invisible energies that serve as powerful catalysts to propel us toward healthy actions if they are used constructively. Emotions serve us for good if we act upon them in a godly manner. They become a problem when we have an ungodly or traumatic response to our emotional state or if we harbor destructive emotions and trauma within our bodies and their organs and nerves.

As long as we understand this and how we may release and resolve such emotions, we will have a very powerful tool for our health. There is a large body of evidence, especially in Chinese constitutional medicine, that unresolved emotions become trapped and stored in the body as invisible stressors and that this impacts organ function, much as a toxin does. This information stems from over three thousand years of Chinese medical assessments on body-emotion connections. Their conclusions correlate in principle with biblical teaching on emotions and their physical impact.

Additionally Chinese medicine has identified correlations between certain emotions and the specific organs they affect. For instance, the liver and gallbladder are affected by anger; the heart and small intestine are affected by joy (as well as its lack); the spleen and stomach are affected by overthinking, anxiety, or worry; the lungs and large intestine are affected by grief; and the kidneys and bladder are affected by fear.[5] It is much more complex than this short overview, as we have many emotions, but you get the idea.

When we release negative emotions and trauma by speaking their names and commanding them to leave, our minds often become clearer and more at peace and our bodies relax. It also appears that the ability to release toxins greatly improves. Every experiment I have done for years supports this. I am so convinced of this that I believe almost all dysfunction in the body and mind has an emotional and/or traumatic component as its root. In America we are just beginning to understand how our emotions interact with our bodies.

The model I have developed for clearing away negative emotions is the biblical concept of speaking to our mountains and commanding them to move through declarative prayers. It has served as a wonderful and very dramatic way to release all types of stress within the body systems.

What might the processing of our emotions look like? For starters, the healthy expression of emotion includes acknowledging it and expressing it to God and others with the intent to release it in a constructive, gentle, loving manner. However, many people, especially those who are ill, do not handle their emotions in a healthy way. Some people handle emotions by blowing up (venting). Others silently chew on their emotions for a while, then swallow them back down, suppressing them into their bodies.

When we vent our emotions, we obsess over the issue and continually feed our concern until the emotions push to the surface and erupt. Those who vent tend to do it with friends and family, who may try to assist until they see the person prefers to grumble and complain instead of trying to solve the issue in a healthy manner. Stress is being managed through a cycle of eruption that exhausts others, who often respond over time by creating distance.

When we suppress our emotions, we chew on them silently and swallow them down, into our bellies, where they find a place to dwell in our organs. This may add stress and compromise the affected organs until we choose to face the emotion and evict it. Burying an emotion never truly gets rid of it, and our bodies respond with stress and discomfort. No amount of medication truly resolves this issue. The emotions must be released and faced.

We weren't made to continually vent or suppress our emotions. God has healthy ways to resolve all our emotions properly—even ones caused by traumatic events, which often involve terror, shock, and injury of some type. Trauma may be any event that blindsides us without warning—such as an accident, death, divorce, abuse, wartime event, animal attack, or the like—and it often happens so quickly that we do not have the time or tools to defend against it. It may form a strong blueprint of stress that keeps our bodies in bondage for years if we don't release it. (See appendix C for a demonstration of how one might release trauma.)

I work most often with three basic groupings of emotions: the anger family, the sorrow family, and the fear family. One important offshoot from the anger family is unforgiveness, which often includes resentment and bitterness. Let's explore each in turn.

Anger

Anger is generally a response to some kind of injustice, where boundaries are crossed. Godly anger teaches us to fight against injustice and to restore healthy boundaries and relationships. Ungodly anger, hatred, and rage can stem from our selfish ambitions and may push us to seek revenge and destroy relationships. Anger may especially affect the liver, colon, and any organ where inflammation and heat are present. It is a hot emotion and, in many cases, may be a factor related to chronic inflammation and the holding of the toxins that spark it.

God's solution for anger is for us to forgive and ask forgiveness, to pray for those who treat us wrongly, and to restore relationships in a gentle and humble manner. He says to turn all injustices over to Him, promising that He will take care of them properly. If we do all of these and fail in reconciling a relationship, at least we are at peace, knowing we did our best. We must move on.

Resentment, bitterness, and unforgiveness

When an unjust situation is not resolved properly, the result can be resentment, bitterness, and unforgiveness. This may occur when we are waiting for the other party to make things right, which may never happen. Then we have to decide what we are going to do with our destructive thoughts and feelings.

If a person has sinned against you, there is a natural law of consequences that takes care of the injustice. People don't truly escape the offenses they have committed. On some level the injustice will be righted. Any method of revenge only poisons the person committing it. Let the Lord's natural law of consequences, which may or may not include the legal system, take the issue off your shoulders so you can forgive (release them), be at peace, and move on.

Sorrow

Sorrow is a response to loss. We learn from sorrow, grief, and heartbreak that all things in this life are temporary and that we must look to God as our true source of peace, comfort, and hope. Godly sorrow teaches us how our sin negatively affects our lives and the lives of others. It is a catalyst for repentance and restoration.

Ungodly sorrow is a prolonging of grief and heartbreak to the point that it keeps us in bondage physically, mentally, and emotionally. Prolonged sorrow can make our bodies and immune systems sluggish and depressed. We may retreat from God, our families, and our responsibilities in this place. Maybe this is why in the Old Testament, God often set a period of thirty days for mourning.

In response to sorrow God promises to bind up the brokenhearted, to give beauty for ashes, and to give us a hope and a future. We are to offer comfort to one another. The best antidote to sorrow is gratefulness and praise for the blessings we enjoyed for a season, even though the giving of gratitude and praise may not feel natural at first. When I first acted upon this information, I was surprised how fast my heart healed.

Fear

Most fear is produced when we take our focus off of God and His love for us. The only approved fear in the Bible is described as fear of the Lord, which respects God for the great and powerful being He is and follows with our being obedient to Him because of His position.

Ungodly worry, anxiety, and fear are tormentors that rob our peace and war against our faith. These can keep us from trusting God enough to receive His promises for our health. When we live in fear, we have placed our faith in the devil's ability to hurt us and make our lives go badly.

Fear of people is a snare to us and will rob us of opportunities to serve God. Prolonged fear, worry, or anxiety is unhealthy and stressful to our immune systems, kidneys, nervous systems, and more. It may manifest as a tightening, constricting force within our bodies.

God's answer to fear is to remember who we are in Christ and how much He loves us. He wants us to learn courage and peace by exercising our faith and activating His power by speaking His promises. Many Scripture verses tell us God promises to be our protector and shield and that we can take courage in His presence. And finally, as far as death is concerned for the Christian it is an upgrade!

Here's an example of how dealing with fear can look. I once had a hair-raising encounter with fear when I was followed by an obvious mugger while walking alone through an industrial area in Hawaii. I started out walking with a group of strangers from a conference center, but a strange character was in our midst. The two men in the group took notice. The stranger wore a hoodie, ball cap, and sunglasses in 80-degree weather. His face was partially obscured and unrecognizable.

In the first ten minutes the group melted away to different destinations, and I found myself alone, heading for a hotel that was still several blocks away. My large computer was sticking halfway out of my bag, and there was no question this guy wanted my computer and purse.

He dogged my heels persistently. Then he disappeared for a short time, and I took the advantage to run a very long block that was bordered by industrial buildings with no visible entrances on my side. Suddenly he appeared again, no more than a foot behind me.

I took a deep breath and visualized myself protected by God's angels. Then I verbally whispered over and over, "My God is my shield and protector." I looked straight ahead and not back at him. He followed on my heels for five long blocks. I kept hearing in my mind, "Don't turn around," and I didn't. When I finally arrived at a small store, I ducked into it, and he disappeared.

As I reflected on this situation later, I came to believe I activated God's protecting power on my behalf through verbally speaking God's Word over my circumstance, and choosing to "see" God's reality and promises over what my senses screamed brought me confidence and peace.

God has all the provisions we need for dealing with all of our emotional challenges—anger, sorrow, fear, worry, bitterness, resentment, unforgiveness, trauma, and more. We can take the liberty to command these from all of our cellular blueprints—from any stories of our lives, from our gestation and birth, and from any carryover our ancestors gave us. This may sound unusual, but I have found much evidence that especially difficult challenges appear to carry a strong connection to birth trauma, gestational stress (likely from the mother), and ancestral connections. In fact, some of the toughest patterns seem to emanate from this last place.

As we study body-system healing in the next chapters, I will note the issues that, when verbally released, seem to most favorably impact the body system listed. All my clients are successful in using these. You can do it also! Don't even waste a second in doubt over this.

CHECKLIST REVIEW

Let's take a moment to review what we have covered in this section. Put a checkmark next to the items you have engraved within your thoughts and heart.

❑ I have learned what it takes to be a son or daughter of God, and knowing this allows me to partner with God in my pursuit of health. I have accepted His invitation and am committed to walk with Him in truth.

❑   I have learned God wants me to be well and have memorized some ways I can receive from Him. (This includes everything from adopting a healthy diet and lifestyle to learning healing scriptures and promises from God's Word.)

❑   I have begun to memorize some of God's promises.

❑   I have learned that daily joy and praise center my emotions and elevate my trust in and love for God. I am praising and giving thanks daily.

❑   I believe I have authority over my spirit, my state of mind, my emotions, my body, my actions, my dwelling, and the devil.

❑   I have learned that words are powerful and can be used for health and healing. I am conscious of what I am saying to myself and others.

❑   I am growing in boldness and confidence.

❑   I believe I can speak to my mountains. If I do this with confidence, without doubting, they will move. I am practicing commanding my mountains to vaporize, dumping them into the sea, and commanding them never to return. I always fill the vacancy that's left behind with God's healthy principles and promises from Scripture.

❑   I believe God's report trumps man's report each time. I am beginning to build an arsenal of the good reports of God in order to speak them and place them in authority over any limiting report that comes from man.

❑   I believe God's healing starts in the supernatural and in the invisible blueprints of my being. This is the foundation and root system upon which good or ill health can take hold.

❑   I have learned that when I build a faith foundation by
    hearing and reading the Word daily, it keeps me focused
    and confident. I am driving out fear, doubt, and wavering,
    and providing a foundation for a miraculous life.

❑   I know how to make a case for healing. I am learning
    the scriptures that back me up.

❑   I believe that when I pray according to God's will,
    which is revealed in Scripture, He hears me and
    responds. I know at least ten healing scriptures upon
    which I can stand.

❑   I don't wait until I see to believe. I see the final result in
    my mind first, just as God sees it.

❑   I see myself well and my body moving toward well-
    ness. This lays down a blueprint for change in my being.
    God's words are life and health to all my flesh. They
    cause the worldly reality to bend to His will. I declare
    myself well in body, mind, emotions, and spirit, kicking
    any unwholesomeness to the curb.

❑   I guard my body by eating well. I know that herbs and
    essential oils are good for my health. I am considering
    the use of healing water as an easy starting point.

❑   I am transforming and guarding my mind by focusing
    on what God says, on His good reports, on gratefulness,
    and on love toward God and my fellow man.

❑   I guard my emotions by not letting them fester or bring
    disease into my body. I speak with integrity and resolve
    all issues in a timely manner with grace and gentleness. I
    realize these can be factors in keeping me well and main-
    taining my health after it returns.

PART II

EQUIPPED TO HEAL

Using Your God-Given Authority

CHAPTER 6

YOUR NEXT STEP

OW THAT WE have set down a wonderful foundation of knowledge about the power of healing words—and specifically God's words—to effect healing in our lives, it is time to take the next step. In this section we will get quite practical.

Each chapter that follows gives special consideration to each major system housed in the body. For each body system, you will learn how it was created to optimally function, what factors lead to its compromise, and common illnesses that manifest in that system. We will also gain insight into causes of compromise from Chinese constitutional medicine. Then we will apply the five foundations for optimal health—good food, herbs, essential oils, water, and lifestyle—making them specific for each body system.

Lastly, and most importantly, we will spend time in God's Word. You are given specific scriptures that lay the foundation for how to pray for that particular body system. That is followed by a powerful prayer tailored for that particular body system. The prayer is exhaustive, covering a variety of issues you may encounter related to that body system. You may not need to pray every aspect included in the prayer, as it contains much more than I typically cover in one session with clients. But the broad range of insights are there to ensure that your need is addressed. Last, you are given personalized Bible verses you can use to speak God's promises over that part of your body daily.

Because each chapter is so specific, focused on one body system at a time, you will be able to quickly find the help you need, based on your body's needs at any given time, and easily begin to apply the related truths to your life.

Before we dive in, let me share a few guidelines that will serve you as we move forward.

1. Remember to verbally command your mountains from all your deepest cellular blueprints. This is defined as releasing them out of all the stories of your life, including your gestation, birth, and any carryover you've received from your ancestors. By commanding your mountains in this specific way, you will reach the core of your genetic and vital components.

2. Know that you may need to work on a body system over a period of time. Speaking to it once doesn't mean you won't have to speak to it again routinely for a period of time.

3. The Bible says there is a time and season for everything. Accordingly you may only peel a piece of the issue away during your first go around. Persevere, even though it may seem repetitive, until you see the results of peace that you desire and you no longer feel any remnants of the buried emotion, trauma, or physical manifestation. Prayer is very valuable here. Satan may also bring some of your symptoms back, challenging you to fall into a defeated mind-set. Don't do it. Restate your position vigorously.

4. Heed a note of caution about overdoing these releases. After this work the body shifts and rebalances, and it may need two to seven days to stabilize. Do not overdo it by addressing more than one or two body systems in a sitting. Also, do not speak these prayers and promises in your car while driving or while doing any potentially dangerous activity. You could get dizzy or faint, and that would be dangerous! Listen to your body in the beginning, and you will soon know how much you are able to tolerate in a single prayer session.

5. Know that you may feel a toxic release. I make sure I am drinking eight to ten glasses of pure water daily,

and I add nightly Epsom salt baths—I stir 2–3 cups into the bath water and stay in the water for twenty minutes—until these toxic releases pass. You might also enjoy the even more powerful essential oil bath recipes included in each chapter.

6. Rest assured that it is normal to feel emotional after you experience an emotional release. In the beginning I experienced a few days of intense irritability after releasing anger. When releasing sorrow, you may feel sad for a few days and have a good cry. (I have not seen any emotional side effect to releasing fear.) Drink lots of water to allow the body to flush out any toxins that have been let go with these releases.

7. Make the change to healthy lifestyle habits to help maintain healing—and enjoy your transformation!

Lastly, I encourage you to consider creating a structured approach to prayer for your health. The following is an example of what you might include. I find the more thorough I am in prayer, the better the results I see, especially with tougher challenges.

You might wish to copy this sample and put it in your prayer closet as a guideline to begin with before you start to address your specific challenge. Please copy the prayer to release trauma found in appendix C, which may, in many cases, remove the issue at its deepest core.

Sample Prayer

First, give God praise and thanks.

Dear heavenly Father, I enter Your gates and into Your throne room with praise, gratitude, and confidence. You are King of kings and Lord of lords. You have magnified the name of Jesus, the name at which every other name must bow, including the name of any illness. I give thanks for the atonement of Your Son and for all the provisions lovingly made for my healing on

*every level. You have provided forgiveness for all my sins and
healing for all my diseases, and I take You at Your Word.*

Next, clear obstacles of unforgiveness and unbelief.

*I turn from and ask forgiveness for any undealt-with sins,
known and unknown, in my life, including that of any
unbelief in Your Word. [Take a moment to confess anything that is on your conscience.] I forgive all men, all
women, any issue I have with society, and any blame I
harbor toward You. You take care of all injustice in Your
time. I can let it go. I also forgive myself for all my errors.*

Now, dump the devil.

*I proclaim to all dark forces and the devil: Because of what
Jesus accomplished on the cross, you are a defeated foe! I
have submitted to God, and I resist you. You have no power
over me or my body, in the name of Jesus. I bind and bar you
from any attack of any nature on my being, my family, my
animals, my home, and my property. Jesus is the name above
all names. All His enemies are under His feet, including you.
I am a member of the body of Christ, His hands and feet
on earth. What God has put under Jesus's feet is therefore
under my feet also. I stand upon that authority. Go and be
gone! My health and my body are free from you.*

Renounce negative reports.

*I renounce and release all negative reports and pronounce-
ments I have received from others, including my doctors, over
my health that do not line up with Your Word. I command
them from my deepest cellular blueprints; they must go out
and into the sea. It is done. Everything is possible with God. I
will stand upon Your reports, God, and meditate upon them.*

Make a declaration to build your faith.

I command this challenge that has manifested [name your specific challenge] and any painful story associated with it to be bound under the authority of Christ and the power of His Word. I stand in strength, confidence, and boldness upon what You have said, God. All of Your promises are yes and amen, and I can count on You keeping Your Word. Lord, You are my strength, my refuge, and my power. Signs and wonders follow those who believe, and I believe! I give You total glory and honor for my healing.

Affirm God's desire for you to be healthy.

I am awesomely and wonderfully made in all my parts. Therefore, any less than that does not belong within me. I will make a picture of what my wellness looks like and view it daily. I allow others to pray for me and lay their hands upon me. I will see my internal being overflowing with God's stream of healing water. I see myself at His table, in the refuge of His wings, where no sickness or infirmity can dwell, and with my eyes set upon Jesus with patience and endurance. I am improving each day in every good way. I will keep my focus on Christ and reply with scripture to any doubts about my healing that others or Satan hurl my way. They will not take my healing from me. I will run my race to the end and win. I am a child of God, and this is my heritage!

Thank you, Father, for the work You have done. I receive it! I pray in Your Son's powerful name. Amen.

CHAPTER 7

THE IMMUNE SYSTEM

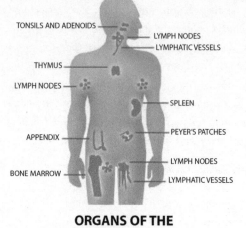

TONSILS AND ADENOIDS — LYMPH NODES — LYMPHATIC VESSELS — THYMUS — LYMPH NODES — SPLEEN — APPENDIX — PEYER'S PATCHES — BONE MARROW — LYMPH NODES — LYMPHATIC VESSELS

ORGANS OF THE IMMUNE SYSTEM

W**HAT IF YOUR** immune system took care of any antagonist that tried to attack your body? What if your lungs felt healthy, vital, and strong? What if any swelling, pain, or inflammation was short-lived? What if you stopped getting sick altogether? As believers we have access to this health plan. It is God's will for us to live victoriously over all invaders.

The immune system is one of the most fascinating and important of all the body systems. When functioning properly, it is a tremendous defensive fortress, complete with its own fighting soldiers—cells that are made to attack and clear foreign organisms, allergens, and all mutated and diseased cells from our bodies.

Our skin is one of our first lines of defense, functioning as a protective barrier, as do our mucous membranes, the slippery moist tissue on the inside of the mouth, nose, lungs, eyes, sexual organs, and intestines. Our stomach and digestive system participate by secreting strong acid and enzymes that can kill invasive germs and parasites. Our digestion houses trillions of friendly bacteria, which are a critical component of our immunity. Beyond this barrier, specific immune cells engulf and attack invaders. The marrow in our bones is even involved in our immunity.

The lymphatic vessels and glands are present throughout our entire body. They contain clear fluid that continually bathes and cleanses our cells, transporting the cellular waste into the lymphatic glands (nodes), where invaders are destroyed. Toxins are then transported through lymphatic vessels and passed into the bloodstream for elimination. The lymphatic system is a type of circulatory system, but it has no heart to pump it. It moves through our chest inhalations and exhalations, and our movement in general. The more efficiently the lymphatic fluid moves due to our movement and exercise, the more we have a sense of well-being and an ability to resist illness. Our lymphatic system includes the tonsils, adenoids, spleen, thymus, appendix, and Peyer's patches lining the intestines.

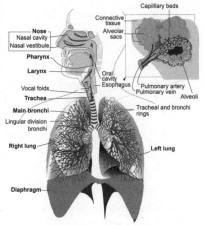

ANATOMY OF THE RESPIRATORY SYSTEM

The good bacteria (friendly flora) within our gut should be well-populated and well-fed with healthy food to keep invaders at bay. These are critical to our entire body and promote healthy digestion, immunity, proper weight, and mental sharpness. Antibiotics, chemotherapy, radiation, certain medications, coffee, alcohol, environmental chemicals, junk foods, and chronic mental and emotional stress may negatively impact these friendly bacteria to varying degrees, diminishing their numbers and resulting in overgrowth of unfriendly bacteria, fungi, molds, viruses, and parasites. These, in turn, may harm our immunity and contribute to various illnesses, including diabetes, mental sluggishness, and obesity.

The bone marrow, the soft, fatty, spongy tissue that lies in the interior of our bones, is critically important for a healthy immune response. The stem cells it produces can develop into white blood cells (fighter cells), red blood cells, and platelets.

Healthy lungs are also a powerful part of our defense system and vitality and a barrier to inhaled invaders. The respiratory system is composed primarily of our sinuses and lungs. The lungs oxygenate the blood and carry away carbon dioxide waste as we exhale.

When all these parts are working properly together, it contributes to a healthy vitality and freedom from illness.

CHINESE CONSTITUTIONAL INSIGHTS

In Chinese medicine the immune system is likened to a strong metal shield used in battle that functions as the protector of the body. It is associated with the lungs and the mucous membranes. The respiratory system is thought to be involved in the healthy circulation of strength and vitality throughout the body. The lungs have a strong relationship with the large intestine, and what affects one may also affect the other. Hunching or rounding the shoulders may be a physical sign that the body is protecting weakened lungs. Those with challenges in this area may tend to have various types of respiratory weakness and congestion. Emotionally there may be a tendency to hold unprocessed sadness, grief, heartbreak, betrayal, rejection, and abandonment.

FACTORS THAT MAY LEAD TO COMPROMISE

Bad bacteria are held in check by friendly bacteria in the gut. If bad bacteria overgrow, they produce toxins that may compromise any organ of the body. Dental infections within the jawbone or from a root canal may be one of the most insidious and destructive forces against immune health and are sometimes silent perpetrators of serious challenges. In any case of cancer of the jaw, neck, or chest, please consider thermography (also known as medical infrared imaging), which detects surface body heat that results from biochemical reactions. A friend of mine had a thermal image taken and was able to see a red line of inflammation leading from an old root canal right down to the site of the breast cancer.

Viruses are unusual entities containing genetic material surrounded by a protein coating, which may make them difficult to detect by the body. They do not reproduce on their own but trick the cells into replicating more viruses. Often the host cell dies in this process.

Yeasts and molds exist naturally in the body, but patterns of overgrowth may be detected when the body struggles with a high-sugar diet, heavy-metal toxicity, or the side effects of certain drugs, including antibiotics. These overgrowths can mimic many diseases and often are a factor in bloating, indigestion, fatigue, brain fog, and skin rashes that involve itching.

Parasites and worms are not as rare as you may think. They are attracted to diseased tissues. There are many recorded cases in the United States.

Chemicals present in cleaning agents, pesticides, and all the elements of industry can be inhaled or absorbed into the body through the skin and may disrupt the immune system and friendly flora.

Heavy metals, such as lead, arsenic, mercury, copper, aluminum, nickel, and cadmium may challenge immune health. Sources of these can include our water pipes, polluted air from industry, pesticides, silver dental fillings, aluminum foil, antiperspirants, toxic food and fish, and certain types of metal cooking pans. There are more sources, but this is a good list to consider and investigate first.

Radiation and electromagnetic pollution includes a spectrum of invisible pollutants that include the emanations from X-rays and scans, cell phones, computers, power lines, and almost any equipment that is plugged into a wall socket. I have many concerns about radiation and scans, and I believe they are overused.

Radiation is an accumulative toxin, a known inflammatory carcinogen, and it especially affects the skeletal system, bone marrow, and thyroid. I see interesting patterns of symptoms that lead me to believe it also may highly impact the pancreas and intestinal flora. Further study needs to be conducted to determine whether it influences the many cases of blood sugar imbalances, chronic fatigue, gut flora disturbances, immune compromise, acidity, and osteoporosis, and to what degree it creates inflammatory and oxidative (aging) damage within the body.

Osteoporosis is rare in third world populations, which can't afford many high-tech diagnostics. Please read up on the CT scan and other forms of radiation and become knowledgeable about what you allow into your body and in what circumstances these tests are warranted. I recommend browsing the American Nuclear Society's website, where you can estimate your personal annual radiation dose.

Certain vaccine additives and ingredients, including foreign DNA, may require more study and have recently been suspected in some types of autoimmune responses, where the body is found to be attacking itself.[1] Who really knows what foreign DNA and some of the metallic and other additives are doing within our bodies? Could any of these make their way into the cells, causing a recognition challenge by the immune system? If your doctor hasn't shown you the ingredient list for the vaccine he or she is recommending so that your consent can be well-informed, please research the vaccines for yourself. Vaccines have been a controversial subject for decades, and it is important for you to be informed and confident in your choices.

GMO foods are another area of concern. We don't know the extent to which genetically altered "food" will affect us. Almost all corn and soy are genetically modified unless they are labeled organic, and there are many more foods on this growing list of genetically modified organisms, including sugar from sugar beets and papaya. We have a right to know which foods have been modified and choose what we are eating.

Any item mentioned previously has the potential to form significant stress within our bodies if the immune system views it as toxic and it isn't eliminated properly. If our lymphatic system becomes devitalized or clogged with debris, symptoms of pain, swelling, discomfort, and fatigue may arise. We may toss and turn more in the night in an effort to properly move the flow of lymph. Illness develops when inflammation cannot resolve properly.

Stress in any form, including trauma and emotional stress, further adds to immune compromise. I have seen much evidence through the years that stress may contribute to various toxins and other invaders piling up and overwhelming the body. Prolonged stress from fear, worry, and anxiety has great potential to sabotage our immune response. Short-term rises in the hormone cortisol assist us in coping with immediate stressors. However, prolonged high levels of cortisol, often called the "death hormone" in these cases, block the production of vitally important interleukin-1 and 2, which are our big-gun protectors against allergens and diseased cells, including cancer. God never intended our immunity to be compromised in this way.

Grief, sadness, heartbreak, betrayal, abandonment, rejection, despair, and depression may contribute to immune, respiratory, and lymphatic dysfunction and fatigue. Unforgiveness, resentment, envy, and jealousy may affect the bone marrow, where stem cells and blood cells are made. Physically the lungs may also become stressed from cold air, shallow breathing, lack of exercise, dehydration, and the poor elimination of waste by the colon. Chronic sinus or lung congestion may indicate a need to cleanse the liver and gallbladder and deal with these emotional issues.

If you have significant immune system challenges, what stressful components in your life are you willing to change? It may be very important for you to think about this in order to get well.

COMMON ILLNESS MANIFESTATIONS

Any sicknesses—from colds to cancer—involve a compromised, weakened immunity. Allergies and autoimmune diseases are related to a hyperactive immune response. The respiratory system may experience flu, pneumonia, emphysema, asthma, excessive phlegm, bronchitis, and infections. Chronic inflammation (heat and pain) may occur in any tissue of the body when there is not enough vitality to clear the causal factors.

APPLYING THE FIVE FOUNDATIONS
OF OPTIMAL HEALTH

Good food

First and foremost, consider the guidelines listed in the food section of chapter 5. Next, make space in your pantry for good food by first dumping any item containing devitalized foods with devitalized refined sugars, which can depress the function of our white blood cells. Toss out the white flour, refined white rice, and all junk foods. Dairy products, especially those that are highly processed, can challenge the lymphatics if you have any reactivity to them. Do you clear your throat of mucus right after eating any dairy product? If so, consider omitting dairy until you change your health habits to encourage the body to have a more neutral response.

Emphasize nut milks and bone broth, raw goat and sheep milk cheeses if tolerated, and green leafy vegetables to nourish your marrow. Include omega-3 oils found in salmon and other oily fish, walnut and flax oil, and vitamin C-rich and lymphatic-friendly foods, such as apples, pomegranate juice and seeds, lemon juice, grapefruit, and peppers. Enjoy carrots, onions, garlic, ginger, horseradish, cayenne pepper, and turmeric to feed the entire immune system.

Herbs

Read about and consider using dandelion, chlorophyll, astragalus, cat's claw, pau d'arco, paw paw, Oregon grape, and slippery elm. A general rule that I often follow is to choose three to six of these herbs and take two capsules of each twice daily with meals.

Essential oils

Here is one of my favorite therapeutic baths, which I call Power Baths, to assist my body in detoxification to improve immune system health:

Pine Needle Oil and Ginger Powder Power Bath

Place 2 cups kosher salt, ¼ cup powdered bulk ginger, and ¼ teaspoon of pine needle oil in a bowl and mix well with a fork. This makes one bath. Soak in this bath eighteen minutes, keeping the neck and chest submerged. Afterward you might choose to apply five drops each of lemon and eucalyptus oil mixed with 1 tablespoon of walnut oil onto the chest. Consider taking two of these baths weekly until any immune challenges have cleared.

One may also find it helpful to experiment with lemon oil—four to ten drops mixed with a tablespoon of carrier oil such as grape seed applied to the chest each day—to nourish healthy lymphatic drainage.

Note: Avoid essential oils when pregnant or nursing.

Water

Drink eight to ten glasses of pure water daily. Remember, the powerful healing water that is imprinted with biblical truths, affirmations, and specific scriptures can further aid in improving your well-being.

Lifestyle

If you smoke, please stop. Keep chemicals and toxic cleaners out of the home and off your lawn. (There are many alternatives to these that you may investigate or make yourself.) Limit antibiotic use as much as possible to avoid developing resistant strains of bacteria and to prevent cycles of sickness from weakening gut immunity.

Consider using a minitrampoline for lymphatic stimulation for about thirty minutes daily. Start off with a soft, gentle bounce and work into a comfortable routine.

Add dry skin brushing toward the heart using a natural vegetable bristle brush before showering. This, along with taking therapeutic Power Baths using essential oils, has been reported by clients to help reduce cellulite. Getting regular massages and exercise, and daily cultivating heartfelt joy and peace all help care for the immune system, as does making it a priority to rid yourself of all trauma and buried emotional baggage.

Forgiveness is critically important. Forgive everyone, either in person or while in prayer in your closet, and do it verbally. Command off all cellular blueprints of resentment, bitterness, and unforgiveness that could have come into your body from any source. Change your behavior and words toward those you have forgiven so your behavior reflects your decision to see them as another of God's creations who is a work in progress, as you are.

Practice lung-strengthening breathing exercises: While walking, swing your arms by the sides, palms inward. Take two breaths in through the nose, take a quick pause, then exhale through the mouth. Consider doing this for thirty minutes daily to build strong lungs.

Enjoy the outdoors. Treat yourself to a walk on the beach, in the forest, or by waterfalls, where the air is fresh and full of healing ions. Open the windows at night and air out the indoor pollution from your carpets and furniture. Practice singing to exercise the lungs and diaphragm. Have a wonderful plan for your future. God already does—agree with Him!

BIBLICAL PATHWAY TO HEALING

These are some scriptures that form the partial basis for our verbal prayer for this body system. The rest of the prayer is based on my experiences with patients during biofeedback sessions. Notice how emotions and mind-sets can affect our body parts.

+ Evict all grief: "Be gracious to me, O LORD, for I am in trouble; my eye wastes away with grief, yes, my soul and my body" (Ps. 31:9).

+ Verbally expel all forms of evil and plagues. You are limited only by your imagination. If you have any concerns about anything, name it and put it into this group: "No evil shall befall you, nor shall any plague come near your dwelling" (Ps. 91:10, NKJV).

+ Evict all wrath, anger, and jealousy: "Wrath is cruel, and anger is outrageous, but who is able to stand before envy?" (Prov. 27:4).

+ Evict all trauma, shock, extreme fear, and terror: "The soldiers shook for fear of him and became like dead men" (Matt. 28:4).

+ Evict all worry and anxiety: "Who of you by worrying
  can add one cubit to his height?...And do not seek
  what you will eat or what you will drink, nor be of an
  anxious mind....But seek the kingdom of God, and all
  these things shall be given to you" (Luke 12:25, 29, 31).

+ Evict all revenge and the resentment behind it. Forgive
  and give the injustice over to God: "Beloved, do not
  avenge yourselves, but rather give place to God's wrath,
  for it is written: 'Vengeance is Mine. I will repay,' says
  the Lord" (Rom. 12:19).

+ Dump all addictions: "'All things are lawful for me,' but
  not all things are helpful. 'All things are lawful for me,'
  but I will not be brought under the power of anything"
  (1 Cor. 6:12).

+ Evict all guilt and shame and their harmful side effects.
  Ask forgiveness for any offenses you may have committed against others: "Fight a good fight, keeping faith
  and a good conscience, which some having rejected
  and suffered shipwreck in regard to their faith" (1 Tim.
  1:18–19)

+ Evict all bitterness and any of its side effects: "Lest any
  root of bitterness spring up to cause trouble, and many
  become defiled by it" (Heb. 12:15).

HEALING PRAYER

Speak this prayer aloud with boldness and confidence. Take your
time and envision what you are saying. Exert the authority that has
been given to you in Christ. In Him all things are possible.

> *Dear heavenly Father,*
>
> *In the name of Your precious Son, Jesus, I thank You*
> *for Your wonderful promises of deliverance, protection,*
> *and safety. I do not have to be sick! No plague shall come*

near my dwelling, as I have been given Your authority and power over them.

You have given me these promises so that I may have peace and not anxiety. I set my mind on the things above and not on the things on this earth. Your Word teaches that I, as Your child, sit in heavenly places with You and at Your bountiful table. I abide under Your almighty shadow and under Your wings, where no disease dare live. I will say to You, Lord, You are my refuge and my fortress, and I will see this protection around every cell in my being. I place the powerful name of Jesus into all my cellular blueprints. I will proclaim that evil and toxic substances and patterns cannot dwell or reenter any longer. They all must all bow to Jesus's mighty name!

I praise you, heavenly Father, that the things that are impossible with men are easily possible with You. You have given good counsel to guide me. You are for me. Who can prevail against me or my immunity? Absolutely nothing!

With the powerful name and words of Jesus, I am fully equipped to receive healing. I command and evict from all deep cellular blueprints of my immunity, lymphatics, skin, bone marrow, lungs, sinuses, all breathing centers, their nerves and circulation mechanisms:

All forms of emotional stress

All wrath, hatred, anger, resentments, bitterness, envy and jealousy, and revenge

All depression, sadness, grief, heartbreak, despair, rejection, and abandonment

All self-condemnation, conflict, and guilt

All types of trauma, terror, fear, worry, and anxiety

All addictions to food, alcohol, chemicals, inhalants, and anything else that is damaging to my immunity or respiratory system

All pestilence and plagues [You may name any sickness or invasive organism you are concerned about.]

All side effects or painful stories associated with any of these things

All scar tissue, all accidents, all injury, and any side effects, including that of surgery and all traumatic words from any person, including my doctor

All toxic allergens and all improper allergy responses to my air, environment, and food

Any stored medication toxicity and side effects

All stored pollutants and chemicals from outside or inside my home, especially cleaning supplies and industrial pollution

Any vaccine side effects, including those from metallic additives and foreign DNA

All absorbed radiation from scans, X-rays, mammograms, cell phones, computers, power lines, or any other source and all side effects

All toxic metals, including aluminum, lead, mercury, copper, nickel, cadmium, and any side effects

All bacteria, viruses, yeasts, molds, parasites, worms, and any other type of plague and any side effects

All negative or toxic cellular programming or blueprints of any type, from any source

I command these mountains and all painful stories that may be connected to them to vaporize and completely leave all my cellular blueprints and parts —they must all go with none remaining. I command them into the sea, never to return. I declare them gone. I am finished with them.

To fill the vacancies these created, I take a seat at the bountiful table the Lord has prepared for me. I partake of all His remedies for my perfect immunity. This includes perfect cellular immunity, perfect lymphatics, perfect respiratory parts, perfect skin, and perfect bone marrow.

I drink in love, hope, peace, mercy, compassion, acceptance, Your faithfulness, and my ability to extend forgiveness toward all. I accept Your Word into all my deepest parts, as it is health to all my flesh. I will live to declare the

Lord's works! You are my shield and protector against anything that would harm me. No plague shall come near my body or home as I stand within Jesus's mighty name.

All sickness is gone, anything opposing me is made to submit, and I declare all attacks of the devil to be quenched. My breath is held in Your hands, and I breathe in easily and receive my fill of Your joy.

Your beauty and good plans for my future fill the hollows of any destroyed dreams or goals. All my needs are supplied.

I continue to taste and drink these wonderful remedies from the Lord's table daily until I see myself filled from the soles of my feet to the top of my head, making me complete and well. I choose to see myself living in divine health and blessed immunity. I praise You daily, heavenly Father. Amen.

HEALING DECLARATIONS

These personalized scriptures will feed the new seeds you have planted. Declare these powerful verses daily.

> I shall serve the Lord my God, and He will bless my bread and my water. He will take sickness away from me (Exod. 23:25).

> I am saved by the Lord, the shield of my help and the sword of His people's majesty! My enemies shall submit to me, and I shall tread down their high places (Deut. 33:29).

> In Your hand is my life and breath (Job 12:10).

> The Spirit of God has made me, and the breath of the Almighty gives me life (Job 33:4).

> I have breath, and with it I praise the Lord (Ps. 150:6).

> My soul is satisfied as with marrow and fatness, and my mouth praises You with joyful lips (Ps. 63:5).

> I shall not die, but live, and declare the works of the Lord (Ps. 118:17).

I consider the poor and am blessed; the Lord will deliver me in times of trouble. The Lord will preserve me and keep me alive, and I will be blessed on the earth. You will not deliver me to the will of my enemies. The Lord will strengthen me on my bed of illness; You will sustain me on my sickbed (Ps. 41:1–3).

I give attention to Your words and incline my ear to Your sayings. I do not let them depart from my eyes; I keep them in the midst of my heart, for they are life to me as I find them, and health to all my flesh (Prov. 4:20–22).

You, Lord, think thoughts of peace and not evil toward me. You give me a hope and a future (Jer. 29:11).

Above all, I take the shield of faith which will be able to quench all the fiery darts of the wicked one (Eph. 6:16).

God will supply all my needs according to His riches in glory by Christ Jesus (Phil. 4:19).

Your Word is living and powerful, and sharper than any two-edged sword, piercing even to the division my soul and spirit, and of my joints and marrow (Heb. 4:12).

CHAPTER 8

THE ENDOCRINE SYSTEM

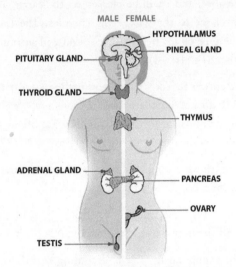

MALE FEMALE

HYPOTHALAMUS

PINEAL GLAND

PITUITARY GLAND

THYROID GLAND

THYMUS

ADRENAL GLAND

PANCREAS

OVARY

TESTIS

MAJOR ENDOCRINE GLANDS

*W*HAT IF EVERY morning you could rejoice in your strength, youthfulness, and vitality, just as the tremendous, godly, faith-filled men of Scripture did, men who were vital and strong into their old age, living lives dedicated to God and His promises? What if you could count on healthy sexual function and ease in conceiving and bearing children?

Each of these blessings resides within the health of our wonderful endocrine (hormonal) system and are within the scope of God's will for our strength and vitality.

The endocrine system is a group of glands that produce hormones that regulate how we grow, the shapes of our bodies, our hair growth, how we gain weight, how we digest and utilize our food, how we metabolize, how we respond sexually, and our quality of sleep. These glands communicate with our cells and affect cellular and tissue function, proper blood sugar, vitality, well-being, strength, youthfulness, and mood. Think of them as a symphony led by the master conductor: the pituitary gland, located in the brain. When all the glands are working properly, the symphony sounds harmonious. When even one becomes out of tune, it affects the performance of all the others. This system is closely entwined with the nervous system and how we perceive our lives.

The pituitary gland is a tiny, pea-sized gland located at the base of the brain. It is commonly called the "master gland" because it oversees the function and hormonal output of the other glands in the body.

The pineal gland is a small gland located deep within the center of the brain and is primarily known to control our body rhythms and sleep cycles by producing the hormone melatonin.

The hypothalamus is a gland located just above the brain stem that connects our nervous system to the rest of our glandular system. It processes our perceptions of life and assists in arranging the proper physical response. If we perceive life as stressful, the hypothalamus will assist our bodies by responding with an influx of stress hormones. This is why we need to learn to be at peace regardless of our environment. Otherwise we may be up and down emotionally, feel burned out, and be in constant need of hormonal support.

The pancreas is not technically an endocrine gland, but it does regulate our blood sugar with the help of insulin. Healthy blood sugar is also supported by the adrenal glands and liver.

The thyroid, parathyroid, and adrenal glands control our vitality and metabolism. The thyroid and adrenal gland work together for energy production, sexual balance, and much more. The thyroid also influences hair growth and quality and the function of the female system.

The sexual glands include the testes and prostate (for men) and the ovaries and breasts (for women). God wants us to be fruitful and be able to reproduce. God designed us to be healthy in these organs and not suffer stress and unpleasant symptoms. Sexual health is also entwined with the health of our thyroid, adrenal glands, and liver.

It is interesting that the foods for the thyroid are often the same foods that feed the ovaries, especially in the world of herbal foods. To possess a healthy head of hair, it will always be ideal to have a balance between all the glands.

CHINESE CONSTITUTIONAL INSIGHTS

Healthy female cycles, menstrual regularity, proper menstrual flow, healthy breasts, and healthy adrenal function are associated with healthy liver function. A tired or exhausted liver may be associated with PMS, scanty menstrual flow, and menopausal distress. A healthy heart and circulatory system is associated with virility. The opposite may lead to impotence. A healthy digestive system is associated with a healthy metabolism as well as comfort in the menstrual cycle. Urinary system health is associated with a healthy prostate and healthy blood sugar balance within the pancreas.

FACTORS THAT MAY LEAD TO COMPROMISE

How you perceive your world matters. We must apply a filter, or we will have stressful, hormonal ups and downs due to knee-jerk responses to the unpredictable world around us. When we allow our minds and emotions to react without control, our hormonal system, specifically the hypothalamus, takes note and our bodies mirror that reaction. We cannot allow anger, sorrow, fear, resentments, and other mind-sets and emotions such as these to dominate or we may stress our hormonal system continuously. Unhealthy relationships, especially with the opposite sex, and the conflicts that may arise from them may also create a source of continual stress, especially upon the sexual organs. We must be able to speak to each other with love and respect and not stuff our words, which may stress our throats and thyroids. Our focus must be on Christ and His promises, and we must receive the peace that comes from that. Our hormonal system will thank us!

As far as environmental factors, I grow concerned about excessive X-rays, especially because no one keeps a record of how many you have had, as well as cell phone and computer use. I'm also concerned about electrical pollution in general and how this affects our glandular function. Thyroid cancer is on the rise, and this gland is easily affected by radiation.

Because mercury vapor releases from silver-colored fillings even when brushing our teeth, I have concerns that this toxic metal may move into the lymphatic system and drain downward, affecting the body, including the thyroid and breast tissue. Investigate the facts and consider the alternatives that dentistry has to offer.

Our lifestyle is important. A lack of seeds and nuts in the diet affects the health of the glandular system. These contain key components that nourish our hormones.

Water infiltrated with chemicals from factories has been correlated in certain communities to disease and infertility issues.

Of course, poor diet, skipping meals, lack of exercise, junk food, and overuse of sugar, salt, and fat contribute to diabetes and a host of glandular imbalances. Many people stress their glands regularly with stimulants. We must return to our Creator's guidelines for a healthy diet of real food.

COMMON ILLNESS MANIFESTATIONS

Common manifestations of a compromised endocrine system may include sleep disturbances, feeling too hot or too cold, hair loss, hypoglycemia, diabetes, inability to heal properly, high cholesterol, visual disturbances, growth challenges, weight challenges, poor energy, fatigue, feeling faint or jittery between meals, irritability, headaches upon arising, falling asleep in the afternoon due to ups and downs in energy, stress, PMS, hot flashes, infertility, polycystic ovaries, uterine fibroid tumors, low sex drive, impotence, and breast diseases of all types—and this is just a partial list! Our hormones affect all of our body systems.

APPLYING THE FIVE FOUNDATIONS
OF OPTIMAL HEALTH

Good foods

Follow the guidelines in chapter 5 for a healthy, biblically based diet and rid your pantry of refined, processed foods. Emphasize healthy raw or freshly roasted nuts and seeds and their oils, such as grape seed, walnut, almond, coconut, avocado, and olive oils. This doesn't mean you should just cook with these oils; it would actually be preferable for you to drizzle the unheated oil on your food. Consider adding 2 tablespoons daily to your diet. Rotate the oils so you benefit from them all. Keep them fresh in a cool place or in your refrigerator. A side effect of using these can be beautiful skin!

In addition, include legumes and organic whole grains as tolerated, and enjoy healthy proteins. You may find you feel best with protein included with each meal, some from animals and some from vegetarian sources. Iodine-rich foods such as fish and seaweeds are excellent for supporting the endocrine system. Eat at least three healthy meals daily, filter your water, and exercise regularly.

Herbs

Consider astragalus, spirulina, garlic, ginseng, and bee pollen. These are excellent herbal foods to promote general endocrine health. A general rule I often follow is to choose three to five of these and take two capsules of each twice daily with meals, making adjustments as needed. Consuming these may take care of all your concerns and are the best place to begin. If you have added needs for fertility or sexual vitality, there are certainly more you may consider.

For female sexual vitality, consider including spirulina, liquid chlorophyll, black cohosh, and bee pollen. Limit black cohosh to one to two capsules at bedtime.

For male sexual vitality, consider including spirulina, saw palmetto (for healthy prostate support), ginseng, and maca (for a healthy sexual drive support).

Essential oils

Lavender, lemon, clary sage, and sweet marjoram are excellent for the endocrine system. Two to three drops of each of these may be applied to the bottom of each foot at bedtime or diluted with a tablespoon of carrier oil and rubbed into the abdomen each evening.

Also consider a Power Bath made with a combination of any of these oils (except lemon). Mix a total amount of a ½ teaspoon oil into 2 cups kosher salt, and enjoy one eighteen- to twenty-minute bath up to once weekly for as long as desired.

Pine Needle Power Bath

This purification bath is often used to target the organs of the abdomen. Mix 2 cups of kosher salt and ½ teaspoon of pine needle oil with a fork, then dissolve it into the bath water. Keep the abdomen and legs in the water for eighteen to twenty minutes. Evening baths are ideal. The goal is to use this bath once weekly for four weeks and then reevaluate your progress.

Pine Needle, Lavender, and Eucalyptus Power Bath

This alternate bath uses ¼ teaspoon of pine needle oil, ¼ teaspoon of lavender oil, and ½ teaspoon of eucalyptus oil premixed into 2 cups of kosher salt as the contents of one bath. This may be used for more stubborn challenges. Keep the neck in the water.

Note: Avoid essential oils when pregnant or nursing.

Water

Drink eight to ten glasses of pure water daily. Remember, the powerful healing water that is imprinted with biblical truths, affirmations, and specific scriptures can further aid in improving your well-being.

Lifestyle

Always ask for lead shields to protect the thyroid or any other vulnerable, exposed areas of the body when receiving any medical

X-rays. This should also be the norm in the dental office. You may be able to request bite-wing X-rays when needed as a possible alternative to the more extreme dental scans that go around the head.

Protect the pineal and pituitary glands as much as you can by holding your cell phone away from your ears. Use the speaker feature if possible.

You may wish to investigate thermography or ultrasound of the breasts as a possible screening tool that is radiation free.

Keep your computer off your lap and your cell phone out of your bra and pants pockets. I believe more investigation should be made into the link between cell phones in men's pant pockets (or clipped on the belt) and male hormonal challenges and concerns. This applies equally to women. In general, avoid as many radiation and electromagnetic pollution sources as possible. Some medical professionals are now recommending CT scans for only life-threatening circumstances or if no other workable alternative is present. Again, investigate these for yourself and be informed. Thyroid stress-related hair loss and more may be related to radiation absorption over time.

Please respect God's teaching for your sexuality and treat your sexual organs with respect. Be careful of medications that disrupt their natural function, as they can have side effects. Avoid any practice that brings you guilt and shame.

Aim for eight hours of sleep in a well-ventilated room that is dark, as light can stimulate the pineal gland and disrupt sleep. Keep any plugged-in device away from your head to minimize stress from electromagnetic pollution. I always suggest keeping these and digital clocks at least eight feet away from the body while sleeping.

Enjoy daily quiet time and prayer. Don't vent hateful words. Take a moment to cool off. Master respectful, truthful, loving emotional expression.

Rid yourself of all worry and anxiety, or at least relegate it to only ten minutes daily. Worry doesn't make anything better and is a colossal waste of time. Give all your concerns to God as you make your own reasonable efforts to live a healthy, productive life for His glory.

Organize your life to decrease stress. Rid your home and office of clutter, keeping only the items that give you joy.

BIBLICAL PATHWAY TO HEALING

These are some scriptures that form the partial basis for our verbal prayer for this body system. The rest of the prayer is based on my experiences with patients during biofeedback sessions. It is interesting to note what God says affects our energy and strength.

+ Root out pride: "I will break the pride of your power.... Your strength shall be spent in vain" (Lev. 26:19–20).

+ Evict all trauma and all patterns related to disaster, oppression, and obsession about the past and any side effects: "Your sons and your daughters will be given to another people. Your eyes will look and fail with longing for them all day long, but there will be nothing you can do. A nation that you do not know will consume the produce of your land and all your labors, and you will be nothing but oppressed and crushed all the time" (Deut. 28:32–33).

+ Evict all extreme stress, fear, and dread, as well as neglect of proper nourishment with healthy food and water: "Saul immediately fell full length upon the ground because he greatly feared the words of Samuel. Also there was no strength in him, for he had eaten no bread all day and all night" (1 Sam. 28:20).

+ Avoid skipping meals, which causes faintness of spirit: "And they gave him a part of a cake of figs and two cakes of raisins. When he had eaten, his spirit came back to him, for he had not eaten bread or drunk any water for three days and nights" (1 Sam. 30:12).

+ Evict all grief, all character faults, all generational curses, and all sinful side effects that may sap your strength: "For my life is spent with grief, and my years with sighing; my strength fails because of my iniquity, and my bones waste away" (Ps. 31:10).

+ Evict trust in man over trust in God due to fear of anything, including the future: "Thus says the LORD: Cursed is the man who trusts in man and makes flesh his strength, and whose heart departs from the LORD" (Jer. 17:5).

+ Turn from all sexual impurity and release all sexual abuse and its side effects: "They committed harlotries in Egypt. They committed harlotries in their youth. There their breasts were pressed, and there their virgin bosom was handled" (Ezek. 23:3).

+ Repent and turn from all past and present sinful sexual activity: "Bring charges against your mother, bring charges; for she is not My wife, nor am I her Husband! Let her put away her harlotries from her sight, and her adulteries from between her breasts" (Hosea 2:2, NKJV)

+ Evict all horror and shocking visuals: "All the crowds who came together to that sight, witnessing what occurred, struck their chests and returned" (Luke 23:48).

HEALING PRAYER

Speak this prayer aloud with boldness and confidence, taking time to consider its meaning. Exert the authority in Christ that has been given to you. In Him all things are possible.

Dear heavenly Father,

In You, I live, move, and have my being and health. You are my strength and song. You are my salvation. You are my God, and I will praise You. You have promised that as I wait patiently upon You, I shall renew my strength. I shall mount up with wings as eagles. I shall run and not be weary. I shall walk and not faint.

I receive from You a strong, healthy body filled with stamina and energy, with healthy glands and healthy fertility. I remind You of Your Word: "The God of your father who will help you, and by the Almighty who will bless you with blessings from heaven above, blessings from the deep that lies beneath, the blessings of the breasts and the womb" (Gen. 49:25). I rest in faith that I shall have what I have prayed for. Thank You for your promises and Jesus's powerful name.

With the powerful name and words of Jesus, I am fully equipped to receive healing. I command and evict from all deep cellular blueprints of my entire glandular system, including my pituitary, pineal, hypothalamus, thyroid, parathyroid, adrenals, pancreas, blood sugar balance, breasts, all sexual parts and virility, fertility, all mechanisms of hair growth, as well as all of the nerves and circulation process of each of these parts:

All prolonged grief, character faults, and generational curses and any side effects of these

All extreme stress, fear, and dread

All neglect and side effects from failing to nourish my body with proper food and water

All extreme trauma, disaster, horror, terror, shocking visuals, worry, and anxiety related to the past, present, or future

All forms of mental stress, including obsessions, oppressions, negative thinking and reacting, vengeful thinking, and trusting in man over God

All stressful thoughts, words, and emotions that I have held onto and stuffed

All wrath, hatred, anger, resentments, bitterness, envy and jealousy, and all acts of revenge, especially against the opposite sex

All self-condemnation and self-hatred, conflict, and guilt that I may be holding on to

All sexual guilt, impurity, or abuse of any nature and any side effects

All addictions to food, alcohol, chemicals, inhalants, and anything else that is damaging to my hormones and glandular system

All forms of pride or wanting to be the boss of my own life, all complaining, and all side effects of sin

All scar tissue, all accidents, all injury, and any side effects, including that of surgery and all traumatic words of doctors or anyone else

All toxic allergens and all improper allergy responses to the air, environment, and food

All stored medication toxicity and any side effects

All pollutants and chemicals from outside or inside my home, especially cleaning supplies and industrial pollution

Any vaccine side effects, including those from metallic additives and foreign DNA

All absorbed radiation from scans, X-rays, mammograms, cell phones, computers, power lines, or any other source and any side effects

All toxic metals, including aluminum, arsenic, lead, mercury, copper, nickel, cadmium, and any side effects

All bacteria, viruses, yeasts, molds, parasites, worms, and any other type of plague and any side effects

All negative or toxic cellular programming or blueprints of any type and any side effect

I command these mountains and all painful stories that may be connected to them to vaporize and completely leave all my cellular blueprints and parts. They must all go with none remaining. I am done with them, and I command them into the sea, never to return. I declare them gone!

To fill the vacancies created, I take a seat at the wonderful and bountiful dining table You have prepared for me. I partake of all of Your perfect remedies for my endocrine *system function. This includes perfect blood sugar balance, sexual function, fertility, child-bearing ability, breast health, and hair growth mechanisms.*

I drink in Your cups of love, hope, peace, courage, patience, mercy, compassion, and forgiveness toward all. I receive Your food for perfect strength, vitality, and a long life just as Joshua, Moses, and Caleb did. I taste and drink these wonderful remedies daily until I see myself filled from the soles of my feet to the top of my head, making me well.

I commit to receiving proper food and water daily. I declare into my cells the desire for healthy food and pure water. You, Lord, are my rock, my fortress, my deliverer, my strength, my shield, my salvation, my stronghold, my power to do all things, my joy, the source of my long life and vigor, and provider of power in Christ to do all things. I will say, "I am strong" in all circumstances.

I see children as my heritage and reward. I commit myself to serving You and teaching my children to also walk in Your ways. I pray these things in Jesus's name. Amen.

HEALING DECLARATIONS

These personalized scriptures will feed the new seeds you have planted. Declare these powerful verses daily.

My Lord is my pillar, my fortress, and my deliverer; my God, my rock, in whom I take refuge; my shield, and the horn of my salvation, and my high tower (Ps. 18:2).

I accept God's power and strength to fill all my weaknesses. He gives power when I am faint, and if I am exhausted, He increases my strength (Isa. 40:29).

I release all grief and declare the joy of the Lord is my strength (Neh. 8:10).

I will declare at any age, just as Joshua did, that my strength and vitality have endured, just as when I was in my prime: "Here I am this day, eighty-five years old. I am still just as strong today as I was on the day that Moses sent me. My strength now is just like my strength then, both for battle and for going out and returning" (Josh. 14:10–11).

"I can do all things because of Christ who strengthens me" (Phil. 4:13).

I instruct my body and sexual organs to be fruitful and bear children in alignment with the Word (Gen. 1:28).

I shall serve the Lord my God, and He shall bless my bread and my water, and He will remove sickness from my life. I shall not miscarry or be barren in my land. God will fulfill the number of my days (Exod. 23:25–26).

God is able to transform me from any state of infertility into a joyful mother of children. (Ps. 113:9, NAS).

Children are a gift of the Lord, and the fruit of the womb is my reward. As arrows in the hand of a mighty warrior, so are the children of my youth. My quiver shall be full (Ps. 127:3–5).

Just as Hannah did, I place my case before You, Lord. You are not a respecter of persons. Please look upon my sorrow and lack of fertility as You did in the account of Your servant Hannah. Remember me. Give me a child, and I will devote my life to training him or her in Your service (1 Sam. 1:9, 10–11, 20).

As a woman, I instruct my body to align with God's words for healthy fertility, proper height, and healthy breasts and hair growth (Ezek. 16:7).

Lord, it is Your blessing that my breasts function correctly in Your design to nourish my infant. I command them to align with Your Word for this purpose (Songs 8:1).

As a woman my hair is a glory to me, for my hair is given to me for a covering (1 Cor. 11:15).

I proclaim and envision my hair full and thick daily as I meditate on this amazing scripture: "When he [Absalom] cut the hair of his head (and at the end of every year he cut it, for it was heavy on him), he weighed the hair from his head at two hundred shekels, according to the king's standard" (2 Sam. 14:26).

CHAPTER 9

THE HEART AND CIRCULATORY SYSTEM

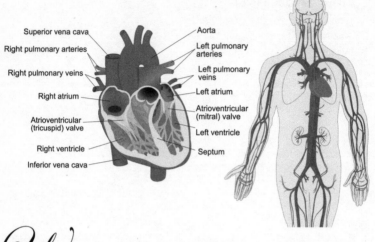

W HAT IF YOU could walk and run with energy and stamina, have excellent circulation, warm fingers and toes, and be focused and alert? What if you felt strong and vital in your daily exercise routine? These are the characteristics of a healthy heart and circulatory system.

Your heart is a miraculous organ about the size of your fist that pumps five quarts of blood each minute and beats a hundred thousand times each day, thirty-five million times per year. It ensures that oxygen- and nutrient-rich blood reaches every cell and that waste products and carbon dioxide are properly channeled to the lungs and eliminative organs.

Your heart has four chambers. The right and left sides are separated by a wall of muscle called the septum. It has four different valves that regulate the direction of blood flow as well as its own electrical mechanism to pace the heartbeat. The heart is encased

Heart image source: ZooFari

within a sac called the pericardium, which supplies lubricating fluid for this important pump. The arteries transport blood away from the heart, and the veins return it. Tiny capillaries branch off the blood vessels to bring blood into the cells. Only the arteries can accumulate plaque and cholesterol deposits; the veins do not. We now know that it is the oxidized (spoiled or rancid) LDL cholesterol that is one of the key risk factors for cardiovascular disease. The health of the nervous system, adrenal glands, kidneys, and liver may be easily entwined with this system.

The parts we will address within this system consist of the heart muscle, heart valves, the heartbeat mechanism, blood, arteries, veins, capillaries, and their muscles and nerves.

Chinese Constitutional Insights

The heart and circulatory system are said to be full of fire and passion and are associated with joy, love, excitement, and vitality. The organ associated with healthy heart function is the small intestine. When imbalanced, a person may tend to be high strung, with ruddy cheeks and a tendency toward insomnia and heart palpitations. The person may also, if exhausted, veer toward the opposite and have low sexual and mental energy. The tongue is the sensory organ related to the heart.

Factors That May Lead to Compromise

A diet of fast food, processed foods, refined salt and sugar, and unhealthy fats such as those found in many commercial products, especially candies, cookies, cakes, and chips, can directly impact this system. These foods may raise our unhealthy cholesterol (LDL) as well as our triglycerides, which are factors related to cardiovascular disease.

The emotions of heartbreak, abandonment, rejection, resentment, and betrayal, as well as intense fear and terror, may compromise the ability of the heart and circulation to have optimal wellness. Any radiation therapy conducted over the chest may have a negative effect on the health of the heart, requiring the need for extra attention. Again, explore your options. Investigate mammotherms, which are gaining in popularity and may serve to reduce routine radiation from mammograms. Infected teeth, gums, and root canals may add to the risk of heart disease.

COMMON ILLNESS MANIFESTATIONS

Illnesses rooted in this body system include fatigue, light-headedness, confusion, heart disease, heart attack, stroke, aneurysms (ballooning of blood vessels that may break), erratic heartbeat or heart murmurs, heart valve defects, angina (heart pain), high blood pressure, poor circulation to the hands and feet (Raynaud's syndrome), circulation compromise from plaque and cholesterol deposits, discoloration of the lower legs, pooling of blood and fluid in the legs, varicose veins, hemorrhoids, blood clot formation, chronic cough, wheezing, and shortness of breath.

APPLYING THE FIVE FOUNDATIONS OF OPTIMAL HEALTH

Good foods

Follow the guidelines for a healthy, biblically based diet outlined in chapter 5. Additionally a diet rich in antioxidants is important, as well as a rich daily supply of omega-3 fats and fat-soluble nutrients, such as those found in wild-caught salmon, flax, and walnut oils, which may lend support to healthy cholesterol (HDL) levels, circulation, and arteries. Antioxidant-rich, fiber-rich, unpeeled organic fruits and vegetables—especially pomegranate seeds and juice—are excellent tools for this body system.

Consider tomatoes and foods rich in potassium and magnesium, such as leafy greens, broccoli, and unsulphured blackstrap molasses. You may wish to omit caffeine if the heart and circulation is overstimulated, marked by an erratic heartbeat and high blood pressure. You may invigorate circulation by adding capsicum, ginger, and garlic to your recipes.

Herbs

Consider spirulina, hawthorn berry, and capsicum. A general rule I often follow is to take two capsules of each twice daily with meals.

Essential oils

Experiment with clary sage and ginger. I like mixing ¼ teaspoon of each of these oils into 2 cups of Epsom salts and dissolving them into a bath for one twenty-minute session. Consider doing this once weekly until you see the results you desire.

Note: Avoid essential oils when pregnant or nursing.

Water

Drink eight to ten glasses of pure water daily. Remember, the powerful healing water that is imprinted with biblical truths, affirmations, and specific scriptures can further aid in improving your well-being.

Lifestyle

Build exercise at the proper pace and aim for at least thirty minutes daily if your doctor offers no objection. Speak to any of your stress mountains at the end of each day. Emotional and mental stress, which overstimulate the adrenal glands, are taxing on the heart. Don't be a workaholic. We don't have to say yes to everything asked of us.

Taking peaceful refuge in the Lord each day is one way to nurture heart health, as God is our true security. See the rewards of the Lord and of eternity outweighing even your largest life challenges. Visualize yourself held in His hands, with your heart being protected and filled with the beauty and peace of God.

Remove stressful clutter from your home and office. Explore new hobbies and enjoy quality music. Get a good night's sleep. Enjoy nature. Play, smile, laugh, and have fun. Express daily gratitude.

Build healthy, trusting, loving, giving relationships. Make a conscious choice to move from any heartbreak and to release the hurt of betrayals. Focus on your blessings and move forward.

BIBLICAL PATHWAY TO HEALING

These are some scriptures that form the partial basis for our verbal prayer for this body system. The rest of the prayer is based on my experiences with patients during biofeedback sessions. Notice how emotions and mind-sets can affect our body parts.

+ Expel all shock and disbelief: "They told him, 'Joseph is still alive, and he is governor over all the land of Egypt.' And Jacob's heart stood still because he could not believe them" (Gen. 45:26).

+ Expel all hardness of heart: "Pharaoh's heart hardened so that he would not listen to them, just as the LORD had said" (Exod. 7:13).

+ Expel all hatred toward others: "You shall not hate your brother in your heart. You shall surely reason honestly with your neighbor, and not suffer sin because of him" (Lev. 19:17).

+ Don't discourage others from doing good: "Why would you discourage the hearts of the children of Israel from going over into the land which the LORD has given to them?" (Num. 32:7).

+ Expel all intense trauma, worry, fear, and anxiety for the future: "Strengthen the weak hands, and support the feeble knees. Say to those who are of a fearful heart, 'Be strong, fear not'" (Isa. 35:3–4).

+ Expel addictions and anything that exerts control other than God: "The Spirit of the Lord GOD is upon me because the LORD has anointed me to preach good news to the poor; He has sent me to heal the broken-hearted, to proclaim liberty to the captives, and the opening of the prison to those who are bound" (Isa. 61:1).

+ Expel all discouragement: "He told them a parable to illustrate that it is necessary always to pray and not lose heart" (Luke 18:1).

+ Expel extreme fear and anxiety regarding the future: "Men fainting from fear and expectation of what is coming on the inhabited earth. For the powers of heaven will be shaken" (Luke 21:26).

+ Expel carousing, drunkenness, and worry: "Take heed to yourselves, lest your hearts become burdened by excessiveness and drunkenness and anxieties of life, and that Day comes on you unexpectedly" (Luke 21:34).

HEALING PRAYER

Speak this prayer aloud with boldness and confidence. Exert the authority in Christ that has been given to you. In Him all things are possible.

Dear heavenly Father,

Jesus, the healer, is welcomed and living within my heart. Anything that would harm me is forbidden to stay in His presence. I receive Your beauty for ashes, Your oil of joy for any mourning, and Your good plans for my future. You are able to do exceedingly and abundantly above all that I ask or think, according to Your miraculous power that You have given me and that works within me.

With the powerful name and words of Jesus, I am fully equipped to receive healing. I command and evict from all deep cellular blueprints of my heart muscle, heart valves, heartbeat mechanisms, blood pressure components, blood, arteries, veins, capillaries, and all their muscles and nerves:

All forms of fear, including intense shock, worry, fear, anxiety, and trauma

All disbelief, hardness, and stubbornness of heart toward God

All hatred toward anyone

All broken-heartedness, including all depression, betrayal, rejection, abandonment, and all physical, mental, or emotional wounds

All carousing, drunkenness, addictions, captivity, and imprisonment due to anything that exalts itself above God, including false beliefs and the worries of this life

All discouragement and delays in my expectations

All scar tissue, all accidents, all injury, and any side effects, including that of surgery and all traumatic words of doctors and anyone else

All toxic allergens and all improper allergy responses to our air, environment, and food

All medication toxicity and any side effects

All pollutants and chemicals from outside or inside my home, especially cleaning supplies and industrial pollution

Any vaccine side effects, including those from metallic additives and foreign DNA

All absorbed radiation from scans, X-rays, mammograms, cell phones, computers, power lines, or any other source and any side effects

All toxic metals, including aluminum, arsenic, lead, mercury, copper, nickel, cadmium, and any side effects

All bacteria, viruses, yeasts, molds, parasites, worms, and any other type, of plague and any side effects

All negative or toxic cellular programming or blueprints of any type, from any source and any side effects

In Jesus's powerful name, I command these mountains and any painful stories associated with them to vaporize and completely leave all my cellular blueprints and parts within my heart and circulatory system. They must all go with none remaining. I declare them gone from all stories of my life and from my gestation and birth, and any carryover or effect from my ancestry back to the beginning of time. I am done with them, and I command them into the sea, never to return.

To fill these vacancies, I take a seat at Your magnificent and bountiful table clothed with a robe of praise and my heart anointed with Your oil of joy. I fully partake of the perfect remedies You have prepared for my life, health, and perfect programming of all Your created parts of my heart and circulatory system, including my heart valves, heartbeat mechanisms, blood pressure mechanisms, all blood vessels, and their muscles and nerves. I drink Your bountiful cup of love, joy, hope, peace, courage, forgiveness toward all, strength, guidance, and protection. I taste and eat my perfect remedies for any betrayal, rejection, loss, abandonment, or any other heart wounds.

Heavenly Father, I acknowledge that all things are possible with You. My heart is now filled with consolation and praise. All heaviness of spirit is gone because You have good plans for my future. My heart rejoices in Your strength and protection, and my hope is in You. I love You and am cheerful because of Your promises.

I resolve to be pure in heart and faithful, and I now rest in Your perfect healing. I resolve to continue to taste and drink Your wonderful remedies daily until I see myself filled from the soles of my feet to the top of my head, making me well. This I pray in the name of Jesus. Amen.

HEALING DECLARATIONS

These personalized scriptures will feed the new seeds you have planted. Declare these powerful verses daily.

I love the Lord my God with all my heart, with all my soul, and with all my strength (Deut. 6:5).

I wait upon the Lord; I am of good courage, and He shall strengthen my heart (Ps. 27:14).

The Lord is my strength and my shield. My heart trusts in Him, and I am helped. Therefore my heart greatly rejoices, and with my song I will praise Him (Ps. 28:7).

I am of good courage, and He shall strengthen my heart, as I hope in the Lord (Ps. 31:24).

The Lord is near to me when I have a broken heart and saves me when I have a contrite spirit (Ps. 34:18).

God sent His word and healed me and delivered me from my destructions (Ps. 107:20).

The Lord heals my broken heart and binds up my wounds (Ps. 147:3).

I trust in the Lord with all my heart, and I lean not on my own understanding; in all my ways, I acknowledge Him, and He shall direct my paths (Prov. 3:5–6).

My cheerful heart is a good medicine to me (Prov. 17:22).

God gives me beauty for ashes, the oil of joy for mourning, the garment of praise for the spirit of heaviness, that I may be called a tree of righteousness, the planting of the Lord, that He may be glorified (Isa. 61:3).

Peace God leaves with me; His peace He has given to me, which is not like the world's peace. Because of this, I will not let my heart be troubled, neither let it be afraid (John 14:27).

My heart rejoices and my tongue is glad; moreover, my flesh also will rest in hope (Acts 2:26).

CHAPTER 10

THE NERVOUS SYSTEM

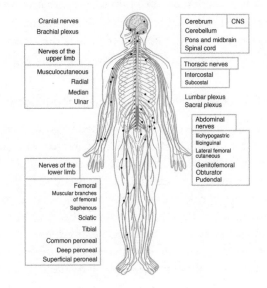

Cranial nerves
Brachial plexus

Nerves of the
upper limb

Musculocutaneous
Radial
Median
Ulnar

Cerebrum — CNS
Cerebellum
Pons and midbrain
Spinal cord

Thoracic nerves
Intercostal
Subcostal

Lumbar plexus
Sacral plexus

Abdominal
nerves

Iliohypogastric
Ilioinguinal
Lateral femoral
cutaneous

Genitofemoral
Obturator
Pudendal

Nerves of the
lower limb

Femoral
Muscular branches
of femoral
Saphenous
Sciatic
Tibial
Common peroneal
Deep peroneal
Superficial peroneal

*W*HAT IF YOU could:

+ Remember what you read?

+ Be cheerful and motivated for your early morning job?

+ React calmly in stressful situations?

+ Stay focused and on task?

+ Look forward to having a good memory in your golden years?

This is the perfect world of healthy nervous system function, which also includes a brain that is well-fed, vital, and strong. We can support these healthy functions by supporting this system each day with healthy lifestyle choices and God's Word. Our wonderful

---

Image source: William Crochot

brain, spinal cord, and nerves foster a vast communication network within our bodies. God's will is that we have a sound mind.

The latest information on the brain suggests that our gut health and its garden of healthy flora is of critical importance to how our brains function. It is important, then, to include the digestive system, which is closely linked to brain and nervous system health.

CHINESE CONSTITUTIONAL INSIGHTS

The ability to focus mentally is linked with the health of the kidneys. A stressed liver is associated with nervousness and tension, including tension in the chest, migraine headaches, and insomnia. A stressed circulatory system may lead to restlessness and anxiety as well as excitability within the mind and heart. A weakened circulatory system may lead to nervous exhaustion and insomnia. Stressed immunity may lead to numbness in the arms and tension in the diaphragm. These are a few examples of how ill health in any system may distort or rob energy from the nerves, spinal cord, and brain.

FACTORS THAT MAY LEAD TO COMPROMISE

The brain's health is highly dependent upon our diet. The average diet feeds the brain only 15 percent of its nutritional needs—but our brains require 85 percent of our nutrition! When you're awake, your brain generates between 10 and 23 watts of power—enough energy to power a light bulb.[1]

Our brain is very vulnerable to imbalanced blood sugar, which is often brought about through chronic overconsumption of sugar and refined foods. This is largely due to the vast soda industry, which understands the incredible addictive properties of sugar. (It appears identical to cocaine in brain response![2]) Blood sugar ups and downs may be the foundation for many brain complaints. We must rid our homes of refined sugars and refined carbohydrates.

Among my clients, I have seen consistent patterns and complaints related to an inability to focus and stay on track. One factor that may be related is the burgeoning use of cell phones. Please keep these away from your head and ears as much as you can. Also avoid dental, sinus, and head CT scans when possible.

We must feed the friendly flora in our gut to have healthy brain function. This information is profound and recent, and you can read more by investigating the writings of Dr. David Perlmutter, perhaps starting with *Brain Maker*. Even autism may have a strong link to poor gut bacteria ratios. Fermented foods, which will be listed shortly, feed these bacteria and should be included in our daily diet.

The nerves and spinal cord are vulnerable to held traumas and emotional baggage, which I believe often compromises this system and may result in the improper elimination of environmental metals and chemicals. It may be critically important to release these traumas and emotions to bring peace and health to this system.

COMMON ILLNESSES AND MANIFESTATIONS

Concerning the brain, common illness manifestations include lack of mental energy, depression, insomnia, mood swings, mental illness, attention deficit, hyperactivity, memory challenges, anxiety, poor use of logic, lack of impulse control (which can link to immoral or criminal behavior), multiple sclerosis, Parkinson's disease, Alzheimer's disease, and more.

Concerning the spinal cord and nerves, compromised nerve function can lead to pain, palsy, paralysis, restlessness, numbness, irritability, subluxations of the spine, hyperactivity, anxiety, and depression.

APPLYING THE FIVE FOUNDATIONS
OF OPTIMAL HEALTH

Good food

Eat salmon; walnuts and walnut oil; and raw, organic egg yolks from brown eggs if you feel comfortable with your egg quality. Raw eggs have the potential to increase the risk of foodborne illness. Support healthy blood sugar balance by ridding your diet of all refined carbohydrates, such as white sugar, white rice, and white refined wheat flours. Rid your diet of all unhealthy fats and sugars too, such as those in fast foods, processed desserts, and candies. Utilize fermented foods daily to nourish the good bacteria in the gut, which has a powerful impact upon the brain. These include kimchi, pickled vegetables, miso soup, sauerkraut, kombucha, and raw apple cider vinegar.

Herbs

Consider gingko biloba, passion flower, chamomile, hops, astragalus, spirulina, and chlorophyll. A general rule that I often follow is to choose three to six of these and take two capsules of each twice daily. Consult your doctor with any concerns.

Essential oils

Enjoy frankincense, lavender, Roman chamomile, clary sage, and pine needle. You may wish to apply up to eight drops of whatever combination you prefer to your brain stem (the hollow space at the base of the skull) once or twice daily. They may also be dropped down the spine, using about ten to fifteen drops of your preferred combination, and rubbed in with 1–2 tablespoons of walnut oil. Avoid getting these essential oils down south into the crease of the buttocks.

You may apply these essential oils daily, ideally in the evenings. Evaluate the results after one to four weeks and adjust the amount as needed to promote stability and maintenance. Avoid essential oils if you are pregnant or nursing.

Water

Drink eight to ten glasses of pure water daily. Remember, the powerful healing water that is imprinted with biblical truths, affirmations, and specific scriptures can further aid in improving your well-being.

Lifestyle

Avoid shocking and traumatic images or sounds. Stop or avoid smoking. Avoid aspartame, which is suspected to interfere with brain and nerve functions. Keep cell phone use to a minimum—better yet, use the speaker feature. Avoid tooth fillings made with mercury if at all possible. Choose to "think on the good" in life. Be thankful.

BIBLICAL PATHWAY TO HEALING

These are some scriptures that form the partial basis for our verbal prayer for this body system. The rest of the prayer is based on my experiences with patients during biofeedback sessions. Notice how emotions and mind-sets can affect our body parts.

+ Evict all anxiety and depression that resides in the heart or anywhere else: "Heaviness in the heart of man makes it droop, but a good word makes it glad" (Prov. 12:25).

+ Evict lack of good sense and all sin: "Come now, and let us reason together, says the LORD. Though your sins be as scarlet, they shall be as white as snow; though they be red like crimson, they shall be as wool" (Isa. 1:18).

+ Evict all anxiety about the present or future: "And do not seek what you will eat or what you will drink, nor be of an anxious mind" (Luke 12:29).

+ Evict all resistance, stubbornness, rejection, or rebellion against God's Word: "Why do you not understand what I say? It is because you cannot bear to hear my word" (John 8:43, ESV).

+ Evict all fear and trauma: "For God has not given us the spirit of fear, but of power, and love, and self-control" (2 Tim. 1:7).

+ Evict all unbelief and all types of impurity from the mind and conscience: "To the pure, all things are pure. But to those who are defiled and unbelieving, nothing is pure. Even their mind and consciences are defiled" (Titus 1:15).

+ Evict all wavering and double-mindedness toward God: "Draw near to God, and He will draw near to you.

Cleanse your hands, you sinners, and purify your hearts, you double-minded" (James 4:8).

HEALING PRAYER

Speak this prayer aloud with boldness and confidence. Exert the authority in Christ that has been given to you. In Him all things are possible.

Dear heavenly Father,

I will magnify Your name and Your greatness because of Your provision for me to have an amazing brain, nervous system, and spinal cord knit together with power, love, and a sound, reasoning mind. I reside in Christ as Your new creation. The old is gone, and all things have become new. I agree with this and release all old patterns and blueprints that have tried to invade this holy place. I pray blessings over my food and water, that they may nourish my entire being perfectly, especially my brain and nervous system. No weapon formed against these parts of my body, including any fear, shall prosper.

I choose to focus my mind upon You and have perfect peace. I praise You, Lord, that any cellular programming contrary to these will be destroyed today and Your patterns reestablished. In all these things that I speak to, I am more than a conqueror through Christ. I will release all mental and nervous stress and rest in Your love, as I am confident in Your Word—that neither death nor life, nor angels nor rulers, not things present nor things to come, nor powers, nor height, nor depth, nor anything else in all creation can separate me from Your love in Christ Jesus.

With the powerful name and words of Jesus, I am fully equipped to receive healing. I command and evict from all deep cellular blueprints within my brain, spinal cord, and all nerves:

All lack of reason and good sense and any sins that have contributed to a lack of mental soundness from any source

All unbelief and impurity from any source that resides in my mind and conscience

All anxiety about the past or future

All depression and any focus on negative outcomes or events

All wavering and double-mindedness concerning the truths of Your Word

All unbelief, dislike, stubbornness, rebelliousness, or rejection regarding Your Word

All forms of criticism I am holding onto toward others

All addictions to drugs, alcohol, food, pornography, TV, video games, or any other destructive activity or substance

All foggy thinking and poor insight

All inability to set goals for my future

All tendencies to be distracted

All roots of a poor memory and poor attention span

All instability of moods and resistance to healthy change

All challenges with remembering names, learning, math, language skills, and following directions

All dental trauma from any source, including injections, extractions, root canals, drilling, and dental metals including mercury, copper, and nickel, and any surgery that may affect my nervous system or anywhere else

All scar tissue, all accidents, all surgeries, and all injury, including traumatic brain injuries, and any side effects and all traumatic words of doctors and anyone else

All traumatic visuals or sounds

All toxic allergens and all improper allergy responses to my air, environment, and food

All medication toxicity and any side effects

All pollutants and chemicals from outside or inside my home, especially cleaning supplies and industrial pollution

Any vaccine side effects, including those from metallic additives and foreign DNA

All absorbed radiation from scans, X-rays, cell phones, computers, power lines, or any other source and any side effects

Other toxic metals, such as aluminum, arsenic, lead, and cadmium, and any side effects

All bacteria, viruses, yeasts, molds, parasites, worms, and any other type of plague and any side effects

All negative or toxic cellular programming or blueprints of any type, from any source, and any side effects

In Jesus's powerful name, I command these mountains and any painful stories associated with them to vaporize and completely leave all my cellular blueprints and parts—they must all go with none remaining. I release all of these perfectly from all stories and events of my life, from my gestation and birth, and from any carryover or connection from my ancestry back to the beginning of time. I command these into the sea. The Son has set all of my parts free; they are free indeed. I declare these mountains gone!

To fill the vacancies created, I take a seat at the bountiful table the Lord has prepared for me. I partake of all His remedies for my perfect nervous system and all its created parts. This includes all of my brain, spinal cord, nerves, and the circulation to these parts.

I drink in all remedies for a sound, healthy, clear mind, just as Jesus has, with perfect focus on spiritual truths, insight, memory, and an attention span filled with perfect peace, love, courage, hope, and all God's blessings of wellness. I commit to transforming my mind daily to the will and teachings of God. I taste and drink these wonderful remedies daily until I see myself filled from the soles of my feet to the top of my head, making me well.

Thank You, Lord, that I can accept and agree with You that my mind is accepting a proper blueprint so that it can function as the mind of Christ, with all purity, intent, boldness, belief, faith, wisdom, memory, and reason. I have a sound mind because that is Your provision and Your promise, and I claim it wholeheartedly. Anything else must bow and be evicted because of the powerful name of Jesus, which I place over my brain, nerves, and spinal cord.

I now accept and rest patiently in Your total healing of my nervous system. Each day I focus on and conform my mind to whatever is true, honorable, just, pure, lovely, commendable, excellent, praiseworthy, and of good report. I choose to see the good and the blessings in life. I speak gratitude daily and bless others. Even when others wrong me, I do not take it personally; instead, I see it as a wound within them. I forgive them. I capture all negative, unhealthy thoughts and reject them. I joyfully and lovingly give daily praise to my Lord. In Jesus's name, amen.

HEALING DECLARATIONS

These personalized scriptures will feed the new seeds you have planted. Declare these powerful verses daily.

You will keep me in perfect peace when my mind is stayed on You, because I trust in You (Isa. 26:3).

I shall love the Lord my God with all my heart, with all my soul, and with all my mind (Matt. 22:37).

Those who live according to the flesh set their minds on the things of the flesh, but I live according to the Spirit and the things of the Spirit. To be carnally minded is death, but to be spiritually minded is life and peace (Rom. 8:5–6).

I will not be conformed to this world but will be transformed by the renewing of my mind that I may prove what is that good and acceptable and perfect will of God (Rom. 12:2).

For "who has known the mind of the Lord that he may instruct Him?" But I have the mind of Christ (1 Cor. 2:16).

Let this mind be in me, which was also in Christ Jesus (Phil. 2:5).

I set my mind on things above, not on things on the earth (Col. 3:2).

CHAPTER 11

THE SENSORY SYSTEM

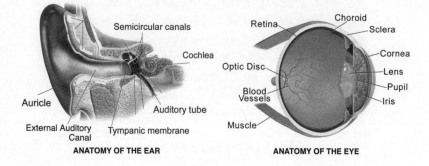

ANATOMY OF THE EAR   ANATOMY OF THE EYE

*W*HAT IF YOU reached your old age with eyes that didn't dim—that could see as well as they did in your youth? What if you never experienced glaucoma, cataracts, or blindness? What if you didn't even need reading glasses? Similarly, what if your hearing was sharp and remained so throughout your life?

Our eyes are most fearfully and wonderfully made. They begin to develop two weeks after conception. They remain the same size throughout our lives as when we were born. The eyes have more than 2 million working parts, and 80 percent of our memories are determined by what we see. The eyes are the second most complex organ after the brain.[1]

Our ears too are amazing structures. The smallest bone within the human body lies within the ear. Your ears are always working, and they are involved in your sense of balance.[2] Sound waves strike the eardrum then are transmitted into the middle ear. Sound waves connect with the inner ear and move tiny, hairlike cells called cilia, which send impulses to the brain and are interpreted as sound.

The Bible contains many scriptures regarding the eyes and ears and offers many promises of healing related to them. In the Bible we also find many testimonies of people regaining their hearing

Images source: BruceBlaus

and sight. It takes faith to receive such healing for ourselves, but remember, God is not a respecter of persons. What He has made available to others, He also makes available to you.

CHINESE CONSTITUTIONAL INSIGHTS

The eyes in general correlate with liver vitality and quality of blood. The ears, specifically the bones of the ear, correlate with kidney vitality and health.

FACTORS THAT MAY LEAD TO COMPROMISE

First and foremost, nourishing healthy eyes requires keeping the liver healthy. The same goes for the kidneys in relationship to the ears. This means that your lifestyle and diet ought to be as pure and healthy as possible. This pays well in keeping these sense organs healthy and nourished.

Subjecting the eyes and ears to violence, gore, horror, or traumatic news may impact these intricate organs in ways we may not yet understand. God asks us to think upon noble, good, lovely, and pure things. We can infer we ought to seek out the same kind of things to hear.

Dental amalgams (silver fillings) give off mercury vapor, even when chewing gum, which may migrate into and negatively impact your eyes and ears.

Avoid staring at your computer for hours. I can often tell when clients have done this, as it shows up as a unique stress response on my biofeedback computer. There is evidence that cell phones may impact the ears as well as the eyes and jaw when they are held against the ears for longer than a few minutes. Loud music and loud noise have been proven to damage hearing.

The majority of people who suffer from hearing loss are under the age of sixty-five. The number-one cause of hearing loss is exposure to excessively loud sounds of 85 decibels or higher. Hearing can be damaged after a single incident of exposure to extremely loud noise, such as a shotgun blast, explosion, or the like.[3]

When it comes to X-rays, think about whether you want your whole head to be scanned with X-rays and CT scans if you do not need that level of intervention. Always ask questions and investigate. Research any dye and its side effects if a doctor wants to do an MRI of your head. Be wise and check things out ahead of time. I have some very regretful clients who wish they would have researched certain tests, scans, or medications before they chose to take them. There are almost always alternatives.

COMMON ILLNESS MANIFESTATIONS

Common illnesses affecting the eyes include near and far vision imbalances, blindness, glaucoma, cataracts, detached retinas, macular degeneration, blood clots, infections, malformations, tumors, and cancers.

Concerning the ears, we see deafness, ringing in the ears, earaches, dizziness, trouble with balance, nerve damage, infections, ruptured eardrums, blocked Eustachian tubes, malformations, and cancers of the outer ear.

APPLYING THE FIVE FOUNDATIONS OF OPTIMAL HEALTH

Good foods

Follow the guidelines for a healthy, biblically based diet outlined in chapter 5. Emphasize high antioxidant berries and fruits such as goji berries, bilberries, blueberries, and black currants. Enjoy kale and leafy greens, carrots, organic grapefruits, lemons, and oranges. Take omega-3 fats in fatty fish such as wild-caught salmon, walnuts, and flaxseed oil, plus leafy greens and veggies. Keep your blood sugar in balance by eating regular meals containing protein.

Herbs

For healthy eye support, consider eyebright, bilberry, and spirulina. A general rule that I often follow is to take two capsules of each of these twice daily.

For healthy ear support, consider bayberry, astragalus, spirulina, and ginkgo biloba. Again I prefer to choose three to four of these and take two capsules of each twice daily. (If you are addressing your eyes and ears together, you don't need to double the spirulina.)

Essential oils

For the eyes, apply three to five drops of clary sage to the brain stem (the hollow place at the base of the skull) twice daily to support healthy function of the brain, nerves, and eyes. Frankincense and helichrysum are popular for applying to the bones surrounding the eyes once daily. (Be careful not to get the oils into the eyes.) Add eight to ten drops of clove and lemon to the bottom of each foot at night.

Ear oil mixtures can be made, but first be knowledgeable. Consult an expert.

For other ear aids using essential oils, I enjoy applying three to five drops of lemon oil to the brain stem twice daily to support the nerves connecting the brain to the ears. This may be mixed into a teaspoon of walnut oil to prevent skin irritation. Additionally, frankincense and helichrysum may be applied the bones surrounding the ears each evening (be careful not to get the oils into the ears). These may also be applied to the brain stem.

Remember to avoid essential oils if you are pregnant or nursing.

Water

Drink eight to ten glasses of pure water daily. Remember, the powerful healing water that is imprinted with biblical truths, affirmations, and specific scriptures can further aid in improving your well-being. I have had good reports in as little as two weeks when a blind woman started using this wonderful remedy.

Lifestyle

Be smoke-free. Take care of your teeth and keep them strong to minimize dental interventions. Consider other filling materials besides silver amalgams, which some countries have now banned.

Choose to see and hear the good in life and on your TV set for you and your family, especially your children.

Look away frequently when doing intense reading or when on the computer. Consider washing your eyes with saltwater drops regularly if you use a computer daily.

Keep music at a healthy sound range.

BIBLICAL PATHWAY TO HEALING

These are some scriptures that form the partial basis for our verbal prayer for this body system. The rest of the prayer is based on my experiences with patients during biofeedback sessions. Notice how emotions and mind-sets can affect our body parts.

+ Evict all images absorbed via pornography and that encourage lust: "I made a covenant with my eyes; why then should I look upon a young woman?" (Job 31:1).

+ Evict all grief and misplaced focus on the oppositions of life: "My eye wastes away from grief; it grows weak because of all those hostile to me" (Ps. 6:7).

+ Evict all images and works of wickedness and do not let them cling to you: "I will set no wicked thing before my eyes. I hate the work of those who turn aside; it shall not have part of me" (Ps. 101:3).

+ Evict all resistance to the words of your conscience or to the cry of the poor: "Whoever shuts his ears at the cry of the poor, he also will cry himself, but will not be heard" (Prov. 21:13).

+ Repent and be reconciled to the Lord so your prayers are heard: "He who turns away his ear from hearing instruction, even his prayer will be an abomination" (Prov. 28:9).

+ Evict all hardness of heart and hardness of hearing toward the truth and healing: "For this people's heart has grown dull. Their ears have become hard of hearing, and they have closed their eyes, lest they should see with their eyes and hear with their ears and understand with their hearts, and turn, and I should heal them" (Matt. 13:15).

+ Turn away from all ungodly talk and music. "'If anyone has ears to hear, let him hear.' He said to them, 'Take heed what you hear'" (Mark 4:23–24).

+ Evict all stubbornness and resistance to hearing God's Word: "You stiff-necked people, uncircumcised in heart and ears! You always resist the Holy Spirit" (Acts 7:51).

+ Evict all words of profanity, any words that glorify Satan or the occult, and all teaching from false religions: "For the time will come when people will not endure sound doctrine, but they will gather to themselves teachers in accordance with their own desires, having itching ears, and they will turn their ears away from the truth and turn to myths" (2 Tim 4:3–4).

+ Evict all lustful, unhealthy images: "For all that is in the world—the lust of the flesh, the lust of the eyes, and the pride of life—is not of the Father, but is of the world" (1 John 2:16).

HEALING PRAYER

Speak this prayer aloud with boldness and confidence. Exert the authority in Christ that has been given to you. In Him all things are possible—even blind eyes seeing and deaf ears hearing!

Dear heavenly Father,

I enter Your throne room with thanksgiving and praise! You inhabit the praises of Your people (Ps. 22:3). You are the Alpha and Omega, the beginning and the end, the King of kings and Lord of lords. You are my Creator, provider, and healer. You are the great physician, Redeemer, and protector. Your words are life and health to all my flesh, which includes my eyes, vision, ears, hearing, and all their connected parts. I am committed to hearing Your Word and what it says about my eyes and ears.

You have said to incline my ear and come to You. You have said in Your Word, "Hear, and your soul shall live"

(Isa. 55:3, NKJV). I place these words into my ears and command them to come in line with this truth.

Romans 8:11 states that if the Spirit of Him who raised Jesus from the dead dwells in me, He who raised Christ from the dead will also give life to my mortal body through His Spirit who dwells in me. Jesus said for Your will to be done on earth as it is in heaven. People see and hear in heaven. I believe this is Your will for me on earth also.

Christ unstopped the deaf ears and restored hearing. He even restored the amputated ear of a man who came to capture Him. He opened blind eyes. Nothing is too difficult for You, Lord. Signs and wonders will follow those who believe. This is the truth, and truth shall make my eyes and ears free.

I ask for forgiveness for any rebellion and sin that included any parts of my eyes or ears. I am done with them.

Jesus always said yes when asked to provide healing and sight to the blind and hearing to the deaf. You are the same, yesterday, today, and forever.

Your Word promises that if I abide in You and Your words abide in me, I may ask anything of You and You will do it, if I will ask in faith without doubting. I ask for perfect sight, both near and far vision as well as perfect eye function, complete with all its parts and connections in total health. I ask for perfect ear function, healing, and hearing, with Your perfect blueprints of health.

With the powerful name and words of Jesus, I am fully equipped to receive healing. I command and evict from all deep cellular blueprints of my eyes, eye muscles, vision, ears, hearing, and all their parts, including the nerves and circulation mechanisms:

All lustful images or desires, including those of all violence, gore, war, and death, all pornography, all addictions, all images glorifying horror and torture, and all images glorifying demonic themes

All greed

All stored sorrow, grief, heartbreak, and oppression from all sources

All stubbornness and hardness of heart toward hearing God's truths

All stubbornness or resistance within my conscience to the plight of the poor

All unrepentance and resistance to God in regard to anything

All words and sounds regarding anything evil or shocking, and all false teachings of any type

All traumatic, terrifying, or shocking sights and sounds

All disdain and arrogance with which I might regard and see others

All side effects resulting from surgeries, dental traumas, and traumatic injuries; all accidents; all injected dyes; and all dental metals

All scar tissue, all accidents, all injury, and any side effects, including that from surgery and all traumatic words spoken by doctors and anyone else

All toxic allergens and all improper allergy responses to my air, environment, and food

All medication toxicity and any side effects

All pollutants and chemicals from outside or inside my home, especially cleaning supplies and industrial pollution

Any vaccine side effects, including those from metallic additives and foreign DNA

All absorbed radiation from scans, X-rays, mammograms, cell phones, computers, power lines, or any other source and any side effects

All toxic metals, including aluminum, arsenic, lead, mercury, copper, nickel, cadmium, and any side effects

All bacteria, viruses, yeasts, molds, parasites, worms, and any other type of plague and any side effects

All negative or toxic cellular programming or blueprints of any type, from any source and any side effects

In Jesus's powerful name, I command these mountains and any painful stories associated with them to vaporize and completely leave all of my cellular blueprints and my eyes, vision, ears, and hearing, and all of their connected parts—they must all go with none remaining. I declare them gone from all stories of my life, birth, gestation, and from any carryover or effect from my ancestry back to the beginning of time. I am done with them and command them into the sea, never to return.

I make an agreement with my eyes not to gaze in lust, seeing people as objects for selfish gratification either in my everyday life or in movies or magazines. I speak to anything wicked that has ever attacked or clung to my eyes and visual parts. I command these all to vaporize and be cast it into the sea now. They are gone from me and forbidden to return.

I speak to anything wicked that has ever attacked or clung to my ears and hearing parts. I command these all to vaporize and be cast into the sea now. They are gone from me and forbidden to return. I stop listening to any enemy and take my refuge in God. Lord, I repent of not wanting to hear Your truths or Your Holy Spirit, not using wisdom in what I choose to hear, ignoring the pleading of the poor, or turning aside to man's false teachings. Please forgive me.

To fill the vacancies these created, I gratefully and with praise sit down at the bountiful table of the Lord, where I partake of Your perfect remedies containing Your divine patterns and blueprints to fill my eyes, vision, ears, and hearing, and all their connected parts.

I am on a path of wellness where I stop focusing on any enemy and take my refuge in God. I commit to hearing what is true with respect and acceptance. I will make my paths straight and in alignment with Your Word.

I drink my fill of Your love, hope, joy, purity, peace, mercy, courage, and strength. I partake of Your guidance and protection. I taste and drink of all your perfect hearing

*and vision remedies daily until they fill me from the soles
of my feet to the top of my head, making me well. In Jesus's
name, amen.*

BATTLE FOR YOUR COMPLETE HEALING

Instead of using only declarations in this chapter, we are also going
to use the Word of God to "make a case" to the Lord. Read each of
the following passages aloud and then reason with the Lord about
them. I have included examples of what I would say if I were going
to battle against anything that was attacking my vision or hearing.
You will even find help for your speech and ability to walk. These
scriptures are life to your eyes, ears, and more. Speak them daily if
you have challenges to overcome.

> Then the eyes of the blind shall be opened, and the ears
> of the deaf shall be unstopped. Then the lame man shall
> leap as a deer, and the tongue of the mute sing for joy. For
> in the wilderness waters shall break out and streams in
> the desert.
>
> —ISAIAH 35:5–6

> The Spirit of the Lord is upon Me, because He has
> anointed Me to preach the gospel to the poor; He has sent
> Me to heal the broken-hearted, to preach deliverance to the
> captives and recovery of sight to the blind, to set at liberty
> those who are oppressed.
>
> —LUKE 4:18

*I thankfully receive this beautiful description of the gospel of
Jesus Christ and command my body to align with it. I sit at
Your table, Lord, and drink in Your miraculous healing for
my eyes and vision, my ears and hearing, even my mobility
and proper speech. I receive Your gospel of good news to
heal my broken heart, Your liberty for any enslavement,
and freedom from all oppression of man and the devil.*

Open my eyes, that I may behold wondrous things from Your law.

—PSALM 119:18

The hearing ear and the seeing eye, the LORD has made both of them.

—PROVERBS 20:12

Then the eyes of the blind shall be opened.

—ISAIAH 35:5

Lord, I make my case that You intended my eyes to see to Your glory, in order that I might see and study Your Word. I rejoice that when I pray according to Your will, You hear me and grant my request to open my eyes and vision, my ears and hearing.

Moses was a hundred and twenty years old when he died. His eye was not dim, nor was his vitality diminished.

—DEUTERONOMY 34:7

The LORD opens the eyes of the blind; the LORD raises those who are brought down; the LORD loves the righteous.

—PSALM 146:8

Then again He put His hands on his eyes and made him look up. And he was restored and saw everyone clearly.

—MARK 8:25

Immediately something like scales fell from his eyes, and he could see again. And he rose up and was baptized.

—ACTS 9:18

Lord, Your Word says You are not a respecter of persons. I remind You of the vision You gave to the blind for Your glory and also the perfect vision You gave to Moses. I am worthy of healed sight, not from my own works, but because Christ has made me worthy. Your Word says I received the righteousness of Christ when I became Your child. I receive Your healing provisions and eyes and ears as perfect as those of Moses. I praise You ahead of time for perfect near vision for reading and perfect far vision for seeing at a distance. This I pray in the powerful name of Jesus. Amen.

Does not the ear test words and the mouth taste its food?
—Job 12:11

He opens their ear to discipline, and commands that they turn from iniquity.
—Job 36:10

Hear, my son, and receive my sayings, and the years of your life will be many.
—Proverbs 4:10

Hear, you deaf; look, you blind, that you may see.
—Isaiah 42:18

Moreover He said to me: Son of man, all My words that I shall speak to you receive in your heart and hear with your ears.
—Ezekiel 3:10

My ears are opened by You to Your Word and to the words of Your Holy Spirit. I love and respect sound doctrine and teaching. I command my ears and eyes to line up with Your commands.

They brought to Him one who was deaf and had difficulty speaking. And they pleaded with Him to put His hand on him. He took him aside from the crowd, and put His fingers into his ears.... Looking up to heaven, He sighed, and said to him, "*Ephphatha,*" that is, "Be opened." Immediately his ears were opened, and the impediment of his tongue loosened and he spoke correctly.

—MARK 7:32–35

They were astonished beyond measure, saying, "He has done all things well. He makes both the deaf to hear and the mute to speak."

—MARK 7:37

When Jesus saw that the people came running together, He rebuked the foul spirit, saying to it, "You mute and deaf spirit, I command you, come out of him, and enter him no more."

—MARK 9:25

I remind You of the hearing You gave to the deaf and have made available to me. I receive Your provisions for healing, and ears and hearing as perfect as those that You healed. I proclaim release from any deaf and dumb spirit and command it to be evicted, come out, and be gone, in the name of Jesus. I say to it, "You have been conquered and crushed under the feet of Jesus, and I am the hands and feet of Jesus on this earth. You have no authority over me." I also consider asking believing friends to put their fingers into my ears or over my eyes and command them to be opened.

Do those things which you have both learned and received, and heard and seen in me, and the God of peace will be with you.

—PHILIPPIANS 4:9

Lord, I receive perfect hearing and ears, as You want Your followers to continue Your work. I praise You for Your divine blueprint, in which my eyes and ears function perfectly with all purity and Your grace. I magnify Your report over any report of man. Your divine blueprint is working within my eyes and ears right now. Anything else must always bow to the powerful name of Jesus, including anything interfering with my optimal visual and hearing cellular blueprints. I give thanks in Jesus's mighty name. Amen.

Chapter 12

THE DIGESTIVE SYSTEM

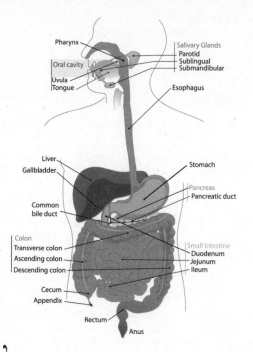

*W*HAT IF YOU had excellent digestion—no bloating, no indigestion, no gas, no pain? Your food turns perfectly into energy and never into unhealthy, excess fat. You have no cravings for junk food, just a desire for pure, healthy food. You have perfect elimination, with the food you eat today exiting your body tomorrow.

I want this marvelous digestive system, don't you?

The digestive system is composed of several important organs: the liver, gallbladder, stomach, pancreas, colon, and small and large intestines. The entire body is dependent on its proper function, which begins in the mouth and ends with the colon. This system breaks down food, digests it, absorbs the nutrients, and eliminates waste and toxins. In fact, what you eat today should be eliminated tomorrow to keep toxic and unpleasant chemicals from forming within the feces.

The intestines also house the majority of our immune system, due to its large lymphatic system and population of trillions of friendly flora, which ward off invaders. If the digestive system isn't at peace, all parts of the body may suffer, including the brain.

In this chapter we will look at the individual organs of the digestive system to increase our understanding of it.

THE LIVER AND GALLBLADDER

The liver is our largest internal organ, and we cannot live without it. It is seated under the right rib cage, just below your right lung. It is a key detoxifying organ and stores nutrients, especially iron. It accomplishes over five hundred tasks, including governing cholesterol, regulating hormones, controlling blood sugar levels, assisting in the processing and absorption of food, fighting infection, filtering blood, neutralizing toxins, and manufacturing bile, which is stored in a hollow organ called the gallbladder. Bile assists in the digestion and processing of fat and is secreted when we eat a meal containing fat. The liver and gallbladder contribute positively to healthy weight management and mood, and assist in the transformation of food into energy.

THE STOMACH

The stomach is located just below the base of the breastbone and is a major digestive organ. When it receives the food we eat, it secretes hydrochloric acid and pepsin for the proper digestion of protein. Stomach acid is an important defense and barrier against parasites and other infective organisms that may be ingested with food.

The stomach is a storehouse of healthy sodium that is found in plants. I am not talking about sodium chloride, which is table salt. Natural plant sodium, which is found in plants such as celery, dandelion, and aloe vera, contributes to a healthy stomach lining. Sodium is one of the four major minerals of the body. Sodium also assists the body in energy production and joint health.

THE PANCREAS

The pancreas is located under the left lower rib cage. It contributes digestive enzymes to the small intestines to process protein, carbohydrates, and fats. It governs proper blood sugar balance with the balanced secretions of insulin and glucagon. When these are functioning as God intended, the pancreas contributes to optimal weight management and vitality.

THE SMALL INTESTINES

The small intestines are located centrally in the abdomen, with the navel as the center. This is where our food is digested and absorbed. Tiny, fingerlike projections called villi line the interior. These function to increase the surface area of the small intestines and aid in the absorption of important nutrients, including proteins, carbohydrates, and fats, into the lymphatic vessels and blood vessels within the villi. These also transport our nutrients into the liver to be processed.

Liver factors are attached to these villi so our nutrients are accepted by our bodies. If the liver is stressed, the body may not accept our absorbed food properly, resulting in allergic responses. "Leaky," swollen intestines that are inflamed or stressed in any manner can allow food particles and harmful organisms to be absorbed directly into the body, creating reactivity and allergy.

The small intestines are a major part of our immunity, as they contain many beneficial bacterial strains that protect us and assist in digestion and brain health.

THE LARGE INTESTINES

Digested food enters the large intestines through the ileocecal valve from the small intestines, and here the water and minerals are absorbed back into the body to make solid waste. If waste remains here too long, toxic chemicals begin to form, and these may be reabsorbed, contributing to sluggishness, brain fog, and toxicity. Good colon transit time is encouraged through the eating of fiber (five or more servings of fresh fruits and vegetables daily) and adequate water intake (eight to ten cups daily). Remember, what is eaten today should ideally leave the body tomorrow.

There is an old saying in the herbal community: "Death begins in the colon." There are good reasons we often make it a priority to restore health to this organ. If it's not functioning correctly, it may affect every other organ in the body with ill health.

The intestinal system houses trillions of good bacteria and bad bacteria, which also perform certain valuable functions. This is important and good if they are in proper ratios. Science is finding that proper ratios may affect us in several ways, a few being our clarity of mind, ability to lose weight, and healthy immune response. The problem is that many people do not have the proper ratio of microorganisms. This may be highly related to frequent consumption of processed foods, refined foods, and sugar, coffee, soda, and alcohol. Eating meat and dairy products laced with antibiotics as well as certain medications may pose even greater challenges.

If we hold hot emotions of anger, hatred, and rage in this part of the body, we may unknowingly complicate any situation of concern. Anger and its cousins are hot emotions and may contribute to inflammation if unresolved. Entertaining a fear mind-set is constrictive to our vitality and may contribute to digestive tension and nerve stress. When we tend to the health of our intestines at all levels of spiritual healing—physical, mental, and emotional—we may immediately begin to experience enhanced elimination, mental clarity, and attitude, improved emotional well-being, clearer skin, higher energy, healthier weight, improved digestion, and much more.

The ileocecal valve is a one-way valve in the right lower abdomen that is present where the small intestines connect to the large intestines. It keeps waste from flowing from the colon back into the small intestine. It is not uncommon for people to experience pain here when the colon is stressed.

The appendix is a small, tail-shaped piece of lymphatic tissue that lies at the beginning of the large intestines in the right lower abdomen. Healthy fiber intake supports the appendix.

CHINESE CONSTITUTIONAL INSIGHTS

When the digestive system is strong and balanced, it is associated with a motherly, sympathetic, and nurturing personality type. When out of balance, worry, anxiety, stomach stress, and frequent digestive upset may become prominent. Breaking down food and metabolizing it to form energy may become impaired.

The liver/gallbladder unit is known as the ruler of the blood and assists other organs to function in harmony. When healthy, the liver/gallbladder unit is associated with a smooth, even flow of vitality and movement within the body, as well as with drive and boldness. The liver is directly associated with eye health. Blurred vision, red or dry eyes, or itching eyes are often correlated with liver stress.

Flexible, strong tendons are associated with a healthy liver. When out of balance, the responses of the body are impaired, sometimes to a serious degree. The vitality, instead of flowing properly through the body, becomes erratic. Resulting imbalances may include PMS, blood sugar imbalances, weight challenges, energy highs and lows, menstrual challenges, allergies, headaches, congested sinuses, digestive distress, and disorders of the blood, including abnormal bleeding, bloody noses, hemorrhoids, and varicose veins. Emotionally a stressed liver may lead to a tendency to become irritable and easily angered. An exhausted liver is associated with depression. Additionally the health of the gallbladder may directly affect the health of the joints and shoulders.

The stomach is associated with the health of the mouth and gums and with healthy breath. Its partner is the spleen, and they both control the health of the muscles. The stomach reacts to internalized thoughts and emotions, especially fear, worry, and anxiety. Large intestine health is associated with health of the lungs. It may be more challenging to heal the lungs if the large intestine is toxic and compromised.

Factors That May Lead to Compromise

Overeating and eating poor-quality, processed foods both stress our digestion and may be the biggest physical factors that lead to compromise. Eating heavy starches, such as potatoes, and heavy proteins, such as steak or pork, and finishing it off with heavy fat, such as cheesecake, especially late at night, may overwhelm our digestion to the point that we cannot sleep properly. Eating when upset, angry, or while having a conflict with someone also impairs proper digestion.

The liver may become diseased from alcohol, tobacco, pollutants of all types, medications, heavy metals, parasites, and various infections. Its health may easily affect its partner organ, the gallbladder. The gallbladder is vulnerable to food poisoning, sometimes chronically harboring these organisms if it is weak. It requires a diet rich in fiber and healthy, bitter, bile-stimulating foods such as dandelion and mustard greens. It may become impaired through chronic resentment and bitterness.

Similarly, the liver may become compromised by harboring chronic anger, hatred, and rage. Inflaming substances that are irritants to the liver such as alcohol, chemicals, infections, and some medications may contribute to both emotional and physical irritability. Irritability, angry outbursts, a hot temper, and inflexibility with the flow of life may indicate the need to cleanse this organ. It is wise to properly process our anger and not allow it to fester internally, as this may exhaust the liver over time. This state of burnout may manifest emotionally as sadness and depression.

The stomach functions best when we eat regular meals in a positive atmosphere and push ourselves away from the table when we are satisfied but not stuffed. The stomach is sensitive to emotional stress and may not digest food properly when we feel tension, worry, fear, or anxiety. If these conditions are prolonged, stomach tension, hiatal hernias, and ulcers may develop. Watching violent TV shows or bad news while eating creates mental and emotional tension, which can compromise the digestion of our meals.

Notice the phrases we often use concerning the stomach: "I have butterflies in my stomach," "Don't worry yourself into an ulcer," and

"I am so upset, I have lost my appetite." Clearly we have some intuitive wisdom about the stomach's reaction to our emotions.

Symptoms that tell us the stomach may need support are gum challenges, bad breath, stools with odor, swollen intestines and belly, ulcers, hiatal hernias, feelings of not digesting food properly, and cravings for sweets.

The stomach, in the Scriptures, appears to be affected by trusting in oneself more than God, resulting in self-indulgent behavior as well as worry, anxiety, and stress about what might happen. In Scripture these manifest through placing one's trust in riches rather than God, oppressing and forsaking the poor, and coveting others' property for personal gain. In our society we commonly observe the desire for gain that hasn't been worked for or earned. Self-comfort and indulgence that shows itself in gluttony and the over-exaltation of food and other earthly things may emerge. In biofeedback I have seen that a thorough release of all stored worry, fear, and anxiety often does the majority of work to ease stress in this organ.

From some of the patterns I consistently observe, the pancreas may be vulnerable to the overuse of CT scans and X-rays. It may also become stressed by the overconsumption of sweets, soda, refined carbohydrates, coffee, and alcohol. This organ is not mentioned by name in Scripture but is likely included in references to the belly and inward parts.

In my experiments it appears that despair and depression may affect the pancreas to the point of interfering with its function. Overworking and becoming obsessed with the serious issues of life to the extent that we crowd out lighthearted, simple pleasures may, in some manner, starve this organ that is fed emotionally by playfulness and joy. We must stop to smell the roses and take time to get down on the floor and play with our children and grandchildren. It is healthy to be a kid at times! It's all about living a balanced life with God at the center. Speak to all mountains of depression and despair each day until they go and see how your pancreas responds. In biofeedback I have seen this yield some wonderful releases of stress.

The small and large intestines are negatively affected by dehydration and any food that upsets the balance of friendly bacteria or flora.

These organs must move waste products through in a timely manner to avoid toxicity. When in a state of stressful imbalance, they may succumb to inflammation and infective organisms, including parasites and worms. Experiment with the release of all forms of anger, hatred, and rage from all cellular blueprints in these organs.

COMMON ILLNESS MANIFESTATIONS

Symptoms indicating the liver needs support may include depression, discouragement, irritability, angry outbursts, tenderness or soreness under the right rib cage, muscle tightness around the neck and shoulders, challenges with tendons, darkness around the eyes, visual challenges, skin disorders and breakouts of any type, tumors, restlessness, insomnia (especially around midnight), feeling toxic or sluggish (especially in the morning), hormonal imbalances, PMS, hot flashes, high cholesterol, allergies, headaches, migraines, hyperactivity, chronic sinus challenges, blood sugar challenges, nausea, vomiting, gas, indigestion, being underweight, weak muscles, hernias, prolapsed organs, feeling cold in the arms and legs, being overweight, bloating, constipation or diarrhea, and body odor. Unhealthy menstrual bleeding, bloody noses, and enlarged or broken blood vessels, as seen in hemorrhoids and varicose veins, may evolve from liver stresses. The formation of excess fat and scar tissue in the liver may result from chronic irritation from various toxins, including alcohol and refined sugar.

Symptoms indicating the gallbladder needs support may include tenderness along the inner border of the right rib cage, shoulder or joint distress, nausea, vomiting, allergies, discomfort after consuming fatty food, constipation, diarrhea, cramping, gas, indigestion, bloating, and formation of gallstones and gallbladder polyps. If you often find yourself mired in resentment and bitterness, you may find you have more gallbladder challenges.

Symptoms indicating the stomach needs support may include discomfort after eating, nausea, chronic issues with intestinal infections, parasites and worms, incomplete digestion of food, discomfort below the breastbone, tension in the stomach muscles, and tension in the chest and heart (including palpitations), as well as smelly, foul gas and stools. If you are a chronic worrier, you may need to give extra support to the stomach.

Common ailments that may plague the pancreas include hypoglycemia and diabetes, which are disorders of blood sugar metabolism. Because the pancreas secretes digestive juices to break down all food types, any weakness in this area may result in bloating, nausea, gas, and feelings of fullness and discomfort after meals. We cannot live without our pancreas, which is why there are very limited medical interventions if pancreatic cancer develops. If you have a lifestyle of workaholism combined with emotional seriousness and inexpression, you may have more challenges with this organ.

Disturbances in the small and large intestines can negatively impact every tissue of the body. Most ailments stem from inflammation and toxicity resulting from the overactivity or underactivity of these organs. Diarrhea, constipation, diverticulitis, gluten intolerance, food reactivity, bloating, gas, challenges with weight gain, polyps, and cancer are common plagues affecting almost every American. Lack of nurturing and supportive relationships may create more challenges in these organs.

APPLYING THE FIVE FOUNDATIONS OF OPTIMAL HEALTH

Good food

Good digestive health is dependent on several factors. It requires fiber for proper transit time within the intestines. The basic example of a healthy, biblically based diet found in chapter 5 will serve you well. The digestive system responds well to fermented foods, such as buttermilk, yogurt, kefir, fermented miso soup, sauerkraut, pickled vegetables, raw apple cider vinegar, kimchi, kombucha, and olives. It also receives excellent nourishment from broth-based soups, papaya and pineapple, yams, brown rice, quinoa, garlic, ginger, horseradish, cinnamon, mint, fennel, and herbal teas.

The liver can benefit from eating organic beef liver, grated raw beets, carrots, zucchini, bitter greens such as dandelion and mustard greens, black cherry and concord grape juices, lemon water, and other tart foods, such as grapefruit, green apples, berries, and tart cherries.

The stomach, and especially the stomach lining, thrives on sodium-rich foods, such as dandelion greens, aloe vera, and celery, as well as raw cabbage, fennel, and nourishing papaya. Root vegetables as well as orange and yellow foods are also excellent.

The pancreas thrives on enzyme-rich foods, such as fresh vegetable juices and raw foods. When foods are not cooked, they retain their enzymes, which supports digestion.

Herbs

For the liver and gallbladder, consider milk thistle, Oregon grape, burdock, chlorophyll, rose hips, and hawthorn berry. I generally choose three to six of these and take two capsules of each twice daily. (If I am targeting the entire digestive system, I might choose a couple of items from each group.)

For the stomach, consider chlorophyll, dandelion, fennel, catnip, cat's claw, peppermint (or peppermint tea), and astragalus. As a general rule, choose three of these and take two capsules of each twice daily.

For the small intestines and colon, consider Oregon grape, astragalus, chlorophyll, peppermint, aloe vera, dandelion, burdock, cat's claw, slippery elm, or cloves. Again, as a general rule, I choose three to six of these and take two capsules of each twice daily with meals. If a particular herb is recommended for more than one body part being targeted, you do not need to double the dosage.

Essential oils

Consider lemon, peppermint, clove, and pine needle. I like to take 1–2 tablespoons of grape seed oil and add three to four drops each of lemon, peppermint, lavender, and clove and apply them over my entire belly. I do this nightly until my results stabilize in the digestive areas.

Pine Needle Power Bath

Use ½ teaspoon of pine needle essential oil mixed well into 2 cups of Epsom salts and dissolve the entire mixture into an evening bath. Soak for eighteen to twenty minutes, keeping your torso, hands, and feet in the water. Schedule this once weekly for a month and then as desired.

Remember to avoid essential oils if you are pregnant or nursing.

Water

Drink eight to ten glasses of pure water daily. Remember, the powerful healing water that is imprinted with biblical truths, affirmations, and specific scriptures can further aid in improving your well-being.

It may be helpful to keep water with a meal limited to four to six ounces to avoid too much dilution of the stomach acid. This means the majority of water would be consumed upon arising and between meals. The stomach will often respond best if you consume warm beverages and foods. This may also contribute to healthy weight management.

Lifestyle

At the first sign of any digestive challenge, consider eliminating wheat, bread, and pasta. Wheat is now hybridized and not grown as the Lord created it. It is a challenge for many people to process the gluten within it. If you do eat bread, consider rye, which is a muscle builder, instead of wheat, which is a fat promoter.

Consider a little raw honey, fruit, real maple syrup, molasses, stevia, or dark chocolate when craving sweets.

Enjoy an environment of good conversation, relaxation, and joy. Turn off the TV and any stressful music. Play games with your family instead. Avoid eating while driving. Keep your focus peaceful to promote healthy digestion.

Eat slowly, chew your food until it is liquefied, and stop when you are satisfied, not stuffed. This is when you will digest your food properly. Eat at least three meals daily, and use a nine-inch plate or smaller to prevent overindulging. We eat with our eyes. Big plates often result in mindless overeating.

To further support digestion and healthy weight, consider the mindful combining of food for easier digestion, such as proteins with vegetables or carbohydrates with vegetables, but eat fruits and desserts alone. Avoid eating several types of food at one meal.

To assist with weight management, consider this experiment: Eat breakfast like a king, lunch like a queen, and dinner as a pauper. Or you might try eating six small meals daily. Avoid eating after 6:00 p.m. when possible.

Walk in forgiveness, love, and gratitude. Resolve conflicts quickly. Cultivate courage and peace. Speak truthfully, keeping integrity in what you believe, do, and say. Good humor, happiness, joy, peace, forgiveness, and the Word of God support the entire digestive system.

BIBLICAL PATHWAY TO HEALING

The following outlines a path for experiencing health in your digestive system. Please take time to really think about each of these and why we must speak to their eviction. This system is so important, you may find you need to process through these evictions and the healing prayer that will follow several times, speaking to the mountains and evicting them from one organ at a time. Don't hesitate to speak to any other issue or story related to these that comes to mind that needs to go. See these things leaving your body and it being refilled from the Lord's table with what is good and acceptable and perfect.

General digestion

Our mouth is the beginning of the entire digestive tract, which ends at the large intestines. Any type of hatred or violence in word or deed may affect the mouth and jaw.

+ Eject all fury and anger: "But Queen Vashti refused to come at the king's command delivered by his eunuchs. Therefore, the king grew very angry, and his wrath burned within him" (Esther 1:12).

+ Eject all lying. Confess, apologize, and restore relationships. Lying puts the body into a moderate state of stress: "You desire truth in the inward parts, and in the hidden part You make me to know wisdom" (Ps. 51:6).

+ Evict all violent and hateful words—control your speech: "The mouth of a righteous man is a well of life, but violence covers the mouth of the wicked" (Prov. 10:11).

+ Eject all traumatic and fearful events, fear of the future, and anxiety regarding the criminal element of society, along with all potential invaders: "I heard, and my body trembled; my lips quivered at the sound; rottenness entered my bones; my legs tremble beneath me. Yet I will wait quietly for the day when calamity comes on the people invading us" (Hab. 3:16).

The liver

Two passages mention the liver and how our beliefs and actions may affect it. Through these passages, we learn that sexual immorality may be destructive to the liver. Intense sorrow, hopelessness, despair, defeat, or depression also appear to affect the liver.

+ Eject all improper sexual lust and immoral relationships, and the delusional thinking accompanying them. Ask God for mercy regarding any side effects: "With her enticing speech she caused him to yield, with the flattering of her lips she seduced him. He went after her straightway, as an ox goes to the slaughter, or as a fool to the correction of the stocks, until a dart struck through his liver. As a bird hastens to the snare, he did not know that it would cost him his life" (Prov. 7:21–23).

+ Eject all sorrow and grief over any issue of life: "Consumed by tears have been my eyes, Troubled have been my bowels, Poured out to the earth hath been my liver, For the breach of the daughter of my people" (Lam 2:11, YLT).

The gallbladder

The gallbladder or its contents are called gall in the Bible, and it is associated with holding onto bitterness.

+ Evict all bitterness and its relatives of resentment and unforgiveness: "For their vine is of the vine of Sodom and of the fields of Gomorrah; their grapes are grapes of gall, their clusters are bitter" (Deut. 32:32, NKJV).

+ Evict all unrighteousness of any form and all forms of bondage and addiction: "For in the gall of bitterness, and bond of unrighteousness, I perceive thee being" (Acts 8:23, YLT).

The stomach

Bearing our own burdens creates a stressful life and stomach, as does being in love with the world and its indulgences.

+ Eject all evil talk and deceptive words, all greed, all ungratefulness, all oppression of others, all violent behavior, all stress, all heartburn, all nausea and vomiting and sourness of stomach, and all trust and exultation of oneself over trust in the provision of God: "Though evil is sweet in his mouth, and he hides it under his tongue, though he spares it and does not forsake it, but keeps it in his mouth, yet his food in his stomach turns sour; it becomes the venom of cobras within him. He has swallowed down riches, and he will vomit them up again; God will cast them out of his belly.... He will give back the produce of labor and will not swallow it down. According to his wealth the restitution will be, and he will not rejoice in it; because he has oppressed and has forsaken the poor. He has violently taken away a house that he did not build. Because he knows no quietness in his belly, he will not save anything he desired. Nothing is left for him to eat; therefore his prosperity will not endure. In his self-sufficiency he will be in distress" (Job 20:12–15, 18–22).

+ Eject all antagonism toward God, all gluttony and fleshly overindulgence, and all lusts for power, wealth, and the indulgences of this life: "For many walk, of whom I have told you often, and now tell you even weeping, that they are the enemies of the cross of Christ: whose end is destruction, whose god is their belly, and whose glory is in their shame—who set their mind on earthly things" (Phil. 3:18–19, NKJV).

+ Evict all excessive craving and lack of self-control regarding sweets: "Have you found honey? Eat only as much as is sufficient for you, lest you be filled with it and vomit it" (Prov. 25:16).

The small and large intestines

Two passages in God's Word specifically note the bowel, or intestines, and the character of the men afflicted with maladies in this area. Both were kings, and both entertained aggressive and prideful mind-sets, selfish ambition, and emotions that included fostering anger, hatred, and rebellion against God, man, and their parents. Both ended up with diseased intestines.

+ Evict all murderous hatred and actions, all evil and acts that lead others to evil, and all rebellion toward God: "Then Jehoram rose up over the kingdom of his father and he became strong. And he killed all his brothers with the sword and even some of the officials in Israel.... And a letter came to him from Elijah the prophet, saying, 'Thus says the LORD God of David your father: Because you have not walked in the ways of Jehoshaphat your father, or in the ways of Asa king of Judah, but have walked in the way of the kings of Israel, and have led Judah and the inhabitants of Jerusalem into whoredom, as the house of Ahab led Israel into whoredom, and also have killed your brothers, those of your father's house, who were better than you, the LORD will bring a great plague on your people, your children, your wives, and all your possessions; and you will have great sickness with a disease of your intestines, until your intestines come out because of the disease, day by day'" (2 Chron. 21:4, 12–15).

+ Evict all anger and harassment of others, and the desire for revenge and any thoughts or actions to make or see oneself equal with God: "About that time King Herod extended his hands to harm certain ones from the church. He killed James the brother of John with the sword.... Now Herod was very angry with the people of Tyre and Sidon. But they came to him in unity, and... they asked for peace, because their country was fed by the king's country. On an appointed day, Herod, dressed in royal apparel, sat on his throne and gave a public speech to them. The mob shouted, 'It is the voice of a god, and not of a man!' Immediately an angel of the Lord struck him, because he did not give God the glory. And he was eaten by worms and died" (Acts 12:1–2, 20–23).

HEALING PRAYER

Speak this prayer aloud with boldness and confidence. Exert the authority in Christ that has been given to you. In Him all things are possible.

Dear heavenly Father,

I praise You that I am fearfully and wonderfully made and that You have already given me everything I need pertaining to life. In Exodus 23:25 You stated, "You shall serve the LORD your God, and He shall bless your bread and your water, and I will remove sickness from your midst." My intent is to bring my life into alignment with Your Word so that You bless my food and I have excellent

*digestive health. In Mark 11:24 You said that what things I
desire when I pray, I am to believe that I am receiving them
and I shall have them. I affirm and declare Your abun-
dance and health filling my entire digestive blueprint.*

*I choose to live a life glorifying to You, with full confi-
dence in the truth of Your promises to me. You have given
me power within my speech and the ability to speak to
any mountains in the way of my health and well-being. I
release any obstacles to my prayers by forgiving any who
have wronged me. I will not allow anger and resentment
to fester within, and I especially evict it in any form. With
these in mind, I declare over my entire digestion total
divine health and healing, purging every encumbrance that
stands in the way.*

*With the powerful name and words of Jesus, I am fully
equipped to receive healing. I command and evict from all
deep cellular blueprints within my entire digestive system,
including every part of my mouth and jaw, esophagus, liver,
gallbladder, stomach, pancreas, small and large intestines,
along with their flora, the ileocecal valve, appendix, and all
their nerves and circulation mechanisms:*

*All forms of fury, anger, antagonism, rebellion, harass-
ment, and violence expressed in behavior or words, especially toward God, His truths, my parents, or authorities*

*All stuffed words containing any of these above or any
evil talk that I am still holding in my mouth, jaw, or throat*

All murderous hatred and actions

All evil and acts that encourage others to do evil

All trauma

*All stress, fearful events, worry, fear of the future, and
anxiety, including that focused on extremists, terrorists,
and harmful or criminal elements of society*

*All lying, lust, immoral relationships, and delusions con-
nected to these*

*All sorrow, grief, depression, despair, and hopelessness,
and all stories involved with these*

All bitterness, resentment, and unforgiveness toward God, others, or myself

All unrighteousness and bondage

All greed; all ungratefulness toward God and others; all oppression of others; all heartburn; all nausea, vomiting, and sourness of stomach; and all trust and exultation of myself over my trust in the provision of God

All difficulties digesting protein, carbohydrates, or fats

All gluttony, all fleshly overindulgence, and all addictions to drugs or alcohol

All lusts (cravings), self-serving attitudes, and ambitions for power and wealth

Any lack of feeling emotionally well-fed and nurtured

All excessive craving and lack of self-control regarding sweets

All desire for revenge and all acts of revenge

All disrespect and dishonor of parents and authority

All reliance on and exultation of self rather than God for future provisions

All pride

All scar tissue, all effects from accidents, all injury, and their side effects, including that of surgery and traumatic words spoken by any person, including my doctors

Any stored medication toxicity and any side effects

All toxic allergens and any improper response to my food, air, or environment

All stored pollutants and chemicals from outside or inside my home, especially cleaning supplies and industrial pollution

Any vaccine side effects, including those from metallic additives and foreign DNA

All absorbed radiation from scans, X-rays, mammograms, cell phones, computers, power lines, or any other source, and all side effects of that exposure

All toxic metals, including aluminum, arsenic, lead, mercury, copper, nickel, cadmium, and any resulting side effects

All bacteria, viruses, yeasts, molds, parasites, worms, and any other type of plague and any side effects

All negative or toxic cellular programming or blueprints of any type, from any source

I command all these mountains and all painful stories that may be connected to them to vaporize and completely leave all the cellular blueprints of every created digestive part—they must all go with none remaining. I am done with them and command them into the sea, never to return. I declare them gone!

Heavenly Father, to fill the vacancies these create, I recline at Your bountiful table and partake of Your perfect divine patterns and life-giving blueprints for my entire digestive system, including every part of my mouth and jaw, esophagus, liver, gallbladder, stomach, pancreas, small and large intestines, and their flora, the ileocecal valve and appendix, and all the nerves and circulation mechanisms within this system.

I drink in deliverance, preservation, and strength to fill all of my mouth, jaw, and digestive parts. I taste and eat until I am overflowing with mercy and compassion toward others, and I take in love, forgiveness, peace, joy, and godly blueprints for perfect digestion, absorption, and utilization of food, as well as perfect flora and freedom from all allergies. I accept Your Word into all my deepest parts, as they are health to all my flesh.

I will walk in obedience, humility, respect for others, and self-control, and I will live to declare Your works. All sickness is gone, anything opposing me is made to submit, and I declare all attacks of the devil to be quenched. My mouth is held in Your hands, and I speak only words of life and health toward others. I praise You as my daily provider and claim that all my digestive parts are fearfully and wonderfully made anew. I will continue to partake of all these delights from the table of the Lord until I see myself filled from the top of my head to the soles of my feet. In Jesus's name I pray. Amen.

HEALING DECLARATIONS

These personalized scriptures will feed the new seeds you have planted. Declare these powerful verses daily.

> My body is God's temple and His spirit dwells within me. I will not destroy it, but keep it holy (1 Cor. 3:16–17).

> All things are lawful for me but not all things are helpful. I refuse to be enslaved by anything harmful to me (1 Cor. 6:12–13).

> My body is the temple of the Holy Spirit. I am not my own, for I was bought with a price. I will glorify God in my body (1 Cor. 6:19–20).

> I discipline my body and keep it under control (1 Cor. 9:27).

> Whether I eat or drink, or whatever I do, I do all to the glory of God (1 Cor. 10:31).

> All goes well with me and I am in good health as I nurture and keep my soul (my mind and emotions) in good health (3 John 2).

CHAPTER 13

WEIGHT MANAGEMENT

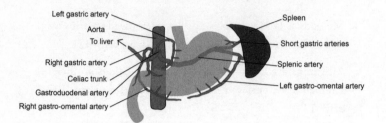

ANATOMY OF THE STOMACH

WEIGHT IS A complex issue. It involves our digestive system, blood sugar balance, glandular system, and lymphatic system, as well as our emotions, mind-set, exercise level, and diet. I believe we have capacity to store much sorrow, grief, trauma, and depression in our fat, weighing our metabolism down and allowing toxins to become mired in the body, which only makes our metabolism even more sluggish.

In addressing this issue, let us remember first that the Lord does not look on the outward appearance and that He deems each one of us valuable. We are not to judge others' value by their outward appearance either:

> Therefore you are without excuse, O man, whoever you are who judges, for when you judge another, you condemn yourself, for you who judge do the same things.
> —ROMANS 2:1

> Who are you to judge another man's servant? To his own master he stands or falls. And he will stand, for God is able to make him stand.
> —ROMANS 14:4

Image source: Mikael Häggström

CHINESE CONSTITUTIONAL INSIGHTS

A stressed digestive system is associated with weight challenges, sugar cravings, abdominal bloating, and feeling uncomfortably full after eating. Emotional indications are nervousness and anxiety. When our liver is stressed by toxins or emotions such as anger, we may react to fats more frequently and not process them correctly. A strong liver is associated with proper fat and cholesterol balances and utilization whether in our diets or in our bodies. A strong urinary system is a tonic to our bodies' vitality. Stress from toxins or fears may result in abdominal bloating and obesity. When the immune system is stressed, our energies may become sluggish and phlegm may accumulate, making the lymphatics overwhelmed, swollen, and sluggish. Fluid retention, difficulty digesting fats, and weight challenges may ensue. Joy is a vibrant, energizing emotion and may be very important to our immunity and to nurture a healthy weight. Depression and grief make us want to stay in bed or on the couch, robbing us of the energy and vitality that may be needed to exercise and properly process our food into energy.

FACTORS THAT MAY LEAD TO COMPROMISE

Weight management is about more than our consumption levels of fat, sugar, salt, and processed foods. We unfortunately consume weight-promoting hormones through commercial animal proteins and dairy products. Certain medications promote weight gain, as do certain chemicals in our environment that mimic estrogen. Our emotional and mental state may be driving these cravings and form the root of many of our symptoms in this area. Please take inventory of these factors as a start in identifying root issues for weight gain.

Eating clean, organic foods and reducing the chemicals we use in our homes and environment are important factors to help us manage our weight.

Look up some recipes to make your own laundry detergent so you don't wear so many chemicals against your skin. Minimize radiation whenever you can wisely do so to protect your thyroid and other body parts. This type of toxic energy can drain the body and promotes exhaustion.

COMMON ILLNESS MANIFESTATIONS

Weight issues can manifest in illnesses such as cancer, heart disease, lung disease, gout, gallstones, diabetes, hypoglycemia, weakening of the joints (especially in the knees, ankles, and feet), poor energy and vitality, infertility, cystic ovaries, poor sex drive, urinary weakness, and imbalanced cravings for junk food, sugar, salt, and fat. All kinds of symptoms can arise.

Weight gain is an epidemic in our society. It can be particularly challenging because negative emotions and mind-sets often partner with poor self-esteem, depression, trauma, anxiety, bitterness, loneliness, and more to perpetuate this issue.

APPLYING THE FIVE FOUNDATIONS OF OPTIMAL HEALTH

Good foods

As always the general healthy biblical guidelines included in chapter 5 provide an excellent start. It is very important to drink plenty of healthy fluids. Green tea is excellent.

Move toward consuming more raw foods, as this can help you shed weight more easily. Consider constructing your meal on a nine-inch plate and fill at least half of it with fresh or lightly steamed vegetables. Omit refined sugars and limit fattening carbohydrates. Enjoy red quinoa frequently as a non-meat source of protein. Emphasize warming spices such as garlic, ginger, horseradish, lemongrass, and cinnamon daily. Cook more with broth instead of oils.

Aim for 100 grams of organic protein daily, evenly divided

between three meals. This may include vegetarian sources, such as healthy protein meal replacement shakes if you are on the go. Remember that skipping meals slows the metabolism.

Consider mixing raw apple cider vinegar equally with raw dark honey in a jar and then mixing 1–2 tablespoons of this combination in 8–10 ounces of water once or twice daily. Squeeze fresh citrus into mineral water with a little stevia as a great soda substitute. Lemon is excellent for the liver and gallbladder. Avoid cold and icy foods and beverages, which slows digestive metabolism.

Herbs

Consider dulse, kelp, chickweed, fennel, and chlorophyll. I prefer to take two capsules of each twice daily, plus 2–4 tablespoons of liquid chlorophyll daily.

Essential oils

Consider red mandarin, clove, grapefruit, lemon, and peppermint. You might try using two to three drops of each in a carrier oil such as grape seed oil and rubbing it into your belly once or twice daily. Also refer to the bath recipes in the chapters on the digestive, immune, and glandular systems, and rotate them so you do at least one bath weekly. These baths are not to be underestimated. They often appear to accelerate results very nicely! Remember to avoid essential oils if you are pregnant or nursing.

Water

Drink eight to ten glasses of pure water daily. Remember, the powerful healing water that is imprinted with biblical truths, affirmations, and specific scriptures can further aid in improving your well-being.

Lifestyle

Pray over all your food and water, declaring it perfect for health, free from toxins, and perfect for your personal fat burning and weight management. At least three times weekly speak to any mountains of glandular sluggishness or toxicity from any source that may be trying to emerge, potentially slowing your fat loss. Center yourself in positive, affirming Scripture each morning. Be positive and joyful, using praise music to elevate your mood.

Buy a wristband that tracks your steps each day and sync it with your phone. It will remind you to stay active.

Begin an exercise program that is smart for you and will coincide with your doctor's advice.

Find out if you are on any medications that promote weight gain. Work on that body system to make it healthier so your doctor can reevaluate what you are taking and possibly reduce or eliminate it when appropriate.

Enjoy hanging out with friends who have similar healthy weight-management goals.

Keep only healthy foods in your pantry and fridge. Eat a substantial healthy snack at home before eating out or going to a party so you have more self-control.

Join a Christian group that is teaching healthy weight management. Be accountable. If you have a setback, don't tear yourself down; just get back on track. Persevere until you reach your goal.

Continue healthy habits and reward yourself with fun activities and other nonfood rewards as you reach your goals.

BIBLICAL PATHWAY TO HEALING

These are some scriptures that form the partial basis for our verbal prayer for weight management. The rest of the prayer is based on my experiences with patients during biofeedback sessions. Notice how emotions and mind-sets can affect our weight.

+ Evict all lack of self-control with food—if you don't want to eat it, don't have it in your home: "And put a knife to your throat, if you are a man given to appetite" (Prov. 23:2).

+ Evict all overeating and overdrinking and associating with those who do: "Do not be among winebibbers, among riotous eaters of meat" (Prov. 23:20).

+ Evict the use of food for selfish ambition: "For such people do not serve our Lord Jesus Christ, but their own appetites, and through smooth talk and flattery they deceive the hearts of the unsuspecting" (Rom. 16:18).

+ Evict a focus on worldly things. Listen to God's good reports instead: "Their destination is destruction, their god is their appetite, their glory is in their shame, their minds are set on earthly things" (Phil. 3:19).

+ Evict all weights and sin that keep you down: "Therefore, since we are encompassed with such a great cloud of witnesses, let us also lay aside every weight and the sin that so easily entangles us, and let us run with endurance the race that is set before us" (Heb. 12:1).

HEALING PRAYER

Speak this prayer aloud with boldness and confidence. Exert the authority in Christ that has been given to you. In Him all things are possible.

Dear heavenly Father,

I thank You over and over, Lord, that I am fearfully and wonderfully made to drive out all negativity toward myself and all judgments of the world. I only speak well of my body and its parts. As I place Your words into my organs and my excess fat cells, I command them to align with Your truth and be in health. I am improving daily with Your truths and with new habits and attitudes. I claim victory even before I see it.

In the name of Jesus, I command and evict from all cellular blueprints of my fat cells and any of my parts governing my weight:

All unwanted weight of all types—mental, emotional, and physical—including all sin and guilt; all trauma from any source; all depressions, addictions, sadness, rejection, abandonment, grief, and heartbreak; all anger, hatred, and rage; any resentment, bitterness, and unforgiveness; and all forms of abuse and its side effects from any sources

All addictions and emotional worship related to food and drink

All overdrinking and overeating and associating with those who practice these things

All negative and hurtful words aimed at my weight or appearance from anyone, including myself, my family, and health professionals

All stored chemicals and medication residue and any side effects

All stored heavy metals, including aluminum, arsenic, mercury, copper, lead, nickel, cadmium, and anything else and any side effects

All toxic allergens and all improper allergic responses to healthy food, drink, and air

All toxic components of junk foods I have eaten

Any stored radiation, electromagnetic pollutions of all types, and their side effects

All bacteria, viruses, yeasts, molds, parasites, worms, and any side effects

All unhealthy cellular debris, excess fat and fluid, and bad cellular blueprints of any type and any side effects

In Jesus's name, I command these mountains and all painful stories that may be connected to them to vaporize and completely leave all the cellular blueprints within my metabolism, fat tissue, and cells—they must all go with none remaining. I declare them gone from all stories of my life, from my gestation and birth, and from any carryover from my ancestry. I command them into the sea, never to return. I am done with them and I declare them gone!

To fill these vacancies, I take a seat at the bountiful table of the Lord, where there is everything pertaining to life, including healthy weight. I eat my fill of God's perfect divine patterns and blueprints of life, vitality, deliverance, self-control, and strength to fill all of my metabolism, fat tissues and cells, my mind, and my emotions. I drink lavishly of God's blueprints for a healthy metabolism, perfect energy, strong muscles, and perfect production of collagen, elastin, and healthy tissues.

Anything opposing me is made to submit, and I declare all attacks of the devil to be quenched. I receive my fill of God's joy and peace, beauty for any ashes of any destroyed dreams or goals, and His good plans for my future with all of my needs supplied. I see myself partaking of these delicacies each day until they fill me from the top of my head to the soles of my feet.

Thank you, heavenly Father, for giving me the proper blueprint for me to see that I am awesome and wonderful as Your creation. You see into my core and view me as valuable and loved. I wait upon Your promises as I stand upon them. I can walk and run symbolically and literally. I lay aside anything that contributes to unhealthy weight and all sinful actions related to this issue. I am committed to serving You and doing what is right and not serving my appetites. I see myself as running in a great race of victory. I commit to not overeat or overdrink. I will control my appetite and mix with other believers who have the same commitments to encourage me. At the right time, I will reap a harvest of blessings as I persevere. I pray this in Jesus's powerful name. Amen.

HEALING DECLARATIONS

Print off the following verse and keep it where you can see it so that you speak it aloud with passion and meaning ten times daily:

> I will praise You, for I am fearfully and wonderfully made; marvelous are Your works, and that my soul knows very well.
> —PSALM 139:14, NKJV

Also refer to the Healing Declarations for the digestive system and declare the ones that address the core challenges you face. Always remember, you are more than a conqueror, bold as lion, and able to do all things through the power God gives you!

CHAPTER 14

THE URINARY SYSTEM

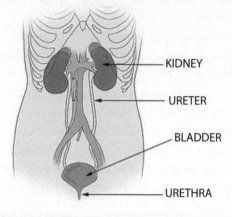

KIDNEY

URETER

BLADDER

URETHRA

COMPONENTS OF THE URINARY SYSTEM

*W*HAT IF YOU slept the majority of the night without being awakened by your bladder? What if you could actually forget about this system of your body until you had to urinate and it was an uneventful experience, with no pain, infection, swelling, or bleeding? God has provided His perfect blueprint of health and healing for this important system.

In the Orthodox Jewish Bible, the kidneys are called both the reins and the inward parts. Their main function is the filtering and processing of blood and the elimination of waste from the body.

The urinary system consists of the kidneys, ureters, bladder, two sphincter muscles, and the urethra. The kidneys are two kidney-bean-shaped organs that sit in the center of the left and right sides of the body, close to the level of the elbows when your hands hang at your side. The ureters channel the urine into the bladder, which holds it until we release it through the channel of the urethra. The kidneys regulate mineral and water balance within the body, which is important for hydration and the health of the bones. Their proper function influences healthy blood pressure, contributing to overall vitality, and the production of red blood cells.

CHINESE CONSTITUTIONAL INSIGHTS

The kidneys are powerhouses within the body, supplying stored energy to any organ running low in its energy reserves. Its partner organ is the bladder. Healthy kidney function is associated with healthy bones, ears, hearing, knees, and sexual organs.

The urinary system is associated with the qualities of water. Water is flexible and flows easily around obstacles and always makes its way almost effortlessly. When this system is strong, a person will often have a flexible, easygoing nature that doesn't get ruffled easily by obstacles. When it is stressed, there will be fluid and mineral imbalances, resulting in urinary weakness, weakening of the bones and spine, and weakened knees.

Emotionally there may be issues with fear, inflexibility, excess concerns with detail, starting a project but getting bogged down in the specifics, and lack of focus, as well as panic attacks and anxiety. "He was so scared, he wet his pants" is a common saying in America that reflects we intuitively match fear with the bladder. When there is a strong response to fright or fear, there may be an instant weakening of the bladder, legs, and knees. If these emotions are not mastered, one might need to continually support kidney vitality.

FACTORS THAT MAY LEAD TO COMPROMISE

It is important to take a careful look at what emotions and mindsets we are entertaining, especially those involving fear (especially of the future) and a general lack of courage.

Physically, we must drink an adequate supply of pure water daily—our body weight divided by two determines the amount of ounces required each day. When we finally feel thirsty, we are often in some stage of dehydration. We need to drink water often throughout the day.

The kidneys thrive on pure water, but in this society, we add significant burden to the urinary system with an overconsumption of acidic coffee, soda, alcohol, and chemically laced tap water. I see many new clients who favor these flavored beverages over pure water.

Tenderness in the soles of the feet, especially upon arising, may be a sign the body is too acidic and needs more pure water. I teach clients to watch for any development of low back pain or knee discomfort and if they develop to consider a reduction in acidic fluids. Bedwetting children, as well as individuals of any age who feel they have any unpleasant urinary symptoms, may wish to consider a return to the simplicity of pure water and gentle herbal teas such as chamomile and peppermint, sweetened only with stevia or a little raw honey.

Refined salt may lead to kidney stress and fluid retention in the tissues and sometimes these may be reflected as fluid-filled bags under the eyes. People may crave salt when the kidneys are fatigued. Many such people are dehydrated. This can lead to a host of symptoms, including leg cramps, lower back pain, and foul, concentrated, dark urine. Environmental chemicals, heavy metals, and medication side effects may significantly burden the kidneys.

High blood pressure may also be positively influenced by addressing the kidneys, adrenals, and their nerves, and by releasing fear, worry, anxiety, and trauma from them as well as from the muscles and nerves of the blood vessels. I have seen blood pressure drop ten points instantly after certain clients chose to release these emotional patterns. Sometimes even bedwetting responds to prayers to release fear. I once had a client who had to assist her son to release fear of his father, and his father also had to make some adjustments. When this was done, the bedwetting soon stopped. These releases may need to be done daily until the brain gets the picture that fear is no longer allowed or needed.

Common Illness Manifestations

Illness in the urinary system manifests as water retention, low back aches, weakness of the knees and legs, impotence, urinary infections, kidney stones, joint and bone weakness, and joint and bone disease.

Applying the Five Foundations of Optimal Health

Good foods

Follow the guidelines for a healthy, biblically based diet as outlined in chapter 5. Emphasize good foods, especially kidney beans and black beans in the diet, which are shaped like a kidney. (God gives us clues.)

The kidneys respond well to minerals. Foods rich in these are nuts and seeds, bone broth, Himalayan salt, and potassium broths made of simmered bones, to which in the last thirty minutes of simmering you add the peelings of organic carrots, celery, potatoes, parsley, and flakes of dried seaweed.

Asparagus, parsley, and watermelon have a healthy diuretic action, supporting the kidney's ability to release fluid properly from the tissues.

Homemade lemonade sweetened with stevia acts as an astringent for the urinary system and may act as a tonic when needed. Pure water is one of the most ideal fluids for the kidneys.

Herbs

Consider burdock, uva ursi, spirulina, parsley, marshmallow herb, juniper, and cranberry. A general rule is to choose three to six of these and take two capsules of each twice daily with meals.

Essential oils

Pine needle Power Baths are excellent. I love taking 2 cups of Epsom salts and mixing in ½ teaspoon of pine needle oil. Make sure the abdomen and legs are in the bath. Do this in the evening for twenty minutes once weekly for four weeks, and then evaluate your progress. Remember to avoid essential oils if you are pregnant or nursing.

Water

Drink eight to ten glasses of pure water daily. Remember, the powerful healing water that is imprinted with biblical truths, affirmations, and specific scriptures can further aid in improving your well-being.

Lifestyle

While addressing any kidney challenge, it would be ideal to stop drinking coffee, soda, and any other sugared or caffeinated beverage.

Cultivate courage and the ability to confront the challenges of life in a healthy manner. Don't just obsess about issues; waste no time after careful prayer and decide to courageously confront your obstacles. Face fears and triumph over them. Release all fear of man, the future, and what other people think. What they think is none of our business. We want to release any of this type of programming from every created part of the urinary system and its muscles, circulation mechanisms, and nerves. Aim to please God. See God as your refuge, strength, and power. Courage and boldness come from your relationship with Him. Be a lion! You can do all things through Christ.

The kidneys respond to reductions in stress. Stop anything that drains vitality from the body. Cultivate restful sleep. Buy good shoes that keep your legs and hips well supported and in proper alignment.

BIBLICAL PATHWAY TO HEALING

These are some scriptures that form the partial basis for our verbal prayer for this body system. The rest of the prayer is based on my experiences with patients during biofeedback sessions. Notice how emotions and mind-sets can affect our body parts.

- Conquer all challenges in life with the Word of God. "Therefore lay aside all filthiness and remaining wickedness and receive with meekness the engrafted word, which is able to save your souls" (James 1:21).

+ Speak the truth. "You desire truth in the inward parts, and in the hidden part You make me to know wisdom" (Ps. 51:6).

+ Evict all lying and poor choices. "I the LORD search the heart; I try the kidneys, even to give each man according to his ways and according to the fruit of his doings" (Jer. 17:10, JUB).

HEALING PRAYER

Speak this prayer aloud with boldness and confidence. Exert the authority in Christ that has been given to you. In Him all things are possible.

Dear heavenly Father.

I have learned that whatever state I am in to be content. You have formed my inward parts and have carefully designed my urinary system. I will not allow terror, fear, anxiety, worry, or discouragement, especially with regard to the future, any place in my being, especially my urinary system and its muscles, circulation mechanisms, and nerves. I will confess any trespasses to trusted believers and receive prayer that I may be healed. I put the matters and cares of each day within Your hands.

With the powerful name and words of Jesus, I am fully equipped to receive healing. I command and evict from all deep cellular blueprints of my kidneys, ureters, bladder, urethra, and all their muscles, nerves, and circulatory mechanisms:

All types of stressful thinking and doing, including doing things my way instead of God's way, which may have resulted in the storage of extreme fear, worry, terror, fright, and anxiety

All lying

All stored fear of my father or parental figure, especially fear related to shame or sin

All secrets, lies, and shame connected to guilt or sin or the shaming of others

Anything that doesn't line up with the Word of God

All scar tissue, all accidents, all injury and their side effects, including that of surgery and traumatic words of any person, including my doctors

Any stored medication toxicity and any side effects

All stored pollutants and chemicals from outside or inside my home, especially cleaning supplies and industrial pollution

Any vaccine side effects, including those from metallic additives and foreign DNA

All absorbed radiation from scans, X-rays, mammograms, cell phones, computers, power lines, or any other source and all side effects

All toxic metals, including aluminum, arsenic, lead, mercury, copper, nickel, cadmium, and any side effects

All bacteria, viruses, yeasts, molds, parasites, worms, and any other type of plague and any side effects

All toxic allergens and any improper reaction to healthy foods, the air, and my environment

All negative or toxic cellular programming or blueprints of any type, from any source

In the name of Jesus, I command all of these mountains and all painful stories that may be connected to them to vaporize and completely leave all the cellular blueprints of every created urinary part—they must all go with none remaining. I release all of these perfectly from all stories of my life, gestation and birth, and from any carryover or connection they have to my ancestry back to the beginning of time. I command these into the sea. It is done! I declare them gone!

No plague of any sort shall come near my urinary system. My God delivers me from all afflictions that try to attack me. The Lord preserves my life when I look to Him and trust in Him. I command my urinary system to line up with the Word of God—*with His courage, strength, power, and life-giving blessings of wellness.*

I thank You, Lord, for preparing me a seat at Your table while I am here on Earth. I taste and fill myself with Your remedies for a perfect urinary system—my kidneys, ureters, bladder, urethra, and all their muscles, nerves, and circulation mechanisms. I drink in love, peace, boldness, courage, and the ability to do all things through You. After making reasonable plans, I laugh at any anxieties regarding the future, knowing Your promises to be my rock, protection, and deliverance. I am at Your table, where no enemy may invade. I see myself partaking of your urinary remedies until they fill me from the bottom of my feet to the top of my head, making me well. Amen.

HEALING DECLARATIONS

These personalized scriptures will feed the new seeds you have planted. Declare these powerful verses daily.

Many are the afflictions of the righteous, but the Lord delivers me out of them all (Ps. 34:19).

No evil shall befall me [or my kidneys], nor shall any plague come near my dwelling (Ps. 91:10).

I will not fear, for You are with me. I will not be dismayed, for You are my God. You will strengthen me. Yes, You will help me. You will uphold me with Your righteous right hand (Isa. 41:10).

CHAPTER 15

THE STRUCTURAL SYSTEM

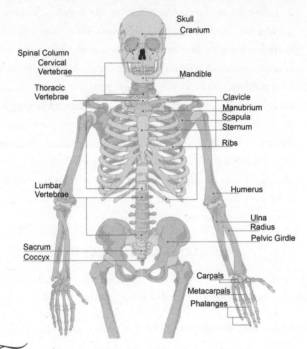

*T*HE STRUCTURAL SYSTEM is best described as a wonderful, supportive framework. It consists of our bones, spinal column, joints, tendons, ligaments, muscles, and teeth, as well as their nerves and circulation processes. I mentioned the skin in the immune system, but it is referenced in some of the scriptures associated with this system, so you will see it included at times.

There are 206 bones in the adult human body.[1] They come in a variety of shapes and have a complex internal and external structure. They are lightweight, yet strong and hard.

The bones provide structural support for the body, protection for vital organs, a storage depot for minerals (such as calcium and trace minerals), and an environment for marrow, where blood cells and stem cells are produced. There are approximately 650 muscles in the human body,[2] which give us the ability to move. Nerves are vital for proper muscle control.

Joints allow the bones to have range of motion while tendons are like a flexible cord of strong, sinewy tissue that attaches the muscle to a bone. Ligaments are similar tough connective tissues that join two bones or bind a joint together.

Baby teeth develop in utero around week six, and permanent teeth develop around the twentieth week. Nutrition is critical at these times, as the lack of it may cause some teeth to fail to develop properly. Each tooth has its own circulatory and nervous system!

CHINESE CONSTITUTIONAL INSIGHTS

In Chinese medicine the kidneys govern the health of the bones, including the bones of the ears. The kidneys are also closely associated with the knees. The digestive organs and endocrine glands are also involved in our mineral balance and the health of the structural system.

It is wise to consider the kidneys and mineral balance when addressing the bones and joints. The joints also have a close association with the health of the gallbladder. Fear and feeling ungrounded or unsupported by life, parents, friends, work, or a spouse may stress this system.

FACTORS THAT MAY LEAD TO COMPROMISE

As storehouses of minerals, our bones have the ability to release important calcium and minerals to buffer excess acidity in the body and keep our pH level in balance. This is important because our tap water is acidic; most grain is acidic; and sugar, soft drinks, and coffee are especially acidic. Our bones may become depleted if we regularly consume an overabundance of acidic foods. Stress can also contribute to acidity in the body.

Consuming poorly constructed calcium supplements may also create problems. Magnesium should be a part of all calcium supplements to ensure proper absorption and assimilation. When magnesium is not included in a calcium supplement, the calcium may process improperly and actually create body responses that deplete the bones. Herbal sources of calcium such as alfalfa and kelp naturally have a wonderful balance of magnesium and calcium.

We may suffer from depletion of vitamin D, which is necessary for strong bones, if we do not expose our skin to enough sunlight. It is now recommended that we receive fifteen minutes of sun daily, with our arms exposed, to assist our body in the manufacture of vitamin D.

Muscles may be compromised by lack of sex hormones, exercise, and protein, and inadequate digestion.

Exercise is also important for the cells of the bones and muscles to build properly. If an elderly person stops standing or walking, his or her bones and muscles may begin to weaken or deteriorate.

Our bones may also suffer if we entertain and hold envy, fear, grudges, resentment, and unforgiveness. We must become mature and apologize for any offense that is rising as a mountain within our relationships. Consider this even if the reason for the dispute isn't your fault. Speak no blame. Blaming another, even if they had a part to play, only escalates the challenge and creates in you the opposite of a bold yet loving lion, which is a complaining victim.

This technique of reconciliation works most of the time to restore relationships. Even if it doesn't, you will know you did your part and you can let it go. If you had a moment of selfishness or poor judgment, identify that in humility. Reaffirm you will do your best to meet reasonable expectations. Be patient with others and their speech. They are a work in progress, just as you are.

COMMON ILLNESS MANIFESTATIONS

Challenges with our bones manifest as osteopenia, osteoporosis, bone cancer, joint inflammations, osteoarthritis, rheumatoid arthritis, frozen shoulder, tendonitis, and carpal tunnel syndrome. Muscles may succumb to diseases, causing them to spasm, tighten, or deteriorate.

APPLYING THE FIVE FOUNDATIONS
OF OPTIMAL HEALTH

Good foods

Follow the guidelines outlined in chapter 5 for a healthy, biblically based diet. Eat less meat and include more vegetarian proteins. Avoid soda and limit coffee, which may severely deplete blood calcium levels, as well as refined sugars, white flour, and white rice. Avoid wheat if wheat allergies are present. Reactivity to wheat can worsen symptoms of rheumatoid arthritis. Emphasize rye bread if tolerated. Learn to use gluten-free flour, especially if any inflammation is present.

The skeletal system thrives on minerals. Foods rich in these are nuts and seeds, especially sesame seeds. These are made even more digestible if soaked overnight in water, rinsed the next morning, and blended in the blender with pure water and then add to smoothies or soups. Enjoy bone broth, Himalayan salt, and potassium broths made of simmered bones, to which in the last thirty minutes of simmering you can add peelings of organic carrots, celery, potatoes, parsley, and flakes of dried seaweed.

Support your health by consuming 2 tablespoons daily of uncooked healthy oils, such as walnut, grape seed, almond, and avocado oils, which can be drizzled over your food. Consume fatty fish such as salmon and cod, plus raw cheeses and dairy products with natural probiotics as tolerated.

Eat plenty of fresh veggies, especially the dark green variety, and fruits daily.

Herbs

Consider horsetail, alfalfa, oatstraw, burdock, ground black walnut hulls, and kelp. As a general rule, choose three to five of these and take two capsules of each twice daily. You may notice that these natural minerals exceed the results you experience with man-made calcium supplements. People often experience better sleep and bone and muscle comfort after one to four months.

Essential oils

I prefer to use ½–1 teaspoon of pine needle essential oil mixed well into 2 cups of kosher salt and 2 tablespoons of powdered kelp for one eighteen- to twenty-minute bath, keeping my neck in the water. Consider doing this weekly until you are satisfied with the results.

Remember to avoid essential oils if you are pregnant or nursing.

Water

Drink eight to ten glasses of pure water daily. Remember, the powerful healing water that is imprinted with biblical truths, affirmations, and specific scriptures can further aid in improving your well-being. Consider assisting the general pH of the body by using a filtration system that produces alkaline water.

Lifestyle

Enjoy healthy levels of sunshine (but avoid burning). You can reap the health benefits without risking overexposure by not spending too long in the sun at any one period of time.

Include calcium- and magnesium-rich herbs and see if your bones and muscles respond to these better than they respond to man-made calcium formulas. Note if you become more flexible and sleep better with herbal formulas.

Exercise and stretch daily to maintain your ability to bear your own weight. See yourself strong for your whole life.

Keep X-rays to a minimum if possible, and request digital X-rays if they are needed. Protect the thyroid and keep your cell phone out of your pockets and bra.

If possible, avoid living near freeways and factories, where you may be exposed to heavy metal and chemical emissions. Avoid all sources of lead exposure.

Don't envy others or hold resentments. Forgive readily. Let God take care of all injustices.

Biblical Pathway to Healing

These are some scriptures that form the partial basis for our verbal prayer for this body system. The rest of the prayer is based on my experiences with patients during biofeedback sessions. Notice how emotions and mind-sets can affect our body parts.

+ Evict all extreme fear from the body: "Terror and trembling came to me, which made all my bones shake" (Job 4:14).

+ Evict all factors that may trouble your bones due to any type of weakness: "Be gracious to me, O LORD, for I am weak; O LORD, heal me, for my bones are terrified" (Ps. 6:2).

+ Evict all grief and any presence of sin and its effects: "For my life is spent with grief, and my years with sighing; my strength fails because of my iniquity, and my bones waste away" (Ps. 31:10).

+ Evict all past times of keeping silent when something should have been said—command those stuffed words out of your jaw and mouth: "When I kept silent, my bones wasted away through my groaning all day long" (Ps. 32:3).

+ Evict all sin and be restored to God: "There is no soundness in my flesh because of Your indignation, nor is there health in my bones because of my sin" (Ps. 38:3).

+ Evict all shame from any source: "A virtuous woman is a crown to her husband, but she who brings shame is as rottenness in his bones" (Prov. 12:4).

+ Evict all envy of what others have: "A sound heart is the life of the flesh, but envy the rottenness of the bones" (Prov. 14:30).

- Evict all isolation, loneliness, and lack of hope: "Then
  He said to me, 'Son of man, these bones are the whole
  house of Israel. They say, "Our bones are dried up, and
  our hope is lost. We are cut off completely."'" (Ezek.
  37:11).

- Evict all extreme fear from the bones: "I heard, and my
  body trembled; my lips quivered at the sound; rottenness entered my bones; my legs tremble beneath me"
  (Hab. 3:16).

- Evict all stubbornness and unwillingness to hear
  God's Word from the shoulders and all cells: "But
  they refused to hearken, and pulled away the shoulder"
  (Zech. 7:11, KJV).

HEALING PRAYER

Speak this prayer aloud with boldness and confidence. Exert the
authority in Christ that has been given to you. In Him all things
are possible.

Dear heavenly Father,

*As Job once said, "Did you not…clothe me with skin
and flesh, and knit me together with bones and sinews? You
have granted me life and favor, and Your care has preserved
my spirit" (Job 10:10–12, NKJV). Remember the blessings
You instructed Ezekiel to speak over old dried bones: "I will
cause breath to enter into you so that you live. And I will
lay sinews upon you and will grow back flesh upon you and
cover you with skin and put breath in you so that you live.
Then you shall know that I am the LORD" (Ezek. 37:5–6).
Father, I am Your faithful child, and I ask for and declare
these same blessings of restoration.*

*You care about the smallest details. The very hairs of
my head are all numbered. You have promised to guide
me continually and satisfy my soul when my life is moving
through a desert of difficulty. You strengthen all my bones*

and cultivate my life and health like a watered garden and an eternal spring of water. I praise You for arming me with strength, perfect movement, and full function for the battles of life. You have already subdued all my enemies. You have taken all my burdens—including those in my skeletal system, shoulders, muscles, and joints—upon You, and I release them in peace and gratitude. I thank You for all the healing provisions You have made available to me.

With the powerful name of Jesus, I am fully equipped to receive healing. I command and evict from all deep cellular blueprints of my bones, spinal column, posture, joints, tendons, ligaments, muscles, skin, and teeth, and all their nerves and circulation mechanisms:

All forms of shame, sorrow, and grief from my own actions or those of others

All sin, iniquity, and stubbornness against or toward God

All forms and feelings of being unsupported, ungrounded, or worried

All forms of extreme fears, terror, and traumas

All forms of envy, weakness, and trouble, and any refusal to speak up when injustice occurs

All forms of hopelessness, isolation, and loneliness

All forms of bitterness, resentment, and unforgiveness

All accidents, scar tissue, misalignments, and injury to any portion of my skeletal system

All toxic allergens and all improper allergy responses to my air, environment, and food

All stored medications and any side effects

Any vaccine side effects, including those from metallic additives or foreign DNA

All negative effects of any dental procedures or the words of my dentist

All negative effects of surgeries or the breaking of bones

All scar tissue

All traumas experienced during birth

Any trauma or negative effect from any chemicals used within my home, yard, or elsewhere

All X-ray, cell phone, computer field, or electromagnetic residue of any type from any source and any side effects

All toxic metals, including aluminum, arsenic, lead, copper, mercury, nickel, cadmium, and lead and any side effects

All bacteria, viruses, yeasts, mold, parasites, worms, and any other organisms that are trying to attack me and any side effects

All negative, toxic cellular programming or blueprints of any type, from any source

I release all of these and any pain surrounding them perfectly and completely from all stories and events of my life, gestation and birth, and any carryover from my ancestry back to the beginning of time. I declare these no longer able to dwell within any created part of my skeletal system and muscles, including their nerves and circulation.

I evict all of these and their blueprints and command them into the sea. The Son has set all of my parts free, and they are free indeed. I am done with them, and I declare them gone!

I repent of holding unforgiveness toward anyone. I will also say, "Bone, spine, posture, joints, sinews, skin, teeth and jaw—you have good news: you are strong in the strength of Christ." I commit to speak my mind and emotions in love and gentleness and not bottle them up. I set as my goal the restoring of relationships when I speak. I love the Word of God, and I obey it with joy.

I now see myself sitting at the bountiful table of the Lord, which is more than adequate to fill these vacancies that remain. I gratefully partake of God's perfect healing and blueprints for a sound, healthy skeletal system and all its created parts, including my bones, posture, muscles, joints, tendons, ligaments, spinal column, teeth, jaw, and all their created parts. I taste and eat His remedies for perfect recovery from falls and all tendencies to stoop, and His provisions for strong hands and knees. I drink abundantly of all of the perfect blueprints He intended for me. I am filled with His comfort, love, support, peace, joy, courage, and strength, and all His blessings of wellness. I see myself partaking of these wonderful remedies and promises each day until they fill me from the soles of my feet to the top of head, making me well.

Each day I will meditate on the Lord—His promises, good reports, comfort, and might, which create joy and rejoicing and make my bones flourish. I choose to be with pleasant and positive people and speak the same to others. Amen

HEALING DECLARATIONS

Declare these promises to your structural system and command it to line up with the Word of God in the mighty name of Jesus. As you speak these powerful, personalized verses daily, they will feed the new seeds you have planted.

- As one whom a mother comforts, so God will comfort me. Then my heart shall rejoice, and my bones shall flourish like an herb; and the hand of the Lord shall be known to His servants (Isa. 66:13–14).

- They are brought down and fallen, but I arise and stand upright (Ps. 20:8).

- "The LORD upholds all who fall, and raises up all who are bowed down" (Ps. 145:14).

- I will not be wise in my own eyes; I will fear the LORD and depart from evil. This will be health to my body and strength to my bones (Prov. 3:7–8).

- The light of the eyes rejoices my heart, and a good report makes my bones healthy (Prov. 15:30).

- Pleasant words are like a honeycomb to me, sweetness to my soul and health to my bones (Prov. 16:24).

♦ Therefore I lift up my tired hands and strengthen my weak knees because of His promises (Heb. 12:12).

BATTLE FOR YOUR COMPLETE HEALING

In addition to the previous declarations, in this chapter consider using the Word of God to "make a case" to the Lord. Read each of the following passages aloud and then reason with the Lord about them. I have included an example of what I would say if I were going to battle against anything that was attacking my bones or skeletal system. Speak this daily if needed.

Your words have raised up him who was falling, and you have fortified the feeble knees.

—JOB 4:4

You have clothed me with skin and flesh, and have knit me together with bones and sinews.

—JOB 10:11

A righteous one keeps all his bones; not one of them is broken.

—PSALM 34:20

Upon God alone, O my soul, rest peacefully; for my expectation is from him.

—PSALM 62:5, DARBY

Your teeth are like a flock of shorn ewes that have come up from the washing, all of which bear twins, and not one among them has lost its young.

—SONG OF SONGS 4:2

The LORD shall guide you continually, and satisfy your soul in drought, and strengthen your bones; and you shall be like a watered garden, and like a spring of water, whose waters do not fail.

—ISAIAH 58:11

Thus says the Lord God to these bones: I will cause breath to enter you so that you live.

—Ezekiel 37:5

So I prophesied as I was commanded. And as I prophesied, there was a noise and a shaking. And the bones came together, bone to its bone.

—Ezekiel 37:7

Make straight paths for your feet, lest that which is lame go out of joint, but rather be healed.

—Hebrews 12:13

Heavenly Father, Your Word states that You restore dead bones, guard against broken bones, restore bones that are not connected or are dislocated, restore tendons, nerves, and ligaments for proper function, restore feeble knees and other joints, and give them the proper strength for proper gait and movement. The king compliments his bride in the Song of Songs, which is symbolic of Your bride, the church, on her full set of clean, white teeth. You are not a respecter of persons, and I ask for your creative miracle restoring any tooth loss or damage to my teeth, as I am a living part of the bride of Christ, the church. I speak and stand upon these strong foundations daily, and I will not waver. I rest peacefully as God partners with me. In Jesus's name, amen.

PART III

HEALING HANDS

Ministering to Others

CHAPTER 16

SHARING THE
MINISTRY OF HEALING

*S*OMETHING WONDERFUL AND beautiful happens as we begin to equip ourselves to heal: we become equipped to minister healing to others!

A good first step when ministering to others is to take some time to build the person's faith by sharing God's will to heal. As we share what God's Word says about healing, our faith also will be strengthened in the process.

I cannot overemphasize the importance of faith when ministering in the area of healing. Faith is an actual invisible substance that brings into reality the hope upon which we are standing, as the following verse attests:

> Now faith is the substance of things hoped for, the evidence of things not seen.
> —HEBREWS 11:1

Our faith grows when we hear God's truth:

> So then faith comes by hearing, and hearing by the word of God.
> —ROMANS 10:17

We each have been given a measure of faith, as Romans 12:3 proclaims. It is up to us to grow that measure into a mighty force by learning God's Word and drawing close to the Lord so we build our confidence in His power to heal. Faith is critical when we are ministering to others because it is what empowers us to stand firmly upon God's truth and speak to the situation at hand.

I sometimes relate faith to a small, invisible muscle that I can nourish and exercise as I hear the Word of God and boldly speak it with expectation. As I take the time to build faith, it can grow large and strong, becoming the vital tool needed for healing to manifest. The Holy Spirit partners with me, releasing His power as I act upon what I have learned in His Word.

It may take years to grow your faith, or it may take only a few minutes. Whatever the case, God's Word needs to become more real to you than the seemingly impossible situation.

The original generation of Israelites wandered for years in the wilderness after leaving Egypt with Moses and were not able to receive their promise—entering into the land of Canaan—due to their unbelief. They had more confidence in the obstacles they faced than faith in the mighty power of God.

Even Jesus asked those who were unbelieving to leave the room before He healed certain people. In some towns He was unable to do many miracles because of the high level of unbelief residing there. This is why we must be wise regarding what we take in through worldly media. If we consume a steady diet of this, we can take on the doubts, worries, cares, and negative mind-sets that are presented.

We must remember that faith is the key to seeing healing become a reality as we pray for others, so we must carefully guard what we allow into our hearts and minds:

> Jesus said to them, "Because of your unbelief. For truly I say to you, if you have faith as a grain of mustard seed, you will say to this mountain, 'Move from here to there,' and it will move. And nothing will be impossible for you."
>
> —MATTHEW 17:20

> He said to them, "Why are you so fearful? How is it that you have no faith?"
>
> —MARK 4:40

And without faith it is impossible to please God, for he who comes to God must believe that He exists and that He is a rewarder of those who diligently seek Him.

—Hebrews 11:6

This is what a lifestyle of faith produces:

A faithful man will abound with blessings.

—Proverbs 28:20

Now Stephen, full of faith and power, did great wonders and miracles among the people.

—Acts 6:8

I want this type of faith, don't you?
The Bible tells us faith works through love:

For in Christ Jesus neither circumcision nor uncircumcision means anything, but faith which works through love.

—Galatians 5:6

This tells me that we must have an intimate relationship with our heavenly Father and compassion for those we serve. Knowing who God is and that He loves us empowers us in this respect. Daily praise and gratitude water this love and keep it vibrant.

Remember, we speak to the mountains of ill heath in faith, seeing it with our minds before it comes to pass. So what do we do while we are waiting for the results? We might see the results instantly, sure, but what if we don't? Many times in Scripture, a time lag was present between the time a person prayed and when he received the response. Sometimes evil forces delayed the result, as in the case of a prayer of Daniel. (See Daniel 10.)

We will grow weak and weary if we start thinking like the world or listening to the pessimism of others and the devil while we wait for someone we are praying for to be healed. Instead, we must keep our focus on God's good promises and reports:

So that your faith should not stand in the wisdom of men,
but in the power of God.

—1 CORINTHIANS 2:5

Watch, stand fast in the faith, be bold like men, and be strong.

—1 CORINTHIANS 16:13

My brothers, count it all joy when you fall into diverse
temptations, knowing that the trying of your faith develops
patience. But let patience perfect its work, that you may be
perfect and complete, lacking nothing.

—JAMES 1:2–4

Patience and endurance are a perfect work that occurs while you
are standing in faith waiting for healing to manifest, or while that
mountain is starting to break up and go. Stay focused on the prize
ahead. Share with supportive friends what you are doing. Keep your
thoughts and words in line with your goal to see healing manifest in
people's lives:

Above all, taking the shield of faith, with which you will be
able to extinguish all the fiery arrows of the evil one.

—EPHESIANS 6:16

That the sharing of your faith may be most effective by the
acknowledgment of every good thing which is in you from
Christ Jesus.

—PHILEMON 1:6

Do you see how faith worked with his works, and by works
faith was made perfect?

—JAMES 2:22

These are the works that perfect our faith. Acknowledging every
good thing that is placed within us as believers feeds it. This is how
we experience victory as God's faith-filled children.

The Commission to All Believers

"Go therefore and make disciples of all nations, baptizing them in the name of the Father and of the Son and of the Holy Spirit, teaching them to observe all things I have commanded you. And remember, I am with you always, even to the end of the age." Amen.

—Matthew 28:19–20

Some pastors have taught that the previous passage is more literally translated, "As you are going, make disciples," meaning that we should be perceptive and aware of who needs to hear the good news as we go about our daily tasks. Isn't it good to witness in our communities as well as when we leave our communities or our country? Both serve the Lord and spread the good news.

As believers we are to develop the type of love that desires for others to experience what we are discovering—that the Lord loves us, that He wants us to have a full, vital life, and that He wants us to live as family with Him in heaven:

Then the master said to the servant, "Go out to the highways and hedges, and compel them to come in, that my house may be filled."

—Luke 14:23

For God so loved the world that He gave His only begotten Son, that whoever believes in Him should not perish, but have eternal life.

—John 3:16

The Lord is not slow concerning His promise, as some count slowness. But He is patient with us, because He does not want any to perish, but all to come to repentance.

—2 Peter 3:9

We are those servants mentioned in the previous passages, who look for those who need healing at any level and make a case to them to come to the table of the Lord, where every good thing they will ever need is provided.

THE LAYING ON OF HANDS

The laying on of hands is a foundational and elementary teaching of the early church. Ideally it would be taught as an elementary truth of our service as a son or daughter of God. The Bible includes it within the foundational teachings on faith, baptism, the resurrection of the dead, and the judgment of God upon the devil and the ungodly:

> Therefore, leaving the elementary principles of the doctrine of Christ, let us go on to maturity, not laying again a foundation of repentance from dead works and of faith toward God, of instruction about washings, the laying on of hands, the resurrection of the dead, and eternal judgment.
> —HEBREWS 6:1–2

In this passage the author of Hebrews is asking the people why they still want to be in grade school when high school is ready for them. If each day we keep pouring the foundation of our home, we will never get to the walls and roof! We need to progress and become mature.

> These signs will follow those who believe: In My name they will cast out demons; they will speak with new tongues; they will take up serpents; if they drink any deadly thing, it will not hurt them; they will lay hands on the sick, and they will recover.
> —MARK 16:17–18

Signs follow those who have grown in their belief in the promises of God and make claim to those promises. If we do not believe in signs and wonders, then signs and wonders will not follow us.

We are told to lay hands on the sick because it accomplishes the will of God. We have a part to play. We must be able to share Jesus with the sick, sharing our faith and the fact that God loves them and wants them saved and healthy.

Again, the Holy Spirit is partnering with us in this process. As we lay hands on a person, we are speaking aloud and releasing the power the Holy Spirit provides. It is God who is doing the healing and God who is to be praised and thanked. We fulfill our role as the hands of Jesus on this earth as we allow that healing power to flow through us and into others.

We don't have to worry about what is happening or how divine healing works. Trying to figure it out may just get in our way. We do our part, and we leave God's part in His hands. After we pray for others, we may see a miracle, or we may "see" nothing, but that doesn't mean nothing happened. I find in biofeedback, something is always happening, but sometimes we must be persistent and repeatedly speak life and health, sometimes on all levels—physically, mentally, emotionally, and spiritually.

Recently I was doing biofeedback with a client who had developed asthma after receiving inhaled medication at the hospital. We had to address some mountains: the side effects and residue of the medications, the side effects and residue of the inhalants, and fear. We had to do this before the stress released totally. This happened as I laid my hands on her (with permission, of course), spoke to the mountains in her life, and thanked God for doing His part and releasing His power. We spent about fifteen minutes speaking to three different organs in her body, and she felt the difference afterward.

Recently a client who had received cancer therapy and was experiencing a blood disorder afterward came for biofeedback. I put my hands on her, and we both spoke to the side effects of the radiation and medication she had been receiving, and all negative proclamations over her health. Then she sat at the table of the Lord, systematically drinking in all the remedies for perfect cells; perfect immunity; a perfect respiratory system and sinuses; a perfect urinary system; perfect blood and marrow, liver, and gallbladder; perfect intestines; a perfect balance of healthy microorganisms; a perfect balance of thyroid, adrenal, pancreas, and blood sugar; a perfect brain, nerves, and spine; perfect bones and joints; a perfect female system; and perfect nutritional balance. With joy, peace, love, and courage, she went on to fill all the ensuing vacancies. We did this right at the beginning of our appointment, and after this brief exercise, the computer said we were finished with the session!

Sometimes it takes just a few seconds or minutes, and sometimes it takes thirty minutes to an hour for a person to sense a change of some sort. Never say healing prayer didn't work when you've prayed for someone to be healed for only a few minutes. You may have just gotten started. Plan to spend some time doing this.

Other times we must do battle over time, as there may be much to clear away from years of accumulation. Sometimes we need only to say little except, "Be healed and whole in the name of Jesus"—that may take care of everything.

It is different for each person. Keep in mind that a person must also be ready to receive healing. Skepticism, feelings of unworthiness, a lack of knowledge, or previous false teaching may block them from accepting healing until those strongholds are torn down. For example, I once saw a video testimony of a paralyzed woman who had received prayer and had hands laid on her for years. When nothing seemed to happen, she gave up. She didn't even go forward anymore when prayer for healing was offered. But one day she accompanied her husband to an event, decided to accept the laying on of hands and prayer, and felt something change. She arose from her wheelchair and has been walking ever since. Never give up!

THE PRAYER OF FAITH

It helps to know what you might say during the laying on of hands. Almost all of the body system prayers offered in this book are based on the prayer of faith in Mark 11:22–24, where we are told to take authority and control over any mountain that dares stand in our way. You may always add more tools. We are battling an enemy, and God has given us many choices concerning the weapons we use for victory.

When laying hands on others to pray for their healing, you can follow these steps:

+ Praise God, repent of any sin that may encumber you, repent of any unbelief or fear, and boldly speak any scriptures you have studied and that the Holy Spirit brings to your mind to build faith in the promises of God.

+ Affirm your confidence in God's Word and remind God of His promises.

+ Agree in prayer with the person you are praying for and speak the words of healing, resting assured that God will partner with you, backing His Word in heaven and making provision for what is needed.

+ Declare with boldness that you believe the healing is done and that the new pattern is set and established, even if you don't immediately see it.

+ Rejoice and rest in the fact that God always fulfills His part. Continue to affirm your healing with scripture.

The following scriptures are all strong promises of God and can be adapted into prayers of faith to ignite His flow of healing power.

"Again I say to you, that if two of you agree on earth about anything they ask, it will be done for them by My Father who is in heaven. For where two or three are assembled in My name, there I am in their midst."
—MATTHEW 18:19–20

Jesus answered them, "Have faith in God. For truly I say to you, whoever says to this mountain, 'Be removed and be thrown into the sea,' and does not doubt in his heart, but believes that what he says will come to pass, he will have whatever he says. Therefore I say to you, whatever things you

ask when you pray, believe that you will receive them, and
you will have them."

—MARK 11:22–24

If you remain in Me, and My words remain in you, you will
ask whatever you desire, and it shall be done for you.

—JOHN 15:7

Is anyone sick among you? Let him call for the elders of the
church, and let them pray over him, anointing him with oil
in the name of the Lord. And the prayer of faith will save
the sick, and the Lord will raise him up. And if he has committed any sins, he will be forgiven.

—JAMES 5:14–15

Here is a sample of a wonderful healing prayer that I often share
with others. It is a prayer of faith, taken from Matthew 18:19–20
and combining principles from Mark 11:

Dear heavenly Father,

*We praise You for the opportunity to share Your Word
and the privilege of laying hands upon [your friend's name].
Without You, we can do nothing. With You, everything is
possible.*

*We repent of any sins that are standing in our way, espe-
cially any fear or unbelief. We evict these and send them
into the sea, and replace them with total trust in Your
promises. Thank You for Your forgiveness.*

*We now bring this challenge of [whatever the challenge
and symptoms are] to Your attention under the powerful
name of Jesus. We command this mountain into the sea,
never to return. We also speak to all physical, emotional,
and mental causes, and any side effects and evict them now
into the sea, never to return. [Take the time to name specific concerns.]*

*We submit to your Word, Lord, and its promises and
resist any part Satan has played in this issue. He must flee,*

along with any bondage he has put upon [your friend's name] and this situation. Go, and be gone now!

We believe in what You have promised in Your Word, Lord, that if two of us agree concerning anything we ask, it will be done by You within the context of Your will. We know it is Your will to heal this [name the issue] perfectly. We release the power of the Holy Spirit to heal and provide perfect restoration, and we believe it is done. We believe a new blueprint of health and healing is present now. We give all credit for this healing to You, and we are grateful to participate. We rejoice and praise You as King of kings and Lord of lords. In Jesus's name, we pray in gratitude. Amen.

Now, rejoice, follow up, encourage, feed Scripture, and give the person any additional help he needs to build him up in the faith, that he may completely receive, maintain, and keep his healing.

CHAPTER 17

MORE HEALING PRAYERS

S YOU PRAY for your own healing and that of others, you will no doubt encounter circumstances that require a unique approach—more than what has been covered already in this book. This chapter is meant to support you in those unique circumstances.

I'll begin by saying that over the years, I have observed many people, just babes in this new journey, who took a few steps into this biblical form of healing prayer but stopped after a few days because they hadn't felt or seen anything yet. This is unfortunate. If you were told to take an important medicine, would you quit after a few days if you weren't yet well? Of course not. You may not feel or see an immediate change, but you know eventually you will.

In the same way we must keep speaking God's Word over our health daily until we see healing manifest in our physical reality. While we are waiting, we have the opportunity to learn patience and endurance. We must learn to believe and rest in peace that a change is occurring, even if we don't feel a difference instantly.

Don't stop or give up because your results aren't immediately visible. Sometimes people stop just before seeing a tremendous victory. Instead, simply switch your approach. If your enemy doesn't yield with a strong punch to his face, bring out the machine gun. Find more healing scriptures to speak over your body. God's Word contains all the fire power you need.

PRAYERS FOR TOUGH CHALLENGES

Greg Mohr, author of *Scriptures to Live By*, had a fifteen-month-old son who appeared to be fine until his joints swelled up to twice their normal size. This was accompanied by a rash until his son could no longer walk or crawl. The child cried profusely and was in constant pain. Medical professionals offered no cure, only drugs. Greg and his wife rejected this approach, as they found no peace in the idea of viewing this as an incurable condition that would require long-term drug management.

Greg and his wife took their son for healing prayer but saw no improvement. The challenge seemed overwhelming. However, they had faith in the power of the spoken Word of God. They decided to put their faith into action and found a cornerstone verse to base their faith upon and build their case:

> Forever, O Lord, Your word is established in heaven. Your faithfulness is for all generations.
> —Psalm 119:89–90

They personalized this verse to their son Michael's generation. They found a total of *seventy* scriptures to stand upon and spoke them aloud over their son daily, often several times a day. They didn't do this for just a day or two or a week or two. They were committed. They were patient; they endured. They knew that the Word they spoke over Michael never returned void or empty. It always accomplished something.

They didn't see anything at first, but then encouragement came. Greg writes in his book:

> Within a month...Michael's condition began to improve. The swelling in his joints gradually went down. The rash was not as dominant as it once was. One month later he began to crawl again. Four months after this he began to walk. Six months later he was completely whole without any symptom of that dreaded disease. Praise be to God.[1]

When we speak God's Word, it never returns without a result. God says so! Our faith—believing and speaking the Word—activates the power of God over ourselves and others. See the healing result as you speak, and see your loving God's compassion toward you. Resist any temptation to stop praying in faith. Speaking God's Word is bringing supernatural remedies into your very core.

These are ways to transform and renew your mind to fight a

victorious battle, tossing out contrary worldly programming and evicting all things that try to exalt themselves above the truth of God's Word. Stay in the present and in a state of peace by keeping your focus fixed on Jesus and His promises, no matter what the circumstances and others say. God's Word trumps all of these. Remember: when the Apostle Peter's eyes were fixed on Jesus, he was able to walk on water! (See Matthew 14:22–33.)

WHEN A CHILD IS IN NEED OF PRAYER

Now, if you know a child in need of serious prayer, here are steps you can take to help him recover and receive the healing God wants for him:

- Speak to the mountains you know exist. Put the powerful name of Jesus over the child. See God clearing the illness or imbalance out now and proclaim it done.

- If any sin of the parents could have opened a door to allow Satan to attack the child, ask the parents to search their hearts, repent of anything that comes to mind, and ask forgiveness of the Lord.

- Next, ask for forgiveness of any doubt or unbelief in order to clear that out of the way.

- Boldly rebuke the devil and any demonic influence that torments or produces infirmities. Inform Satan that you know he and his cohorts have been cast down in total defeat by Christ. They must subject themselves to His power. (Remember, the devil counts on people being ignorant of this in order to wreak his havoc.) Satan and his demons have no legal right of influence, as you have repented and stand forgiven before God. Command any demonic influence to leave and never return. Don't let them speak to you. Don't get caught in that trap. Instead, silence them and send them away.

- Remind the child and his or her parents that Jesus has taken on any curses that may have come their way and to verbally acknowledge and lay claim to that truth. (In the Old Testament disease is called a curse.) Make sure they realize that Jesus took all disease, all curses, upon Himself at the Cross.

PRAYERS FOR INHERITED PATTERNS AND GENETIC DEFECTS

As we enter this next subject I wish to make absolutely clear that I do not believe we inherit another person's sin, either from our parents or lineage. However, through many client sessions I have come to believe that certain strange side effects of sins committed by our parents and ancestors can pass down to us within our cellular blueprints. The sins of others and of the world affect us also.

You have learned by now that whatever mountain I speak to, I often speak to the story it connects to, from any event in life, gestation, birth, or ancestry. I command it out of the deepest cellular blueprints of the body. In biofeedback I have seen the importance of progressing through each stage of this process. When clients first experiment with releasing things from their lives, they sometimes see no change. As they move on to releasing things from their birth, they still may see no change there either. It may be the same with releasing things from their gestation. However, when they speak to specific mountains passed through their ancestors, which is the stuff of our deepest cellular imprints, we often see surprising changes occur on the computer screen. It's fascinating!

This is my general rule after years of experience and observation: If a challenge is easy to release, it likely came from events in my life. If it is a moderate-to-severe issue, it may have roots in my birth or gestation. But if it is a stubborn, difficult, and lengthy issue, I've found it is often rooted in the ancestral blueprints.

These deep cellular patterns seem to manifest the most after age fifty if they have not yet been eliminated. Working at this level may be necessary in order to pull a large stress out by the roots for good.

Here is an additional prayer you can use to address the many possible consequences you or another person may be carrying due to what others have done, especially in your family and ancestral line. You can pray it aloud over yourself and personalize it for your entire family as another tool for your health:

Dear heavenly Father,

I acknowledge Your hand in my life and the purposes for which Christ came—to truly set me free at every level of my being, including freeing me from fear and any unbelief. This also includes freedom from any sin and the curse of any illness or infirmity. Christ took all of these upon Himself out of love for me. As a believer and Your child, I fully accept these promises.

I, therefore, in the power of Jesus's name, cast off all mountains of unhealthy oppressions, satanic involvement, curses, unhealthy spiritual patterns, bindings, strongholds, addictions, compulsions, negative thinking patterns, unresolved emotions, physical ailments, and genetic imperfections and the stories associated with them that cling to any of my deep cellular blueprints from any and all iniquities of my male and female generational lineage, including any stepparents or anyone who raised me, back through all generations.

I acknowledge Christ's sacrifice for my sins and total freedom from its effects. The Son has set me free, and I am free now. This was provided by Jesus's death and resurrection and by my belief in these. I rejoice in these holy provisions.

In the vacancies that were just created, I receive into my deep cellular blueprints the development of Your mind and character within my own, with healthy physical, mental, emotional, and spiritual patterns as You originally intended for me. I am grateful for all blessings my earthly parents and lineage passed onto me. I forgive them for any mistakes as I ask forgiveness for my own.

Thank you, Father, for Your loving mercy and forgiveness. In Jesus's name, amen.

911 Emergency

Sometimes an emergency comes upon us that gives us little or no time to prepare. Gathering God's words for these times is best done in advance, while we are well.

So, picture this. You are at home and you receive a call. Someone you know and love was involved in a terrible accident and is in the hospital. You are asked to come right away. The news isn't good. What is your first response?

+ Panic

+ Hysterical crying

+ Grabbing a Valium

+ Racing down the road at eighty miles per hour

+ Calling others and reinforcing the terrible tragedy and agreeing with a bad outcome

+ All of the above

+ None of the above

Jesus doesn't want us to be traumatized, emotionally damaged people, living our lives as victims of our circumstances. He wants us to rise above these things, proving ourselves steadfast, calm, courageous, and at peace, resting in His power and promises. He would never ask this of us if it wasn't possible to do. Claim these promises:

God is our refuge and strength, a well-proven help in trouble.

—Psalm 46:1

Let not your heart be troubled. You believe in God. Believe also in Me.

—John 14:1

Peace I leave with you. My peace I give to you. Not as the world gives do I give to you. Let not your heart be troubled, neither let it be afraid.

—John 14:27

What if we responded in this manner to all of our emergencies instead? Here is the process I would use in any family emergency:

+ I take time to control my mind and emotions by stopping and acknowledging who my amazing God is. I praise Him for being the King of kings and Lord of lords and for promising to never leave or forsake me. I remind myself that He can heal every disease and raise the dead. There is nothing this world can throw at me that can overcome God's bigger and better arsenal of response.

+ I continue to praise and be thankful for these things, even if it takes fifteen to twenty minutes, until I regain my composure and can keep my sole focus on Jesus. This will assist me in leaving my fear behind so I avoid wavering back and forth in my mind. When it comes to reality, I remind myself that I see only 5 percent of it. The supernatural, invisible realm is 95 percent of reality, and a big God lives within it. He is on my side and has given me every weapon that I need for victory if I have prepared ahead of time. I allow my heart to calm down, release any fear, and remain in peace, recalling, "You will keep him in perfect peace, whose mind is stayed on You, because he trusts in You" (Isa. 26:3).

+ I find out the report. I will want to understand the reality of it, but I never agree with this report as being the final say. This is very important. If I do, I will agree with the devil that he has a right to be involved. I agree only with the Word of God; it has the final say.

+ I inform the doctor that I respect his help and knowledge but that his report, the hospital report, the scan report, and the blood report are not the final reports. I am firm in my testimony that I serve a God who can do *anything* because He says He can. Total recovery is possible because everything is possible with God.

+ I don't back down. I stay in this mind-set with all my trust and hope in God. I do not speak or meditate on anything but His promises. I speak them aloud all through the day. I rebuke the devil and any doubt, discouragement, despair, or self-condemnation that even dares to rear its ugly head, and I send them to drown in the sea. I continue to praise God for who He is, what He is going to do in this situation, and for the might of His power. I enlist others who are full of faith in these matters to come and speak healing verses over my loved one when I cannot be there. I keep the following words of God in front of me, and I don't waver from them: *"Whatever things are of good report, if there is any virtue, and if there is any praise, think on these things"* (Phil. 4:8, emphasis added).

You will only know the good reports of God if you have taken the time to find them. You must stay focused here. Go to God's promises and start believing and acting upon what they tell you.

Read this verse back to God and remind Him that *all* means *all*:

> But my God shall supply your every need according to His riches in glory by Christ Jesus.
>
> —PHILIPPIANS 4:19

Thank Him for having the healing remedy that is needed. He has thought of everything in advance! If your loved one is a Christian, personalize and proclaim this verse over his or her life:

> "The right hand of the LORD is exalted; the right hand of the LORD is valiant." I shall not die, but I shall live and declare the works of the LORD.
>
> —PSALM 118:16–18

Make your case that this person has more glory to give to the Lord and more to accomplish for Him. Remind the Lord that they are needed to do good in His name and that they are a blessing to others. See yourself at the Lord's table with His remedy available to you or your loved one. Speak to the healing occurring and see it done within your mind.

> This is the confidence that we have in Him, that if we ask anything according to His will, He hears us.
>
> —1 John 5:14

"We" are the believers in Christ. Healing is God's will for His children. This verse is meant to give you great joy and expectation.

> Whoever eats My flesh and drinks My blood remains in Me, and I in him.
>
> —John 6:56

We symbolically do this during communion at church, when we remember what Jesus did for us with honor and gratefulness. We see Him as in our hearts, living within us. We also examine ourselves for any conscious sin and repent of it and forsake it. If you are doing this regularly, you remain and abide in Him and He remains and abides in you:

> I am the vine, you are the branches. He who remains in Me, and I in him, bears much fruit. For without Me you can do nothing.
>
> —John 15:5

We acknowledge that all power and glory and healing is a work of the Lord through us, not of ourselves. We glorify and praise Him for His goodness.

Now, verbally ask for the results you want to see while acknowledging this verse:

> If you abide in Me, and My words abide in you, ask whatever you wish, and it will be done for you.
>
> —John 15:7, nas

Perhaps you ask for all organs to be perfect, all wounds healed, all scars gone, perfect brain function, perfect flexibility, vision, hearing, and anything else that needs to happen for wholeness to be restored.

Remind the Lord of your faithfulness and study. Remind Him of your trust in Him and that He can do anything. Remind yourself to be bold in speaking the Word and of the power released in laying your hands upon your loved one, coupled with the name of Jesus.

Jesus healed all who came to Him. He made no exception. He always said yes. Remind the Lord of this and thank Him that He is no respecter of persons:

> His fame went throughout all Syria. And they brought to Him all sick people who were taken with various diseases and tormented with pain, those who were possessed with demons, those who had seizures, and those who had paralysis, and He healed them.
> —MATTHEW 4:24

> But when Jesus knew it, He withdrew from there. And great crowds followed Him, and He healed them all.
> —MATTHEW 12:15

Jesus wants to know if you believe you can move mountains. Say, "Yes, I believe!"

> They will lay hands on the sick, and they will recover.
> —MARK 16:18

> Truly, truly, I say to you, he who believes in Me will do the works that I do also. And he will do greater works than these, because I am going to My Father.
> —JOHN 14:12

Now thank the Lord for the healing blueprint your loved one has received. Continue speaking life-giving, healing Scriptures several times daily and wait expectantly, in patience and perseverance, for the finished work.

LIVE LONG AND PROSPER

*T*RULY BELIEVE THAT if God put His amazing and incredible work into His wondrous creation, with us being His masterpiece, He certainly cares whether we live long or die young. The devil has made it his job to kill, steal, and destroy, but Christ gave you power over him. Don't let him in your life to accomplish any of these tasks.

The Scriptures are our greatest weapon, and they have a lot to say about length of our days.

> You shall walk in all the ways which the LORD your God has commanded you, so that you may live and that it may be well with you, and that you may prolong your days in the land which you shall possess.
> —DEUTERONOMY 5:33

> Moses was a hundred and twenty years old when he died. His eye was not dim, nor was his vitality diminished.
> —DEUTERONOMY 34:7

> But Jehoiada grew old and full of days and died. He was one hundred and thirty years old when he died.
> —2 CHRONICLES 24:15

> So Job died, being old and full of days.
> —JOB 42:17

> Because he has set his love upon Me, therefore I will deliver him; I will set him on high, because he has known My name. He shall call upon Me, and I will answer him; I will be with him in trouble, and I will deliver him and honor

him. With long life I will satisfy him and show him My
salvation.

—PSALM 91:14–16

The righteous shall flourish like a palm tree and grow like
a cedar in Lebanon. Those that are planted in the house
of the LORD shall flourish in the courts of our God. They
shall still bring forth fruit in old age; they shall be filled
with vitality and foliage, to show that the LORD is upright;
He is my rock, and there is no unrighteousness in Him.

—PSALM 92:12–15

Happy is the man who finds wisdom, and the man who
gains understanding; for her benefit is more profitable than
silver, and her gain than fine gold. She is more precious
than rubies, and all the things you may desire are not to
be compared with her. Length of days is in her right hand,
and in her left hand riches and honor.

—PROVERBS 3:13–16

Even to your old age I am He, and even to your graying
years I will carry you; I have done it, and I will bear you;
even I will carry, and will deliver you.

—ISAIAH 46:4

For I know the plans that I have for you, says the LORD,
plans for peace and not for evil, to give you a future and a
hope.

—JEREMIAH 29:11

Children, obey your parents in the Lord, for this is right.
"Honor your father and mother," which is the first com-
mandment with a promise: "so that it may be well with you
and you may live long on the earth."

—EPHESIANS 6:1–3

God has a future and a plan for you, and you may have the long
life he intended for you when you align with Him. He takes into

account how you honor your parents, your love toward Him, and your honor of His name. He wants you to call upon Him and declare Him righteous and your rock. He wants your life to be full of wisdom and understanding.

A life "full of days" is not complete at age eighteen, thirty-five, fifty-eight, or even sixty. We are to have a long, fruitful life, seeking the deliverance of the Lord when illness attacks to preserve our health until that season arrives to go home. Don't see yourself according to society's standards—someone who will become a frail, achy, immobile, old-aged man or woman. See yourself like Moses, who had vigor and great eyesight until the time of his death. Call those things that aren't as though they were, and let the power of these truths allow you to look forward to your golden years. Stand upon the scriptures I quoted previously. Speak them until they are a part of you and expect victory.

YOUR DAILY COMMITMENT

If you desire to live the life of health and vitality that God desires for you, I encourage you to make the following commitments each day. Doing so will transform your health—physically, spiritually, and emotionally.

- I arise each day rejoicing that I have on the armor of God and am equipped to heal myself and others.

- I choose to make every day count for the Lord.

- I have authority and power from Christ, the healer, who lives within me. I see myself living in the shadow of the Most High and in His refuge, where no disease may dwell. I speak His truths until they firmly live in my heart and overshadow earthly reports.

- I spend time in the Word daily. I continue my treasure hunt for even more healing scriptures and promises present in God's Word.

+ I envision the kinds of transformations my family would experience if we cut out thirty minutes of TV and started studying the Word of God together.

+ I incorporate praise music into my drive to work to frame my day, feed my joy, and keep my emotions mastered.

+ I watch or listen to teachings on healing to learn more and build my faith in God's promises of healing.

+ Every few weeks I tape favorite scriptures up in the bathroom, on the refrigerator, on my desk, or in my car that I want to memorize, and I read them daily.

+ I experiment with healthier foods and some favorite herbs to boost my diet, and I consider using essential oils. I read to understand more about these additional remedies of Scripture.

+ I remember to pray a prayer of gratefulness over my food and drink. I make and drink the word of the Lord in the form of healing water, especially with tough challenges that war with my emotions.

+ I boldly speak against any mountains in my body, my emotions, and my thinking patterns that come to mind, and I replace them.

+ I walk in love and kindness toward all and ask for forgiveness when I stumble. I keep my conscience clear with my Lord as a powerful way of keeping the door closed to attacks by the devil.

+ As I become stronger, I choose to let others know how I am growing in the Lord and using His divine remedies for my health. I expect some questions and possible criticism but know that it exercises my spiritual muscles to be able to stand firm in my position with gentleness and love.

- I cultivate a sense of expectation for divine appointments to come my way, where I can be a positive influence and mentor in someone else's life.

- I ask permission to lay hands on anyone who shares their troubles with me, and I pray for them. Practice makes perfect in this area.

- I enlist a friend who wants to take this journey with me.

- I give thanks to my heavenly Father ahead of time for blessing my day. I expect it to be a great one, regardless of any surprises. I will have a healthy, productive day in His service.

BECOMING A SON OR DAUGHTER OF GOD

*W*HEN THE APOSTLE Peter told his Jewish audience who Jesus truly was, this was their question and Peter's reply:

> When they heard this, they were stung in the heart and said to Peter and to the rest of the apostles, "Brothers, what shall we do?"
>
> Peter said to them, "Repent and be baptized, every one of you, in the name of Jesus Christ for the forgiveness of sins, and you shall receive the gift of the Holy Spirit. For the promise is to you, and to your children, and to all who are far away, as many as the Lord our God will call."
>
> —ACTS 2:37–39

The gospel has not changed. Our response also must be the same. In order to experience all the benefits of God's Word and His healing promises, we must come into a personal relationship with Him by repenting of our sins.

The Bible tells us that "all have sinned and come short of the glory of God" (Rom. 3:23) and that "all unrighteousness is sin" (1 John 5:17, NKJV). No matter how nice a person you are, all means all, so no one is exempt.

God is holy and righteous and perfect, and sin separates us from Him because He cannot fellowship with sin. But, as we have seen, all of us have sinned. So what are we to do?

Because of God's great love for us, He sent His Son, Jesus, to pay the penalty for our sin, enabling us to be made righteous before

God. This free gift of salvation is available to anyone who would choose to accept it.

The process is easy. The Bible says, "If you confess with your mouth Jesus is Lord, and believe in your heart that God has raised Him from the dead, you will be saved, for with the heart one believes unto righteousness, and with the mouth confession is made unto salvation" (Rom. 10:9–10).

If you've never accepted Christ as your Savior, allowing Him to be in charge of your life and your future, simply pray the following prayer:

> *Lord Jesus, I want to know You as my Savior and Lord. I believe You are the Son of God and that You died for my sins. I also believe You were raised from the dead and now sit at the right hand of the Father praying for me. I ask You to forgive me for my sins and change my heart so that I can be Your child and live with You eternally. Thank You for Your peace. Help me to walk with You so that I can begin to know You as my best friend and my Lord. Amen.*

Once you have accepted Christ into your heart, making Him the Lord of your life, I would strongly encourage you to do the following:

+ **Get baptized.** Acts 22:16 says, "And now why are you waiting? Arise and be baptized, and wash away your sins, calling on the name of the Lord" (NKJV). Water baptism is a symbolic burial of our old life, doing in type what Christ did in reality. He died, was buried, and rose again. We die to our old life and rise up out of the water to live a new life with a clear conscience. Baptism helps us see and feel that our past is truly gone and forgiven.

+ **Invite the Holy Spirit to direct your life.** It is the Holy Spirit who guides us, empowers us, and enables us to understand and apply what is taught in the Word of God. It would be tragic to try to live this Christian life without His direction. He empowers us to walk in obedience to Christ and live in victory over sickness and defeat. The Bible tells us the Holy Spirit comes and dwells with every believer who asks (Luke 11:13; Acts 5:32). See the sample prayer in chapter 1 for guidance on how to invite Him into your life.

+ **Find a Bible-believing church.** The Bible tells us not to forsake the assembling of ourselves together (Heb. 10:25). This is because the church is where you can grow in your faith by studying God's Word and walking with like-minded Christians who believe in the power of the gospel. God never intended for His children to be lone rangers. It is important that you seek out a healthy fellowship of believers.

When you accept God's gift of salvation, you become God's adopted son or daughter, and He wants you to see yourself as such—a joint heir with Christ, clothed in the righteous of God's own Son:

> If you live according to the flesh, you will die, but if through the Spirit you put to death the deeds of the body, you will live.
>
> For as many as are led by the Spirit of God, these are the sons of God. For you have not received the spirit of slavery again to fear. But you have received the Spirit of adoption, by whom we cry, "Abba, Father." The Spirit Himself bears witness with our spirits that we are the children of God, and if children, then heirs: heirs of God and joint-heirs with Christ, if indeed we suffer with Him, that we may also be glorified with Him.
>
> —ROMANS 8:13–17

Despite our mailing address here on earth, when we become children of God, we become citizens of the kingdom of heaven. Seeing ourselves here is a vantage point of victory:

But our citizenship is in heaven, from where also we await
for our Savior, the Lord Jesus Christ.

—PHILIPPIANS 3:20

He has delivered us from the power of darkness and
has transferred us into the kingdom of His dear Son, in
whom we have redemption through His blood, the forgiveness of sins.

—COLOSSIANS 1:13–14

We have access to the throne room of God, where we can go for
forgiveness when we stumble, to talk with our Creator, and to make
requests of Him. All it takes to do this is to simply envision yourself entering His throne room with praise and thankfulness to talk
with your dad. Our lives are meant to be full and exciting as we
see miraculous transformations occur within ourselves and those we
minister to.

Keep everything in perspective. Even the biggest challenges in
this life fade into obscurity in the face of God's exciting promises for
our future. As the Scripture says, "Eye has not seen, nor ear heard,
nor has it entered into the heart of man the things which God has
prepared for those who love Him" (1 Cor. 2:9).

SAMPLE EMOTIONAL CLEARANCE EXERCISE

*A*FTER YOU COMPLETE the body system work, you may find the following to be an excellent sheet to keep at hand, as it tends to clear out any loose ends that may reveal themselves.

This work circles around a prayer that you can use again and again:

> *In Jesus's mighty name, I command off all mountains of [name your concern] and the story it came from to release completely from all the deep cellular blueprints of all my created parts, especially my [be specific about your concern and wherever there is pain]. They must all go with none remaining. I am done with these and any demonic oppression entwined with them. I command them gone and evict them completely from my total being. Any injustice I am carrying, I give to God to take care of. In these vacancies I accept the Lord's divine, healthy cellular blueprints, emotions, and mind-sets of [whatever you envision your health looking like].*

When saying the above prayer, you can use the following list of emotions, inserting two to three items at a time into the blank spaces. Be careful—don't overdo it and try too many at one time. One to three sections a day may be plenty.

IN PLACE OF...	ASK FOR THE REPLACEMENT OF...
Sadness, grief, heartbreak	Joy and God's good plans for your future
Betrayal, abandonment, unreturned love	God's beauty for ashes and His love and care for you
Discouragement, despair, depression	Hope, joy, and His promises
Rejection, helplessness, lack of control	His strength, power, might, and guidance
Low self-worth, disgust, worthlessness	Being clothed with Christ in His righteousness
Fear, worry, anxiety	Focus on Christ and His peace
Indecisiveness, all stress, tension	What God says about our lives
Failure, all trauma, terror	Victory, safety, total healing, and divine protection
Anger, intense hatred, rage	Forgiveness, compassion, and mercy to others
Lust, shame, guilt	Respect for all as God's creation, self-forgiveness, and the ability to move forward
Blame, jealousy, stubbornness	Taking responsibility, obedience, and seeing God as your source
Addiction, resentment, bitterness	Victory, forgiveness, and knowledge that you can do all things through Christ who strengthens you
Unforgiveness of self, men, women, children, society, and God	Forgiveness, mercy, and compassion

Repeat these prayers as any new layers reveal themselves or as any new health challenges surface. It is not uncommon to have to dump several truckloads of dirt from a complex challenge that contains several facets of trauma and emotional bondage. We may need the Lord's revelation to assist us. Always seek the guidance of His Holy Spirit.

You may choose to make it a regular practice to repeat this prayer exercise to maintain your freedom from life's stresses and to keep peace dominant in your life.

PSALM 91: GOD'S ANSWER FOR TRAUMA

I BELIEVE THAT PRAYING Psalm 91 aloud is wonderful medicine that has the powerful ability to break up the most challenging blueprints—yes, even down the toughest traumas of war and post-traumatic stress syndrome. I have applied and formatted the psalm into a beautiful prayer of healing, safety, and comfort for you. Consider repeating it aloud and with conviction, meditating upon it daily until you have arrived at a place of solid peace and healing.

Dear heavenly Father,

Thank You for meeting all my needs. Whenever I seek You, You are there. You hear me, and You have promised to deliver me from all my fears. I see myself completely delivered and free from every form of fear that has ever touched my being and settled there.

I speak to all traumatic patterns that have captivated any of the deepest cellular blueprints of my body, mind, nerves, and emotions—all birth trauma, accidents, medical proclamations, surgeries, violent attacks, betrayals, deaths, catastrophes, and war atrocities; any intense shock, fear, or fright; any physical, mental, emotional, or sexual abuse; and [name what you need to]. I pull them out by the roots, place the powerful name of Jesus over them, evict them completely, and hurl them into the sea. I am done with them, and they are gone. It is done!

Into those vacancies I fill myself from the soles of my feet to the top of my head with new, perfect cellular blueprints of Your healing, safety, and peace.

I now dwell in the secret place of the Most High, and I abide under the shadow of the Almighty. I say of the Lord, "You are my refuge and my fortress; My God, in You I will trust."

I see and consider myself totally protected and delivered from all traps and snares and from the perilous pestilence. You cover me with Your feathers. Under Your wings I take refuge.

Your truth is my shield, surrounding me entirely. I am not afraid of the terror by night, nor of the arrow that flies by day, nor of the pestilence that walks in darkness, nor of the destruction that lays waste at noonday. My focus is on You and You alone.

A thousand may fall at my side and ten thousand at my right hand, but it shall not come near me. Because I have made You my refuge and my dwelling place, no evil shall befall me, nor shall any plague come near my dwelling. You give Your angels charge over me to keep me in all my ways. I shall call upon Your name and You will answer me. You are with me in times of trouble. You will deliver me and show me Your salvation. You will satisfy me with long life.

I praise You and thank You for all of these promises. In Jesus's powerful and mighty name I pray. Amen.

WHO I AM IN CHRIST

*K*NOWING WHO YOU are in Christ, your mission as a child of God, and the promise of healing and wholeness given to us in God's Word is a first step to walking in the fullness of health and vitality. Declare these promises daily, or as often as needed, to solidify in your mind and heart who you are in Him and what He makes available to you.

I am _____

- Planned (Eph. 1:4)
- Completely forgiven and justified (1 John 2:12)
- Reconciled to Him (2 Cor. 5:18)
- United with Him (1 Cor. 6:17)
- A new creation (2 Cor. 5:17)
- His beloved (Eph. 1:6)
- A chosen nation and a royal priesthood (1 Pet. 2:9–10)
- A child of the King (John 1:12)
- A saint (Eph. 1:1)
- A joint heir of Christ (Rom. 8:17)
- Anointed (1 John 2:27)
- Celebrated by angels (Luke 15:10)
- A child of light and truth (1 Thess. 5:5)
- The salt of the earth (Matt. 5:13)
- In His thoughts (Jer. 29:11)
- Fearfully and wonderfully made (Ps. 139:14)

- The righteousness of God in Christ (2 Cor. 5:21)
- A masterpiece (Eph. 2:10, NLT)
- Blessed with my family (Deut. 28:3-4)
- Listed by name in the Book of Life (Luke 10:20)
- A dwelling place of God (1 Cor. 3:16)
- The body of Christ on earth (Eph. 5:30)
- Seated with Christ in heavenly places (Eph. 2:6)
- A citizen of heaven (Phil. 3:20)
- Chosen and appointed (John 15:16)
- Holy (Heb. 3:1)
- Loved with an everlasting love (Jer. 31:3)
- More powerful than the devil (1 John 4:4)

I live in the throne room of God, empowered with His authority. My road leads to victory.

My mission is to _____

- Believe God (Gen. 15:6)
- Resemble Christ (1 John 3:1–2)
- Walk in truth (3 John 1:4)
- Trust God wholeheartedly (Prov. 3:5)
- Grow in wisdom (James 1:5)
- Be powerful and brave, and maintain a sound mind (2 Tim. 1:7)
- Walk by faith (2 Cor. 5:7)
- Glory in my freedom (John 8:36)
- Bear good fruit (John 15:16)
- Walk in joy (Neh. 8:10)
- Do good works (Eph. 2:10)

- See God as my strength (Ps. 27:1)
- Wear God's full armor (Eph. 6:13)
- Triumph over my circumstances (Deut. 28:13)
- Be more than a conqueror (Rom. 8:37)
- Reside in peace (1 Pet. 5:7; Phil. 4:7)
- Prosper in all I do (Deut. 28:8)
- Bear good news (Isa. 52:7)
- Shine light in the world (Matt. 5:14)
- Minister reconciliation (2 Cor. 5:18)
- Make disciples as I go (Matt. 28:19)
- Baptize believers (Matt. 28:19)
- Be equipped to heal (Matt. 10:1)
- Be bold as a lion (Prov. 28:1)
- Move mountains with my faith-filled words (Mark 11:23)
- Lay hands on the sick and cast out devils (Matt. 10:1)
- Speak life to the sick (Prov. 18:21)

I will never give up, stay quiet, or bow to evil. My commitment stands, and He holds my destiny in His hands.

HEALING DECLARATIONS

- Jesus Christ (the healer) is the same yesterday, today, and forever (Heb. 13:8).
- With God nothing is impossible (Luke 1:37).
- By His stripes my healing has already been purchased (1 Pet. 2:24).
- No weapon formed against me shall prosper (Isa. 54:17).

+ No plague shall come near my body or my home
  (Ps. 91:10).

+ You, God, forgive my sins; You heal all my diseases
  (Ps. 103:3).

+ I speak in faith and victory to move any mountain in
  my way (Mark 11:23).

+ I pray in faith and believe that I receive them, and I will
  have them (Mark 11:24).

+ I take a seat at the Lord's table, which is already prepared, where I can receive healing (Ps. 23:5).

+ I see myself reaching out and taking my remedy. God
  has granted me everything pertaining to life and godliness (2 Pet. 1:3).

I will not waste another moment in sickness and defeat. My God
is a God of victory. He has won the victory over sin, death, and the
devil, who is out to kill, steal, and destroy. It has already been done.
My inheritance is ready and present for me to receive. I reach out
and take it! I see myself healed in my mind, my emotions, my heart,
and my body.

RESOURCES

For further information on Chinese Constitutional Medicine, see S. Dharmananda, *Your Nature, Your Health: Chinese Herbs in Constitutional Therapy* (Portland, OR: Institute for Traditional Medicine and Preventative Health Care, 1986).

For quality, organic, pharmaceutical-quality herbs, essential oils, and more, visit www.mynsp.com/usa or www.equippedtoheal.com.

For quality, alkaline pure water, see the following:

+ The Alkal-Life: www.equippedtoheal.com
+ Water Revolution: www.water-revolution.com/usa or www.equippedtoheal.com

For far-infrared light therapy, see The Original Amethyst Bio-Mat at www.amazingbiomats.com.

These mats capture God's far-infrared light and His healing negative ions in a wonderful technology that also includes the healing power of God's amethyst, which cover the mats. When lying on the bio-mat, people experience a healing light wave that can have an extraordinary impact on the circulatory, skeletal, digestive, immune, and nervous systems.

For personal assistance and a more complete list of available services, visit www.equippedtoheal.com.

NOTES

INTRODUCTION

1. See Andrew Womack Ministries, Healing Testimonies, particularly "Malignant Skin Tumor-Healed," accessed February 15, 2016, http://www.awmi.net/video/healing/.

CHAPTER 1—YOUR RIGHT TO DIVINE HEALTH

1. Englishman's Concordance, "nir·pā," accessed February 16, 2016, http://biblehub.com/hebrew/nirpa_7495.htm.

2. Blue Letter Bible, "sōzō," accessed February 16, 2016, https://www.blueletterbible.org/lang/lexicon/lexicon.cfm?t=kjv&strongs=g4982.

CHAPTER 2—KNOW YOUR AUTHORITY

1. John MacArthur, *The MacArthur Bible Commentary* (Nashville, TN: Thomas Nelson, 2005), 273.

2. This story is drawn from Thurman Scrivner's booklet *God's Power*, which is part of the "Fabulous Five" set made available through Sid Roth's *It's Supernatural!* television broadcast, and Scrivner's appearance on *It's Supernatural!* the week of March 2–8, 2015.

CHAPTER 3—THE POWER OF YOUR WORDS

1. James C. Mundt et al., "Voice Acoustic Measures of Depression Severity and Treatment Response Collected Via Interactive Voice Response (IVR) Technology," *J Neurolinguistics* 20, no. 1 (January 2007): 50–64, doi: 10.1016/j.jneuroling.2006.04.001; Deutsche Welle, "Voice Analysis: An 'Objective' Diagnostic Tool Based on Flawed Algorithms?", accessed February 16, 2016, http://www.dw.com/en/voice-analysis-an-objective-diagnostic-tool-based-on-flawed-algorithms/a-17187057.

2. Eileen McKusick, "The Therapeutic Use of Sound in Alternative and Conventional Medicine," Foundation for Alternative and Integrative Medicine, accessed February 16, 2016, http://www.faim.org/complementaryalternative/therapeutic-use-sound-alternative-conventional-medicine.html; Stephanie Rosenbloom, "What's the Buzz? Sound Therapy," *New York Times*, November 24, 2005, accessed February 16, 2016, http://www

.nytimes.com/2005/11/24/fashion/thursdaystyles/whats-the-buzz-sound
-therapy.html?_r=0.

3. Timothy Ferris, "Dark Matter," *National Geographic*, January 2015,
accessed February 23, 2016, http://ngm.nationalgeographic.com/2015
/01/hidden-cosmos/ferris-text.

4. *Merriam-Webster Collegiate Dictionary* Eleventh Edition (Spring-
field, MA: Merriam-Webster Inc., 2003), s.v. "energy."

5. Ferris, "Dark Matter."

6. Ibid.

Chapter 5—The Five Foundations of Optimal Health

1. "10 Leading Causes of Death by Age Group, United States—2011,"
Centers for Disease Control and Prevention, accessed February 23, 2016,
http://www.cdc.gov/injury/wisqars/pdf/leading_causes_of_death_by
_age_group_2011-a.pdf.

2. Nicholas Staropoli, "A Reader Asks: Is Life Expectancy in
America Declining?", American Council on Science and Health, June 3,
2015, accessed February 16, 2016, http://acsh.org/2015/06/a-reader-asks
-is-life-expectancy-in-america-declining/.

3. See, for example, www.boughtmovie.com.

4. Jeff Donn, Martha Mendoza, and Justin Pritchard, "An AP Investigation: Pharmaceuticals Found in Drinking Water, Pharmawater I,"
accessed February 23, 2016, http://hosted.ap.org/specials/interactives
/pharmawater_site/day1_01.html.

5. Jeffrey Traister, "What Emotions Affect Different Organs in the
Huma Body?", LiveStrong.com, March 19, 2011, accessed February 23,
2016, http://www.livestrong.com/article/193234-what-emotions-affect
-different-organs-in-the-human-body/.

Chapter 7—The Immune System

1. Joseph Mercola, "HPV Vaccine Linked to Nervous System Disorder
and Autoimmunity," Mercola.com, October 21, 2014, accessed February
25, 2016, http://articles.mercola.com/sites/articles/archive/2014/10/21
/gardasil-hpv-vaccine-adverse-reactions.aspx.

Chapter 10—The Nervous System

1. "100 Fascinating Facts You Never Knew About the Human Brain,"
Nursing Assistant Central, December 31, 2008, accessed February 25,
2016, http://www.nursingassistantcentral.com/blog/2008/100-fascinating
-facts-you-never-knew-about-the-human-brain/.

2. Abigail Wise, "What's Worse for Your Brain: Sugar or Cocaine?", Huffington Post, accessed February 15, 2016, http://www.huffingtonpost .com/2014/05/07/fed-up_n_5281670.html.

Chapter 11—The Sensory System

1. "Twenty Facts About the Amazing Eye," Discovery Eye Foundation, June 10, 2014, accessed February 25, 2016, https://discoveryeye.org /blog/20-facts-about-the-amazing-eye/.

2. "Ten Cool Facts About Hearing," HearingAids.com, accessed February 25, 2016, http://www.hearingaids.com/about-hearing-loss/how-we -hear/10-cool-facts-about-hearing/.

3. Ibid.

Chapter 15—The Structural System

1. "Bones...How Many, and What Do They Do?", MedicineNet.com, accessed February 25, 2016, http://www.medicinenet.com/script/main /art.asp?articlekey=6884.

2. "Everyday Mysteries," Library of Congress, accessed February 25, 2016, https://www.loc.gov/rr/scitech/mysteries/muscles.html; Kim Ann Zimmermann, "Muscular System: Facts, Functions & Diseases," *Live Science*, accessed February 25, 2016, http://www.livescience.com/26854 -muscular-system-facts-functions-diseases.html.

Chapter 17—More Healing Prayers

1. Greg Mohr, *Scriptures to Live By* (Woodland Park, CO: Healing Door Ministries, 1989), v–vi.

ABOUT THE AUTHOR

*S*YLVIA ROGERS IS committed to teaching scriptural healing techniques to help people take more responsibility for their health and partner with their heavenly Father to experience wholeness and lasting wellness.

She holds a bachelor of science in nursing and is a certified nutritionist, a natural health consultant and herb specialist, and a national lecturer and teacher for Nature's Sunshine Products. She is also a certified biofeedback specialist who assists her clients in praying biblical promises and principles during biofeedback sessions with eye-opening and astounding results. She has condensed what she has learned into an easy, step-by-step guide to help anyone experience the same wonderful results in their own homes and communities.

Visit www.equippedtoheal.com for more information regarding her business, mission, offered services, and the fine products that can be used as tools in one's healing journey or to help others. Her first book, *The Pearl Box: Breaking the Bondage of Disease Through Biblical Tools for Physical, Mental, Emotional and Spiritual Health*, is also available for purchase.

Sylvia and her husband, Mark, live in Gresham, Oregon, and are blessed with three adult children and eight grandchildren.

CONNECT WITH US!

CHARISMA HOUSE

(Spiritual Growth)

 Facebook.com/CharismaHouse

@CharismaHouse

Instagram.com/CharismaHouseBooks

 **SILOAM**

(Health)

Pinterest.com/CharismaHouse

REALMS

(Fiction)

Facebook.com/RealmsFiction

Ignite Your SPIRITUAL HEALTH
with these FREE Newsletters

CHARISMA HEALTH
Get information and news on health-related
topics and studies, and tips for healthy living.

POWER UP! FOR WOMEN
Receive encouraging teachings that
will empower you for a Spirit-filled life.

CHARISMA MAGAZINE NEWSLETTER
Get top-trending articles, Christian teachings,
entertainment reviews, videos and more.

CHARISMA NEWS WEEKLY
Get the latest breaking news from
an evangelical perspective every Monday.

SIGN UP AT:
nl.charismamag.com

CHARISMA MEDIA